In the Land of the Shoes
A card-carrying optimist reflects on her long life

Nancy Lund

"In the Land of the Shoes: A card carrying optimist reflects on her long life" by Nancy Lund. ISBN 978-1-62137-007-9 (softcover); ISBN 978-1-62137-016-1 (hardcover).

Published 2012 by Virtualbookworm.com Publishing Inc., P.O. Box 9949, College Station, TX 77842, US.

Manufactured in the United States of America.

TABLE OF CONTENTS

1909

Mama — Estelle Therese Lyon Rosenfield 1973

For Mama

Mama, you will appear on many pages of this story. As Mary said in the poem written a few days after your death,

"We were not finished when you took your leave ..."

And that is why I feel compelled to tell you how it all turned out, Mama. You followed the twists and turns of my life, my becoming a radical, my marriage, my kids, my tries at various careers; but you missed these final, these long chapters.

I trust that you knew that I always loved and admired you, although in my early years I made a point of emphasizing our differences. But I knew what a wonderful listener you were. It is a gift — being *simpatico* — a quality that made complete strangers, as well as friends, unload their troubles, sure of your understanding ear.

Your presence here is also because your high standards in art, literature, in everyday speech — and above all in behavior — have stuck with me. So as I write this I am saying, "See how it turned out, Mama? This is what I did with all my energy and good intentions. Too late for your corrections and notes in the margin. You think I could have done more and better? Granted. But at least I am telling it as it really was and that is one of the things you always gave me credit for: Nan's in-your-face honesty!"

So, Mama, here it is.

In the Land of the Shoes

It came to me when I was on my knees, frantically searching for the two one-dollar bills our mischievous three-year-old had thrown into his toy box. All the money we had in the house to last till Friday when I hoped my husband would be paid. All this fuss over two measly dollars. And that is what triggered the memory: "That shoe! I am living in the land of the shoes!"

I grew up a privileged child. Waited on by servants, everything miraculously taken care of by ready hands. We lived in an elegant home, surrounded by lawns and gardens. There was even a miniature forest where our Scottish gardener coaxed a crocus to bloom despite El Paso's desert climate.

Our home sat on the corner of Cincinnati Street and an unpaved alley which we crossed on our daily walks. Four little girls and our nurse, IV. One day I picked up a strange object from the dust of the alley.

"What in the world is this?" I asked IV.

"It's a shoe."

How could this flat, floppy thing be a shoe? Shoes were made to fit a person's foot, little for children and big for grown-ups. Shoes were white or brown or shiny patent leather. They had heels and tongues. They must have shoelaces or else little buttons.

In my six-year-old imagination this shoe must belong to some strange creature who had only one foot. Or perhaps it dropped from the sky where one-footed people flew about.

"Probably dropped off the rag-man's wagon," IV said. "For goodness sake why would you pick up the dirty thing?"

I don't believe I ever thought of it again. But perhaps I did take a look at the rag-pickers drab wagon, piled high with indescribable junk, the next time he made his semi-annual trek down our alley.

And now, all these years later, the scene sprang to mind. How did this cosseted child (one of eight equally loved and cherished), who had never seen a shoe with as much as a run-down heel, never known a person to have a toothache, never learned how to use a broom or as much as held an iron in her hand until she was in her mid-twenties — how had she arrived at what I truly recognized as "the land of the shoes"?

———————

I sailed through a happy, carefree childhood. We were so insulated from the outside world that our parents removed the front page of the paper during the Hickman kidnapping case. Of course we learned the gory details from our classmates and pretended we knew it all along.

I was lucky in my spot in the family hierarchy as third oldest. My brother Leon was six years my senior and I was positioned between Teeta (Louise) and Mary, sisters who were models of orderliness and responsibility — everything I chose not to be. They were the ones who saw to it that I was on time, found my books and jacket, and made excuses for me when I cut up at school. I was incurably dreamy and impractical.

I was probably ten years old when an exasperated teacher called me a Bolshevik. In 1927 the phrase "Iron Curtain" had not yet been coined, but it was a time when our history and geography teachers were very circumspect about anything east of the Urals.

"What's a Bolshevik?

"Someone who never follows the rules, makes things hard for the authorities."

Yes, I had to agree, I am a Bolshevik.

———————

Our comfortable upper-middle-class life came to an end shortly before my nineteenth birthday. My father lost his prosperous grocery business and our lovely house was sold at a terrible loss. I don't remember packing; that was left to professional movers. We just got into our two seven-passenger Packards and drove to Los Angeles, along with Marcial, our chauffeur and handyman. Our first rented house was not too different from our former home, but after a year we moved to an apartment – the ten of us crowded into three bedrooms, with one bath.

I dropped out of UCLA after one semester of my junior year, mostly because I could not see myself becoming either a teacher or a secretary. Those were the only careers my father thought suitable for his daughters and were the paths taken by Mary and Teeta.

I took a variety of temporary jobs – model, nanny, and finally salesperson at a bakery owned by my parents' best friends, the Jacobys. Within months I was made manager of a small branch bakery in Westwood. Jennie, my predecessor, was so obsessed with keeping the glass cases clean and sparkling that the shelves were empty by 3:00 p.m., so I brashly doubled the bakery order on my first day. We sold out and I doubled the order again, and again. I was pronounced a great success and got a ten-cent raise.

Two weeks later Anita, who managed another branch, called me to say that Mr. Jacoby had refused to sign with the Bakers Union and I should ignore the picket line at the market next day.

Though my family still thought of themselves as upper-class, I was making friends and reading books that made me question the system that had wiped out my father. "Sorry," I told Anita without hesitation, "In the long run I have more in common with the bakers than I do with Mr. Jacoby." No, I would not cross a picket line. The pickets never appeared but I was promptly fired.

Thinking that my actions had put my folks in an embarrassing spot, I offered to move out. That was when Mama said, "We taught you children to think for yourselves and now you are thinking for yourself. The choice is up to you."

That choice led me to the Communist Party. Not the Party we have been taught to scorn, but one that stood for good and positive things. Let me tell you about *my* Communist Party. It supported the Soviet Union because it seemed to be a laboratory for a great experiment — to see if a classless society organized for the benefit of the many could succeed. My Communist Party supported the Scottsboro boys and jobs for Negroes ("Black" came later.) My Party believed that a just society could be built by taking from each according to his ability and rewarding each according to his needs.

I wept and still weep for Ethel Rosenberg. I have a feeling that her Communist Party and mine had much in common.

So it seemed incomprehensible to me not to join a group who believed as I did — that greed should not be rewarded, that it was wrong that the color of a man's skin or his religion could bar him from a job, or education or where he could live. Why would I not join with people who believed that man is essentially good and that the world can be improved?

Now I was ready to go to work for the labor movement. First as a Retail Clerk and then for the UAW-CIO, trying to organize Douglas Aircraft in Santa Monica. Though I wrote great leaflets (and made terrible coffee) and eagerly met three shifts coming and going to work, I hardly fit the image of a labor leader. My union buddies loved me but couldn't get over my naiveté, my vocabulary as strange to them as theirs was to me. There was still my warm supportive family and the aura of my special childhood wrapping me in a security blanket of sorts. I had not changed much from the dreamy girl I had always been.

When the war ended, anxious to be a part of the new world that was coming, I took a job as Secretary of the Communist Party of San Diego (at a very low-rate pay). It was in San Diego that I met Dick. Our mutual friends were sure that we would make an ideal couple even though we came from such different backgrounds. We soon found that these differences were insignificant alongside the values we shared. So, buoyed by optimism — and eager to live together — we married in January of 1947.

Dick continued to go to Law School under the G.I. Bill and worked as a laborer when he could. We moved into a bi-racial housing project in November of that year, a few weeks before Eric was born. In June of 1949 our second son, Ben, was born.

We were living on a shoe-string in 1950. I loved being a stay-at-home mother but I was a terrible housekeeper. How could I have left our last $2 lying around — Dick's mother would never have been so careless.So here I was, at the age of 33, on my knees frantically searching for the money I needed for milk for my kids. And at that moment I finally connected the alley of my childhood with my own life. The "Land of the Shoes" was real. It existed. People lived in it, grew up, got married, had kids. And their clothes grew shabby and their shoes wore out, if they were lucky enough to have any. The "Land of the Shoes" was right here, but in a way it was a million miles from Cincinnati Street.

"Here tickets," said Eric, holding up two crumpled dollar bills. I gave a whoop of relief and gave him a big, forgiving bear hug.

Why did I title my memoir "In the Land of the Shoes" and make this the first chapter of the book? It is because that moment of recognition did not make me regret my choice. Yes, my life was now quite different from that of my childhood but casually, almost unconsciously, I had chosen wisely.

And I suppose that was why the first working title of my memoir was "Bo-Peep at 90." I have always been confident that everything will turn out all right, and it usually has. My lost purse has been returned time after time, there are tickets at the box-office although I have neglected to order them, a taxi will get me to my job on time! Bo-Peep's sheep will come home wagging their tails behind them!

What follows, then, is my recall of growing up happy, marrying happily, and happily trying to improve my little corner of the world.

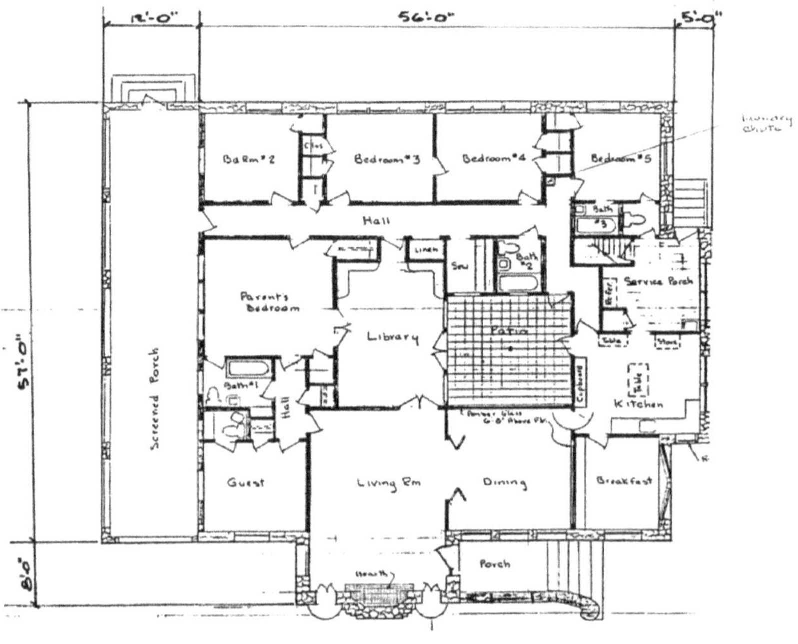
12'-0"
56'-0"
5'-0"
57'-0"
8'-0"
Laundry Chute
Bd Rm #2
Clos
Bedroom #3
Bedroom #4
Bedroom #5
Bath #3
Hall
Linen
Sew
Bath #2
Service Porch
Refer
Parent's Bedroom
Library
Patio
Stove
Table
Cupboard
Kitchen
Bath #1
Hall
Screened Porch
Guest
Living Rm
Dining
Breakfast
Porch
Hearth

700 Cincinnati Street:
A House Designed By A Woman

I grew up in a house designed by and for my mother. It is this house that haunts my dreams and forms a kind of benchmark for the homes I design today.

I was three and a half when the ground was broken for our new house. We lived then a short block away and between mealtimes, naps and baths, I spent many happy hours picking up the lovely smooth black circles which seemed to appear from nowhere. Now I know they were the knock-outs from electrical boxes. And it strikes me how functional everything was, down to the three-way switches, so that you didn't need to cross the room to turn out the lights.

It took me thirty years of working as a steel detailer and structural draftswoman to realize that the house I grew up in had planted the seeds for my true calling. Soon after my husband and I moved to the mountains I hung out my shingle as a Home Designer. And I like to think that in the homes I design today my structural training meets the artist touch of my mother.

Here in the Sierras homes are designed for warmth rather than the coolness of the house I grew up in and I must be ever mindful of my clients' pocket book, a consideration which my parents blithely ignored. But the elements that made our home in El Paso so satisfactory, so memorable, are the qualities which I try to capture. If I suggest a pull-out shelf in the linen closet, built-in sideboards in the breakfast room, finding that perfect spot above the utility room to fit in a laundry chute — all echoes of the house I grew up in — my clients smile with approval. As I sit at my drafting board I feel Mama looking over my shoulder, critical but supportive.

It was the spring of 1921 when ground was broken for our house at 700 Cincinnati Street. My father's grocery stores were doing well and my parents felt it was time to build a home appropriate to their standing in the community. They chose a site on El Paso's "first mesa", only a few short blocks from the towering presence of Mt. Franklin. The Rio Grande, several miles to the west, was a mere glint of silver in the purpling sunset.

In my memories, as in my dreams, there is always light — the clear, sharp crystal light of the desert, for El Paso is more a part of the West than of the South. It was Mama's inspiration to use El Paso's native stone, its ever-so-subtle pinks and grays, lavenders and greens waiting to be illumined by the changing angles of the desert sun. The exterior, with its chimneys and slate roof, was based on a French farm house — not quite a chateau. Rough-hewn timbers formed the window sills and lintels above the doors, and the wrought iron grills of the long screened porch on its north side were repeated in the gate that enclosed a back courtyard.

Early photos of the house do not reflect the landscaping designed by Mama. Besides the de rigueur front lawn and hedges, there was our play area — a huge sprinklered side lawn. Fruit trees and grape vines were planted against the rear stone walls and Papa's vegetable garden, from which he harvested huge tomatoes, was next to the "drying courtyard."

The old blueprints, creased and folded many times, are full of details of window sills and jambs, obviously drawn by the well-known architect whose name is on the plans. But it was my mother, not he, who determined the flow of rooms, the simple but elegant spaces, the way the house worked — shouldn't children awaken to the morning sun — wouldn't screening the long porch provide an ideal place for playing and studying? Her viewpoint prevailed so that 700 Cincinnati became the house, for each of her children, against which all homes would be measured.

We were fortunate to grow up in a home with original paintings on the walls and a library packed with encyclopedias and classic literature. Each of us was encouraged to paint, to write, to dance, never to copy someone else. As for Mama, she had many accomplishments in her life besides the raising of eight children. The only one of her sisters to go to college, she graduated from the St. Louis School of Fine Arts. At the age of fifty she became a professional actress, returned to painting seriously at the age of sixty, and performed on radio, TV and movies into her late seventies. But to me, and I believe in her own estimation, the house at 700 Cincinnati Street was her greatest achievement. Isn't it significant that among the things she saved for me (after fifty years and many moves) were three copies of the architect's plans?

I am looking at the architect's first draft. One small closet in my parents' bedroom? Mama managed to add a long, narrow closet that fitted into the space behind the bookcase in the adjoining library. A pull-out rod brought her dresses into view, a fixture she had seen in my Uncle Max's dress shop. At the back of the closet there was a light and shelves where Christmas and birthday presents could be successfully hidden. In that first draft, the front bathroom is entered through the hall but there is no door from the bath to the master bedroom. Surely a man designed that! Mama saw that by moving the toilet to the opposite wall, there was a way to place a second door into their bedroom.

Margaret Mead has written that most homes are built as though the children will remain aged ten. When we moved into the house there were five children: my older brother was ten; the girls were seven, four, two and six months of age. Fifteen years later there were eight children at home, ranging in age from twenty-five to seven — and the house still "worked." A bedroom designed for two little girls now held three teenagers, a bureau added to augment the two closets with their built-in drawers and upper cabinets for out-of-season clothing. Our grandparents (often visitors) were no longer living, so the guest bedroom became my older brother's. When one of us had a friend over to spend the night there was a daybed in the library for the displaced sister. The three bathrooms (master's, children's, and nurse's) proved to be adequate to the growing family.

As a youngster I thought our house very ordinary, much too practical, so lacking in mystery! By contrast our Aunt Amba's house, a block away, was dark and interesting. With big somber furniture and heavy drapes it was redolent of her perfumes and powder. We loved to go there.

I envied, too, the frilly curtains and frothy coverlets of my girlfriends' bedrooms. No curtains in our bedrooms, or carpets either. Beside each of our beds was a small bright Navajo rug to keep bare feet from the highly polished oak floors. Where did Mama find the floral-printed chintz shades for those extraordinary seven-foot high, double-hung windows? Like the windows and much else in the house, I am sure the shades were made to order, with special rollers to withstand heavy use.

None of our friends had houses like ours. None were as light, as airy. And none, in those days before air-conditioning, were as cool as our house with its eighteen-inch deep walls and recessed windows.

Our daughter, Radia, grew up loving her grandmother's quick humor and her sense of style. When I tell her that I am writing a piece about the house in El Paso she asks me,

"Are you writing about the house or about Grandma?"

"Well, it is not easy to separate the two. In many ways the house reflected the two sides of your Grandma's personality, the practical and the artistic.

"When you think about El Paso and growing up in that house, what pictures come to mind?"

———————

It is a winter evening and we children are already in our pajamas, seated around the pale apricot-colored breakfast room and Mama is reading us stories from Irish Fairy Tales. "Mahoo Roo and Mahoo Beg" she reads in a most believable brogue, an accent she would later use, playing an Irish housekeeper in a movie. The last rays of the sun give the room a special glow. Yee, our Chinese cook, has cleared the table and we sit and listen, entranced.

I see Mama and Papa sitting in their big leather chairs in our library where we are having a serendipitous picnic. Our Sunday morning picnic on Mt. Franklin has been aborted by a sudden furious wind-and-sand-storm. The light that normally floods in from the patio is obscured by sand, filling the sky. We children sit on the floor of the library and happily peel the waxed paper wrapping from our bacon and scrambled egg sandwiches. It would not be a picnic if we ate at our usual places in the breakfast room, or even at the enameled table in the kitchen. Have you never heard of a library picnic?

And I see Mama in a flowing chiffon dress, gracious and laughing at the annual tea she gives for the teachers at the private school we attend. We older girls pass through the swinging door from the kitchen, a plate with petit-fours or delicate cups of tea in our hands. Our teachers never looked as pretty as they do now, sitting on the pale couches and elegant chairs of our living room, or standing at the open patio doors in the library, on this early spring day. We see the house through their eyes and are impressed.

I was nineteen in 1936, it was the depths of the Depression when my father's chain of grocery stores went bankrupt. The house was sold at half the price of what it had cost to build. It was a wrench for me, those moves to ever smaller flats and apartments after we left Texas. I can only imagine what it must have meant to Mama, but she never spoke of it with regret. However, she never gave up designing houses, as if some day we would have money to build again. I remember telling a friend, "It's no use visiting us on Sunday, all we do is watch Mama draw house plans."

When I dream about being in the house — as I often do — my sisters and I are teenagers. And in the time-warp of dreams the little ones are my grandchildren, not my youngest sister and brother. I am busy parceling out chores: who is to clean, who shop, who cook. In today's world there would not be the servants of my childhood, but a large family such as ours would have enough hands to do the work themselves. They would be grateful for the tiled floors and counters, the abundant storage cupboards and the ivory-enameled woodwork that defied scratches.

At different times in the intervening decades, five of us have made trips back to El Paso, fully intending to ring the doorbell to "our house." Only my older brother has done so and his report did not inspire me to take the chance. I would much rather keep the house as I remember it and as it is in my dreams, than face the changes that seventy years has brought to it — and to me.

Note: This chapter was originally written in 1977, entitled "A House Designed by a Woman".

Nancy and Teeta (1919) and Nancy (1927)

Growing Up Happy

I grew up happy! I have always taken my happiness as a given. But now I know it is not that simple. I grew up happy because I had the security of being greatly loved — and more than that — I had no need to do anything, be anything, to be worthy of it! I think each of us Rosenfield children knew that we were loved. Did all of us come to the conclusion that we were, in and of ourselves, lovable? I am not sure. But for me, the confidence that I was loved and lovable — two qualities that are not synonymous — has been the source of my glide through life.

I think of my childhood as drenched in sunshine. El Paso's year-round sunshine. (Summers we spend in Cloudcroft, out of the heat. More of that, later.)

Our life is orderly, predictable, secure. Had Mama read, or was it instinctual, that order is what children need? I am always surrounded by family, but there is space enough to stretch, to run, to tumble head over heels on the sweet-smelling, but ever-so-slightly scratchy grass.

There are sunny walks and naptimes and bath-times and then supper times in the west-facing breakfast room. The setting sun glints through the lowered shades as Mama, in her lovely soprano voice, reads the Pooh stories or many of the delightful poems of A. A. Milne or perhaps an Irish folk tale.

I remember long sunny afternoons that turn chilly toward sunset. We are all playing "Rover, Red Rover" or "Statues" in the side yard. We Rosenfields are joined by Edmund and Herbert, close friends from up the street. Occasionally Rosalyn and her cousins Adelaide and Donald may come from across the street. Our cousins Jimmy and Bobby may be there, too. The games span the years from when I was four to nine or ten, when Leon and Herbert, who are six years older than me, would have moved on to other interests.

Teeta and I are the older sisters, so we will help the little ones who are sure to be caught moving when "It" turns around. They don't understand that now they are out of the game — but of course it doesn't matter. Rosalyn — is she Leon's age? — has trouble understanding why, if there are rules of a game, we don't stick with them. We laugh — it's just a game, silly!

———————

When I was ten or so, I happened on an unfinished letter Papa was writing to his sister, Zerlina, in New York. I wasn't snooping. I had probably gone to the secretary in my parents' bedroom, looking for a pen. But there it was, in his meticulous handwriting, a long letter describing each of his children for her benefit.

Papa had something loving and insightful to say about each of us. I skimmed through the first part until I got to me. For Nancy he used the words *courage and undauntable and full of fun*. I never told anyone I had read the letter but I hugged it inside me, like a gift. My father thought of me in those wonderful words! I had to live up to them.

———————

Growing up in a big family does not guarantee that all will be peaceful and harmonious. Certainly it helps if the house is large and warm, the food is plentiful, everyone is well, and there are no dark secrets hanging over anyone's head.

People who learn that I am one of eight children may visualize us as being like the Waltons of TV or — horrible thought — neglected and lonely like the children in Stephen Zanichkowsky's autobiography *Fourteen*.

Certainly not! The family I grew up in was unique and I believe the central factor that made it so different from the hundreds of homes I have observed since, and most of the biographies I have read — was how much my father and mother genuinely loved each other. My parents, Estelle Lyon and Leon Rosenfield, married for love — their future together was a gamble. Neither had money or position, but they were both optimistic and daring. Reform Jews, secular and moral rather than religious, they had the same outlook toward life. Above all, they shared a sense of humor. Even more, a sense of the ridiculous. Far from being smug, they were at ease with themselves and it made it easy for others to be comfortable in their presence.

I would describe their love as the strongest kind of friendship — in which sex played a role (I know, I know, there were other pregnancies besides the eight of us!) but was not the dominant one. Papa worshipped his bright, witty wife and Mama loved him for the man he was.

My sisters and I always thought of our mother as a quixotic Victorian. She seemed almost prissy about language and certain displays of intimacy, but as a graduate of the St. Louis School of Fine Arts she had done her share of nude studies. She was comfortable with bodies, including her own.

Papa's success as a businessman was almost accidental. He was easygoing, more concerned about his employees than about getting ahead. Tenderhearted, he forgave the bookkeeper's absences (he was wont to go on two-week benders) time after time. Even when Papa learned that the man had been embezzling him for years, he was reluctant to see the guy go to jail.

"It's not him, it's the alcohol."

———————

As Reform Jews we always said we had the best of it all when it came to holidays. We lighted candles for Hanukah and a few days later celebrated Christmas. There was no tree, not due to religious scruples, but because Mama remembered when live candles decorated the tree and the danger of fire was too great to risk. For us Christmas morning was redolent with the smell of the oranges in the lumpy stockings which hung on our different chairs.

The family held a Seder Supper come Pesach and a few days later dyed Easter eggs and put them in baskets. Papa would hide the eggs throughout our garden, us older ones helping the little ones.

We started saying a simple family prayer when Leon was Bar Mitzvah'd, as well as confirmed, when he was twelve, I think, and I would have been six or seven. We didn't gather around Mama but she would come into the hall on which our bedrooms opened and call out, "Prayer." We would stop our chatter and whatever we were doing and repeat together:

> May the Lord bless us and keep us
> And make his countenance to shine upon us
> And give us peace.
> Amen.

In my mind it was more of a family thing than a religious one.

———————

Does your position in the family matter? First child, middle child, baby? It seemed to me then — and still does — that I had the ideal spot, third eldest in a big family. Leon, the first born, and Teeta, two and a half years older than I, were easy children to raise, so my arrival was no big deal. And then along came Mary nineteen months later. She, like Teeta, seemed to like being obedient and following rules. So I was the lucky one, free to be the carefree and irresponsible sister. Being the Po-Peep of the family was comfortable, a perfect fit!

But beyond birth position, my childhood was quite different from that of my younger siblings, especially Julie who was nine years younger than I. By the time Julie was six or eight and I was in my late teens, the Depression (and the bookkeeper) caused my father to lose his once-prosperous business, and the upper-middle-class life we had known in El Paso came to an end. Julie, more than my other sisters, felt the strains and tensions of hard times, of many moves. Gone were the servants, gone was the big house, with its light-filled rooms, the walled garden where we could run around in our slips. The first place my folks rented when we moved to Los Angeles was comparable to our home in El Paso, but after that, the ten of us were crowded into a small one bathroom flat. Now, too, there were problems between our parents that I never saw at her age. I have always been sad that Julie — whose life was wonderful in so many ways — was deprived of the happy childhood memories that have nourished me.

But it is my childhood I am writing about. In my very earliest memory I could not have been more than two, because Mary is not around. I have on a long nightgown, with a drawstring at the bottom. I even remember the feel of the much-washed flannel and its pale tan and blue stripes! (Once I am in bed the hem will be gathered below my feet and the string tied to the bottom rail.) But now it is suppertime. I am at the kitchen table and again I am faced with that awful runny, under-boiled egg. I dawdle as long as possible and then I am inspired. Even though my legs are encased in flannel, I manage to stand up on the chair and turn around. Plop! I sit down squarely on the dish. A most satisfactory sound — and feel — as the egg squishes beneath me and runs onto the table. I am picked up, my dripping gown stripped off, told to finish drinking my milk, sitting there in a skimpy undershirt. Later I will be spanked for such defiance but I think Emma, who was our nurse at the time, is hard pressed to keep from laughing.

Other early memories may be prompted by family photographs, but when I was three and a half I remember clearly the day we went to the hospital, to see Mama and our new baby sister, Josephine. The Hotel Dieu was a big imposing building that we had often driven by, but I had never been inside. I remember the hollow sound of our shoes — Papa, Leon, Teeta, Mary and me — as we walked across the shiny tiled floors. I remember my awe at seeing nuns for the first time, their huge starched headgear like boats sailing ahead of us. I remember how Mama looked, sitting up in bed, her long curly hair in a decorous braid. We walked over to the bassinet in a corner of the room, and there was this tiny red creature. Not anything like I expected. A baby, really? Mama said we might call her Weena, if we found Josephine too much of a mouthful. (Later we would call her Jo.) "More of a worm than a Weena," I whispered to Teeta. Smart ass at three!

Mama did not believe in kindergarten, so I did not start school until a month before I was seven. I do not remember any trauma being left by Mama in Mrs. Norton's 1st and 2nd Grade brightly lit room. I think I did some of my best drawings seated on a low pink chair at a small round pink table. Drawings uninhibited either by teachers or peers or my increasingly self-critical eye.

Mama never drove and for many years we rode across town in Mr. Williams' jitney, along with other students of the El Paso School for Girls (later it became Radford School for Girls). It is to my undying shame that with no teacher present and Teeta silent, I often led the hazing which new girls — or those like poor slow Nelliebelle, who lisped and wore heavy glasses — endured on the ride to and from school. While it was never physical, it was abusive as only language can be. There! Now I have confessed to an ugly trait that fortunately I outgrew.

In a few years Mary was old enough to go to school, followed by Josephine and then Adele. At some point Mr. Williams retired and we were driven by our own chauffeur.

School was a lark for me. I was probably bored and often managed to get myself in trouble. When other girls ran through the sprinklers I sat on one. When I appeared, dripping, in the classroom, Teeta was called out of her 6th Grade class to take me down to her gym locker. (4th graders did not have gym.) There I was stripped of all my clothes and clad in her huge (even for her) white middy blouse and enormous navy blue pleated bloomers. My soggy shoes were replaced by Teeta's high-top gym shoes. Unchagrined, I shuffled through the rest of the day to the exasperation of Mrs. Harris, my teacher, and the giggles of my classmates.

When I was in 5th grade, a classmate and I were hanging on the monkey bars long after the recess bell had rung. One shoe dropped accidentally, then another. Off came our socks. Then why not our dresses? I think we were completely naked, knees bent over the topmost bars, swinging gaily, up-side down, by the time a student was sent out to look for us. She returned — speechless — so it was Miss Daniels who had to come looking for us.

Was that the time that Mama was asked to come to school for a teacher's conference about me? Mama listened to the list of outrages and then quietly told the teacher what kind of a child I was. Miss Daniels, who must have been new to Radford, got the picture.

"Oh. I understand. Nancy is an only child."

"Yes," said Mama. "She is an only child of six only children."

There was discipline. Swift and brief. Not for school misdeeds but transgressions at home. Mama spanked us, over her knee. The dress came up, the drawers came down, bare bottom exposed. A few hard smacks and then Mama rubbed our hot little bottoms with witch hazel, lovely and cool. And the matter was closed.

At the age of ten, when faced with a choice of a spanking or "Having your father talk to you when he gets home," I would say, "Oh please spank me!!" Because Papa could make me feel so ashamed.

"Do you know how many worries your mother has? And how it concerns her when you misbehave?" And then the clincher: "Do you know how proud your mother is of you when you do well?"

"Oh, please, Mama, spank me!"

Nineteen months apart, there was never enough space between me and Mary. Or perhaps too much. Often I wished Mary and I were twins. Then there would be no need to keep ahead of her — and she wouldn't always be trying to catch up, or worse, pass me.

At seven, my classmates teased me about believing in Santa Claus. "Of course," I countered, "I didn't ever really believe in it."

Naturally I came home to Mary, "I know something you don't."

"No you don't." "Yes I do." and on and on until I told her, "There isn't any Santa Claus."

She burst into tears and I got a spanking for making my little sister cry.

What is the age at which one learns long division? 3rd grade? I was enthralled. It was so neat. It worked so well. There was no end to its possibilities.

Again, "I know something you don't." Again, "No, you don't." And, inevitably, I taught Mary long division, only to realize, "Now you know everything I know."

I recalled that moment 30 years later listening to the identical conversation between my sons Eric and Ben. Only Eric was more dramatic than I. He slapped his hand on his forehead, "What have I done? Now you know everything I know."

CODA

Eight children, all following different drummers, disparate interests. I think of each of us in high school and then (some of us) in college, putting our term papers on Mama's pillow, whatever the subject we had chosen. In the morning it would be on our dresser or at the breakfast table. Spelling corrections in the margin. A sentence reworded. A question mark or two. And almost always a note of praise, sometimes in the form of a limerick!

No two of us followed the same path, though we may have started out as Liberal Arts majors. It was social work for Leon, much of it in the Jewish community, then as an administrative judge for the state of California. For Teeta it was teaching, a career she pursued before and after the births of four children and would have followed if only she had lived past the age of thirty-seven. Mary dropped out of Art School to study shorthand and typing, becoming a secretary and the main family bread-winner, in her early twenties. Mary had her own "Letter Shop" in Taos for many years and then, back in San Francisco, she returned to work for the team of lawyers for whom she had worked before. At the age of nine Jo decided to be a journalist, and journalism became her life-long career. Adele, after years as a bookkeeper, went back to college in her fifties to get her B.A. and M.A. degrees, and then as a CPA worked into her eighties. Julie went into nursing right after high school. Later — and with three little kids — went back to college to get her B.S. as well as a degree in Public Health. At the age of 45 Julie became a nurse practitioner, among the very first hired by Kaiser Permanente. She retired after more than 50 years of nursing, at the age of 72. For David it was baseball, first, last and always. He started out behind the plate and has been in the General Manager's seat for a Triple A team for over 50 years. And I, the latest bloomer of all — after many false starts — have spent the last 30 years drawing house plans for pure joy (like Mama) and actually making money at it!

Cloudcroft

The forests of my childhood were those of Cloudcroft, New Mexico, where my family had a summer home. At an elevation of 9000 feet, it was reached by dizzying switchbacks and railroad trestles over deep canyons. Cloudcroft's pines, oaks and aspens, its cosmos-filled meadows, and its towering thunderheads became the benchmark against which my sisters and I would measure all scenery in the future. Years later, our husbands had to reconcile themselves to hearing that the Alps, Norway, even the Andes and Himalayas are "like Cloudcroft."

Life for us in El Paso was bland and predictable: school, the library, Sunday afternoon drives with the whole family stuffed into Papa's vehicle. I remember dibbing to sit on one of the fold-up jump seats in the Ford, preferable to being crowded into the back seat. The Ford had snap-on isinglass windows, handy if we encountered a dust storm. Later we drove more elegantly in a seven-passenger Packard.

But Cloudcroft beckoned with horseback riding, day-long hikes and picnics complete with wild strawberries. Everything in Cloudcroft was different — instead of dresses we wore khakis, we dressed in front of the fireplace on chilly mornings, even our food was unpredictable. But the weather was wonderfully predictable. Dry and dusty until the 4th of July when the first thunderstorm drove us to cover. Then rain every afternoon until the middle of August, though on most days the sun came out later. The last weeks of our vacation were golden, Indian summer weather, heartbreaking to have to leave.

Nancy in Cloudcroft (circa 1925)

Best of all were the stables where there were cowboys. Real cowboys. Not movie cowboys, but real live cowboys in worn dungarees and wide-brimmed dark hats. Hank was the friendliest. He could be counted on for a smile of recognition wherever we happened to see him. But Shorty was our favorite. He had a misshapen foot but that made no difference when he was in the saddle. He was the handsomest, with dark-lashed blue eyes and long dark sideburns. Then there was tall, lanky Hugh, mysterious, a long scar across his cheek, something sad about him. And of course all the cowboys smoked, the cigarette clamped in the corner of their mouth, one eye squinted against the thin column of smoke.

My sisters and I lived for the visits to the stables. The smell of horses, the straw under our feet, saddles and bridles hung haphazardly against the rough walls. We would have liked to hang around all day, but that would be unseemly. We came to order six horses for the next day. My mother insisted that one of the cowboys ride with us, though older brother Leon was an expert horseman and Teeta, Mary and I felt we needed no one. True, sister Jo, at five, needed a gentle horse and help to mount.

Returning from the stables, my sisters and I played a game in which we were the cowboys, walking like them, drawling like them, with twigs in our mouths, taking turns being Hank or Shorty or Hugh. No one wanted to be Guy who actually ran the stables and who we called "Spiteful old grin" because of the times he rode up to tell us that the horses would not be available next day and we would have to wait for the anticipated treat.

Many of our friends from El Paso also summered in Cloudcroft: Gretchen and her family; Joe and Eddie; and, of course, the Givens. Come September Teeta, Mary and I would be attending a private Girl's School, so we would not see most of them until the following summer.

But the summer I was nine, it wasn't a cowboy or a new face that caught my eye, it was Edmund Givens, who I had known all my life. A sturdy ten-year-old, blue eyes, softly curling blond hair, rosy cheeks — he might have been a cherub in a Renaissance painting. And there were his boots!

Though not kin, Edmund's family and mine were very close. In the Southern tradition we called each other's parents Uncle and Aunt. We lived a block apart in El Paso and both families had homes in Cloudcroft. Herbert, Edmund's older brother, was Leon's best friend and they were at our house that afternoon.

We were sitting on the log fence that rimmed our yard when Edmund showed me his new boots. They were very fancy affairs — cream colored leather with heart shaped cut-outs lined in red leather, all along the boot cuffs.

"I'm going to put my sweetheart's name in there," he said.

There were plenty of hearts, room for many names.

"What about me?" I asked.

"Well, maybe."

Suddenly it became very important to have my name in one — or all — of the hearts. "I'll be your sweetheart."

"Then we have to exchange rings," he said, twisting a ring off his finger.

I had to run into the house to get a ring out of my jewelry box, because rings were not worn every day, especially in Cloudcroft. We exchanged rings but his was way too big for me.

"You can put it on a necklace," he said. So back to the jewelry box I went for my favorite blue necklace. I slipped the ring on it and fastened the necklace around my neck.

"Now we're engaged," he announced. How did he know all this? Years before TV, no radio in our homes and I'm sure he wasn't a reader — especially of romance.

"What does it mean — engaged?"

"It means we're going to get married when we grow up and you have to promise not to marry anyone but me."

"Well, I do want to marry you. But I can't promise never to marry anyone but you."

"Why not?"

"Because you might get killed before we grow up and then I'd have to be an old maid."

"Oh. All right."

That should have told us that this was not a marriage made in heaven!

All the conspiratorial whispering was too much for our brothers. They began to serenade us with cowboy laments "Red River Valley" and "You Made Me Cry."

That afternoon and all the days that followed were a blur of excitement. Edmund and I against the world — as represented by Leon and Herbert. We sat together on the log fence and pretended not to hear them. And, oh, it was a delicious feeling, going to bed with a necklace tucked inside my pajamas. I would finger the ring and tell myself, "I'm engaged. The only one in my family to be engaged!"

"I don't think Mama's going to like it," said Teeta, ever the wiser, older sister.

It was Friday afternoon, and my parents, who had been in El Paso for two weeks, leaving us in the care of a cook and housekeeper, were due to drive up before dark. I ran to Edmund, "Here's your ring. Give me mine back."

He surrendered it without a word. The blue necklace and my ring were safely stored in the jewelry box by the time Mama got out of the car. She never mentioned anything about my engagement so I'm sure no one tattled.

But for the rest of that summer, Edmund was much on my mind. When it was my turn to sleep over at their house (a regular event between the two families) Herbert could not let dinner pass without sly remarks about engagements and rings. Edmund barely spoke but there was nothing unusual in that. After everyone was in bed I made several extra trips to the bathroom, so I could walk by Edmund's room and admire those golden curls. A week later it was time to go back to El Paso, to school and life as usual.

The next summer there were new people in Cloudcroft. Most wonderful of all, there were two new boys at the tennis courts. The year before Leon had taught Teeta and me how to play tennis. We knew how to keep score, to alternate between serving and receiving, but beyond that we were hapless.

The new boys were Donald and Greg, not from El Paso, but someplace back east. Donald was the oldest, dark like Teeta and apt to mutter awful curse words under his breath — "damn" not "darn". Greg must have been two years older than me. He was red-haired, tall and skinny, full of awful puns — "I haven't a line to stand on."

Luckily, though older, the boys were not much better tennis players than we, but they were funny and bright and we looked forward to meeting them every morning. Together we would sweep the court, pull the net tight and play the first set. Later, hot and sweaty, we would throw our rackets down and collapse under the nearest tree. I wouldn't say I had a crush on Greg, but I'd be awfully disappointed if he didn't show up.

Though Leon played tennis, neither Edmund nor Herbert was interested in the game, so we didn't see much of them early in the summer. Not until the Fourth of July when all our friends gathered on our porch for the one big event in Cloudcroft — the Annual Rodeo. Our house bordered the long meadow where it was held. We always called it the "ro-day-o" giving it the Spanish pronunciation, accent on the second syllable.

Days before the Fourth, we watched the chutes being set up, temporary fencing erected, and then the cattle herded in. The cowboys from the stables were much in evidence and they came up to our fence for an occasional drink from the hose, tipping their hats in thanks.

We had invited Donald and Greg who had never seen a rodeo, along with the usual summer crowd — Joe and Eddie, Gretchen, Caroline, Frances and a boy (maybe her cousin) and Edmund and Herbert, of course. There were cookies and lemonade for everyone and we watched the usual spills and yelled ourselves hoarse, "Hang on!" "Don't let 'em throw ya!" "Hang on!" Donald and Greg the most enthusiastic of all.

The rodeo was over. It was almost sunset and most of our friends had wandered off when Annie and Angie Chapman came by to deliver the *El Paso Times*, always two days late but welcome, nevertheless. The Chapmans lived directly across the meadow from us, the non-summer part of town. Their dad was the Cloudcroft postmaster and we had known them all the years we had been coming up. We talked about the rodeo; they had seen most of it, saving the last deliveries to the houses along the meadow.

The setting sun was in our eyes when the house across the meadow was suddenly bright. At first we thought it was the reflection of the sun on the upstairs windows but then we saw the flames burst through the roof. And Annie and her little sister stood on our porch and watched their house consumed. It was unbelievably fast, one moment it was a house, then only a skeleton of a house, the posts and rafters outlined against the awful orange of the fire.

Teeta and I were crying, holding on to the weeping girls.

Donald and Greg were yelling. "Can't we do something? Isn't there a fire department?"

And then I heard Edmund's voice. "In Cloudcroft? It was just a shack, anyway."

I looked at him with all the scorn a ten-year-old can muster. My summer of puppy love long buried, curls and boots no longer the things that mattered.

Rosenfield family (1931). Main row: Leon Sr. (Papa), Louise (Teeta), Mary, Nancy (Nan), Josephine (Jo), Estelle (Mama), Leon Jr. Front row: Julie, Adele (Dellie), and David

Changes

In 1932 the depression hit our family. I think Papa had managed to keep us at Radford that last year so Teeta could graduate with all the honors she deserved. It was going to be public school for the rest of us, while Teeta would go to El Paso's Texas College of Mines, not Mills or Scripps as we had dreamed.

Mary and I would go to El Paso High, while Jo and Adele would go to Dudley, the elementary school in our neighborhood. I had skipped an early grade but Mary had skipped two, so she was just one year behind me. That year I was going to be a junior and Mary would be a sophomore. Off we headed to El Paso High with William, our chauffeur, driving Mama, Mary and me. I remember being introduced to the principal, handed a schedule of my classes and assigned a locker before Mama left us.

The stairs alone overwhelmed me — so wide, so crowded with bodies — so daunting. The noise in the halls.... The embarrassment of being the only one to rise when the teacher entered the classroom.... It was all too much. Mary and I braved it a second day. Then we went to bed. We were sick. We were way too sick to ever go to school again.

After the third day, when no colds developed, there was no diarrhea, no fever, we were told to get up and go to school.

"Why can't we go to the Loretta Academy?" we wailed. (A Catholic school we had scoffed at a few months ago.)

We argued with Mama, "What good is school anyway? We can read all the same books at home. Papa quit school when he was 13 and look at how smart he is!"

Finally Papa was called in. "It isn't the same now as when I was a boy. Without a high school diploma, the only job you could get today would be at the 5 and 10 cent store."

That sounded good enough for me.

"Nobody's hiring fourteen-year-old girls when grown men with families can't get a job."

I gave up before Mary. In my first class that day, the girl who sat next to me asked, "Where were you? We thought maybe you had moved away!"

I couldn't wait to get home to tell Mary, "They missed me! School isn't so bad, after all."

So Mary and I survived. It also helped that we knew all the Jewish kids from Temple, kids who were on the school paper and were student body activists. Leon had attended El Paso High and been an honor student six years before, so the teachers had great expectations from us. Mr. Flynn, the Latin teacher, was just as Leon had described him, still smearing his glasses to complete opaqueness, still giving the Aeneid alternate translations; dear Mrs. Frank with her Scottish burr was still teaching English; and the sisters Kelly were still teaching math.

"How can you give me an A-Minus in Trig when I had 100% on all my homework and 100 on all my tests?" I challenged Charlie, the reddest-haired of the Kellys.

"I don't give A's for being the assistant teacher in the class."

Oops! I knew what that came from. Obviously she took exception to my correcting her mistakes on the blackboard. I knew what she meant to write, but I was concerned that other students might copy her occasional slips and be graded down.

Speaking of good grades, when my sister Jo graduated from the elementary school my folks attended the ceremony. The Superintendant of Education spoke, and he completed his remarks by saying, "We had one student who made the highest I. Q. grade ever recorded in Texas — Josephine Rosenfield — and I would certainly like to meet her parents."

32

"Josephine must be an only child," he said when my folks introduced themselves.

"Oh, no, we have eight children. And they're all equally smart."

"No, according to the Mendelian theory with one genius among eight children, there must be six normal and one retarded child. I would certainly like to test them all."

I don't know how the others were tested but Mary and I were taken one Saturday morning to the Education Department. The Supe handed each of us a list of questions and left the room. We were finished quickly and were talking about how easy the questions were when he came rushing into the room.

"What were you saying? What language were you speaking?"

"All we know is English."

"No, no. Children, especially sisters that are that close in age, have their own special language."

We shook our heads and afterwards in the car told Papa that if that man was the head of education, Texas must be in a bad way. In the end our family was supposed to have seven geniuses and I, thankfully, was only a near-genius.

One story, but probably occurred later, concerns my little brother David. He had become an avid baseball player at the age of nine, an activity that kept him out of doors and helped him overcome his allergies. One afternoon Toby, as he was then called, and a teammate were spending an inordinate amount of time in his bedroom, laughing their heads off. As the youngest child he got away with a lot, but Mama thought this bore investigating.

"Just what are you boys up to?"

Finally Toby admitted, "We know some dirty words and we were writing them down."

She stretched out her hand for the paper. "Let me see. Hmm. You've misspelled 'bastid'."

The summer before my senior year was another bummer — the first that we did not go to our summer home in Cloudcroft. Julia Z, who was to become a life-long friend, an honorary Rosenfield, was my lifesaver that summer. I don't think I could have born it without her. We went to the movies. We talked. We read voraciously. We promised each other great careers as artists; we picked out the titles of the novels we would write. We would be women of high moral character and enormous talents!

One of the things I remember about my senior year was that I had I had a terrible crush on Herbert S. He had been in my Confirmation Class. He managed to avoid me, probably (and properly) resenting that the school gossip column had linked our names. I wasn't invited to the Senior Prom, a slight Mama tried to assuage by waltzing me around the dining room table. How awkward I was, how light she was on her feet.

I had dreamed of going away to college — Bryn Mawr or Mills. Instead, the next fall Julia and I followed Teeta to El Paso's Texas College of Mines, now known as University of Texas at El Paso (UTEP). Teeta and I usually walked the few miles between our house and the small campus. I think Leon's class (he graduated in 1932) was the first time Mines offered a B.A. in Liberal Arts. The big difference between Mines and High School, as far as I was concerned, was that you could cut class and no note would be sent home to your mother.

"Let's cut the rest of our classes today," I would say to Julia. She would agree and then before I could dissuade her, would run off to tell the professors that she would not be in class that day. I wanted the feeling that we were doing something naughty; she needed her job at the campus library and didn't want to jeopardize it.

Freshmen at Mines were gently hazed. "No beanie today?" an upperclassman would see that you were without the cap that marked you as a freshman. "Carry my books!"

But we could attend the annual "Dog Patch Dance." The day afterward Mama heard from the Temple matrons how shocked they were that Nancy had taken a non-Jewish boy to the dance.

Mama could have cared less. My invitation launched George B's career as a popular campus stud but failed to provide a future date for me!

One of the college organizations was Dr. Zimmerman's "Quill Club." Teeta was a member and I soon joined. It was a very small group of would-be writers and while I didn't write anything memorable it was a good experience just to hear Dr. Z's terse dismissals of purple prose. Mary, always on my heels, began college at Mines and joined the Quill Club the following year.

———————

Our first year in Los Angeles in 1936, Teeta and I went to UCLA, she to get her teaching credential in California and I ... just to get my B.A. degree. Mary opted to go to the Otis Institute of Art. As an English major, I took English Lit (1700-1865?) and Short Story Writing. It was my first creative writing class. I had not yet found my voice — I was deadly serious — but I did have some facility. I volunteered to write for the Daily Bruin and was assigned the Art beat.

Along with George Papermaster, whom I had met in the English Lit class, I went to some of the galleries in downtown L.A. and wrote short pieces that were printed — without editing.

George had first spoken to me when I changed my seat in the English Lit class. (The only black student in the class was sitting where I usually sat.) "How would you like it if I moved my seat away from you?"

"Why would you?"

"You're Jewish, aren't you?"

"That couldn't be a reason to move your seat."

"Some people hate Jews. They feel the same way about them as you seem to feel about Negroes."

"I don't hate Negroes. It's just that I've never sat with one. I don't know how to act around them."

It must have been Mama's insistence that we speak accentless English that no one ever suspected that we Rosenfields had grown up in Texas!

George recognized that I was not hopeless, that my ignorance was not willful and indeed I was eager to learn. At the Religious Conference Building, the anti-Greek center of the campus, he introduced me to the campus writers, the activists, the radicals.

UCLA had a hefty "out of state fee" and since I wouldn't consider going for a teaching credential, I dropped out after one semester. I always thought I would go back later. But I stayed in touch with George. For a number of months I worked at the bakery in Westwood, and so was able to spend time at the campus.

George could have been painted by his favorite artist, El Greco. Not knowing anything about homosexuals, I had romantic notions about him but eventually decided he was a-sexual. Over the next few years George became "an honorary Rosenfield" and a willing escort if Mary, Teeta or I needed one.

It was George who persuaded me to sit on the Board of the Jewish Youth Division. The J.Y.D. was an arm of the Los Angeles Jewish Welfare Fund, created to get the youth involved in fundraising; but I found it an exciting venue where politics and social issues were discussed.

George soon had me involved with a youth group at Hollywood's Temple Isaiah. Our first project was a puppet show dramatizing the story of Esther, set to one of Prokofiev's dances. We set about making our own paper-maché puppets and before long Mary joined the group. The puppet idea died, unmourned, but the effort morphed into the Drama Group for which Mary and I agreed to write some skits. But the leaders of the Drama Group – Paul, Audrey, Kenny – were "radicals" who wanted to put their ideas into practice. The Drama Group would be a "holistic effort" – everyone was to participate in all the activities, everyone would share in the glory!

The original group of thirty dwindled to twelve, but Mary and I were committed. We spent countless evenings and every weekend for the next year and a half immersed in the Drama Group. We learned the Stanislavsky method of acting from Paul, who hailed from the New York theatre. We took off our shoes and danced barefoot to the original music written by Morrie, one of our members. We learned to move our bodies in new ways, inspired by Esther, a dance teacher from UCLA. We girls dyed the long cotton skirts and tee shirts we would wear and the boys dyed their pants and tops. We looked like a real dance troupe! And we honed our acting skills in skits we had written, working hard to be as professional as possible.

Finally we felt ready to perform an ambitious three part program: the dance, four skits, and an Anti-Nazi one-act play. We were to be one of the six fundraising events sponsored by the J.Y.D., all of which were held at the large auditorium at Rabbi Magnin's well-known Temple Zion.

Two days before the date of our performance, the Youth Rabbi from Zion came to see a rehearsal. He made noises of approval but turned out to be a rat. He brought word back to the Temple elders that we were a bunch of radicals, and that our offering was inappropriate to be sponsored by the Temple. Our dance, titled "Unemployed Youth", was not a Jewish issue; the skit I had written lampooned Aimee Semple McPherson (a Christian religious figure), and the one Mary had written satirized Hollywood (big donors to the Jewish community). Even the Anti-Nazi play was too political for them.

But the J.Y.D. stood behind us. Together we hired a real theater, printed and sold tickets all over town and for two nights we performed — creditably, I might add — at the Ebell, the large theater just off Wilshire Blvd.

A few months later I was fired from my job at the bakery. I quite surprised the "radical" youth from the Drama Group, moving so quickly from their kind of left-wing talk to actually joining the Communist Party!

Clockwise from top left: Julia at college graduation (1938),
Florence Bates (1940's), Nan and Julia (2007)

Mama and Florence, Julia and Me

Florence and Julia — two friendships that began in Texas and carried over to our lives in California.

Born in 1888, a year younger then Mama, Florence Rabe Jacoby (Bates) is listed in "Texas' Remarkable Women." She was the first woman to be admitted to the Texas bar, practicing law there for twenty years; and she also was an accomplished pianist. Unconventional and daring, Florence was already somewhat notorious when Mama met her in 1908. She — an unmarried woman — had gone barn-storming around Texas with a young rabbi! But that didn't deter the two young women from becoming friends — really a special friend — since it was she who introduced Mama to her future husband, my Dad.

By the time I knew her, Florence was handsome rather than pretty. She projected culture but in a loud, brash way, unlike Mama who projected an aura of ladylike refinement. In any setting, Florence became the center of attention. She was a marvelous storyteller with a vocabulary ranging from academia to the stable. Once you met her you would not forget her, nor that voice or her deep, melodious laugh.

Over the years Florence visited us in El Paso a number of times, always creating a stir with her furs, her perfume, her little Chihuahua dog. I think it was 1932 when Florence and Will Jacoby (they were married in 1929) visited us in El Paso. She regaled us with stories of their latest financial disaster but her long shapely fingers still displayed several large diamond rings. The Jacobys were looking for a place to stay and I happened to know that the parents of my high school friend, Ann Person, had rooms to rent.

That turned out to be a fortunate stop for them. Within a few years the Persons moved to Los Angeles, taking the Jacobys along with them. Person was a professional baker and by the time we moved to Los Angeles in 1936 the bakery had become the P & J Bakery. I remember how incongruous Florence looked behind the bakery counter, her considerable girth wrapped in the lilac and yellow bakery smock, a frilled yellow and lilac caplet set at a rakish angle on the masses of her gray hair, and the diamonds still flashing as she guided a loaf of bread through the slicer.

Within a few years Person died or retired. Under Will's management (no union!) the bakery prospered and he opened a number of branches. At different times Jo and Adele as well as I worked for them. The Westwood branch was the scene of my firing in 1941.

While the Jacobys had been happy to leave El Paso, our family's departure was far from voluntary. My father might have weathered the great depression if it had not been for two other factors. My brother Leon believed that the major cause was the theft of tens of thousands of dollars over the years by the trusted bookkeeper. By pocketing a slice off every payment going to the wholesalers, he had destroyed Papa's credit as well as robbing him.

But a major factor had to be Safeway. In the mid 1930's the giant corporation moved in to El Paso. It opened rival markets in every neighborhood where Papa's Piggly Wiggly stores were located. We were told that the loyalty of Papa's customers kept him in business far longer than Safeway anticipated. But by the spring of '36 Papa had no choice but to sell out. One of the terms of the sale of his Piggly Wiggly stores was that my father agreed not to go back into the grocery business for at least five years.

Should we move to San Francisco or Los Angeles? The fact that Mama had gained high praise for her acting in a number of Little Theatre productions made Los Angeles/Hollywood a natural choice. She would recoup the family fortune by breaking into the movies at age 50! Besides she was related to George Jessel and surely he would use his considerable influence to open doors for her. (Let it be noted that he made no move in that direction.)

As soon as we were settled in L.A., Mama made a beeline for the Pasadena Playhouse, where many Hollywood stars had been "discovered." Papa or Leon drove her. She got some small parts in the "Lab", Pasadena's experimental theatre. For a time Mary and Leon got involved there as well. I'm not sure why I didn't ride along. Perhaps by that time I had decided to be a governess/writer. I would spend the quiet afternoons writing the great American Short Story while the obedient children slept.

With the P & J Bakeries flourishing, Florence was no longer working and seemed to Mama to be at loose ends. Why not go with her to Pasadena one evening?

She agreed. It happened to be a "reading" for a new play, one that had been selected for production but not yet cast. The director, warming up the audience, asked everyone to laugh. And then again, laugh. One more time, laugh! Florence's laughter rang out above and over everyone else's and she was immediately cast as "Mrs. Bates" in a production of a Jane Austen play. And it was as Florence Bates that she became known.

Florence's career rocketed while Mama's moseyed along. Florence's success made it possible for the Jacobys to move to a fancy house in the Hollywood Hills, but the two families remained close for many years. They and my parents continued to play bridge together several times a week.

As I wrote in "In the Land of the Shoes" I was manager of one of the P & J bakeries when I was fired because I would not cross a picket line.

A few days later my brother Leon asked Mary and me to come out to Vista Del Mar, the Jewish Children's Home where he was a director. As we had in previous years, Mary and I helped make-up the children's faces for their annual show, a series of skits and musical numbers suited to children ranging in age from four and five to teenagers. After the show we went to Leon and his wife Bobbie's apartment for cake and coffee and to meet the Wintners. Lee had a marvelous tenor voice and (previously unknown to Leon) was a regular performer at left-wing events. His wife was a pianist. They had volunteered to teach the Vista Del Mar children various musical numbers and then provided the music for the show.

That evening when Lee heard my story about being fired he immediately told me about the Workers School in downtown Los Angeles. He also urged me to contact the Retail Clerks Union. Both of which I did. That was August 1941 and by my birthday in October I was an eager recruit of the Communist Party.

Somewhere about here I have to tell you about my skin problems and other momentous changes in my life, before and after Pearl Harbor.

Soon after we moved to Los Angeles my face broke out in a delayed case of teenage acne. I was also plagued by eczema in the crooks of my elbows and behind my knees. Mama took me to a dermatologist and I had ultraviolet treatments, forever it seemed, to very little effect. I was a sucker for every skin cream and finally settled on a product called "Mazon" that seemed to help a little.

I was still working at the bakery when I noticed a spot on my chin that wouldn't heal, but kept oozing. When Dr. Robinson (the dermatologist) saw me, he exclaimed in disgust, "Impetigo! Only infants and adults in very poor health ever get impetigo. They have no resistance to the germs in common dirt."

He prescribed a salve which I applied liberally. A few days later my face was completely broken out and there were blisters in the crooks of my elbows and knees. It must be more impetigo — the disease of dirt — ugh! That night I applied more salve and still more. I woke up early the next morning in agony. I felt that I was on fire. I washed my burning face and all the skin came off.

The mirror revealed mere slits where my eyes should be, surrounded by a face swollen beyond recognition. And my neck — it was swollen past my ears!

"I'm ruined," I sobbed. "Please, kill me. Somebody, kill me. I can't live like this!"

We had to take two streetcars to get to the doctor. Somehow Mama got me dressed, rigged me up with a big hat and some kind of veil. I cringed in the corner of the elevator going up to Dr Robinson's office, sure that I would disgust anyone who saw me.

"Mercury poisoning," Dr. Robinson pronounced. "What did you do, eat it?"

Apparently too-generous use of the salve plus my long use of Mazon, which contained mercury, had tipped the scale.

"You're lucky that we can reverse the mercury in your blood or this could be as fatal as carbon-monoxide poisoning."

Yes, I was lucky. I recovered fairly quickly. It was an extreme instance of the gentler "face peal" administered in beauty parlors. My skin grew back clear as a baby's, petal soft, blemish free. I wouldn't say it was worth the agony but for the first time in many years I felt confident in a close-up.

———————

So it was with this new face that I went to work as a clerk at Ralphs Market and attended Workers School. And it was there in the hall, between classes, that I met my dream man. Marvin, a fellow I knew from the Drama Group, introduced him to me. Handsome, serious, smoking a pipe — he looked like a young Earl Browder (longtime head of the Communist Party) — my ideal in every way. By the time I came home to tell Mary that I had met the man of my dreams, I couldn't remember his name! But I knew he was the one. And there he was the next week at the Workers School. He was talking to Marvin who suggested we go out for coffee after class. Thurman — that was his name!

We sat over coffee for hours. Thurman talked knowledgably about the stock market, world affairs, but seemed a good listener as well. And equally exciting, Thurman had a car. After dropping

Marvin off, Thurman turned to me, "Would you like to study with me? I have quite a Marxist library and I'm free most evenings."

Yes. Yes. Would I ever! And so it began. He came to the house, seemed eager to meet my parents and within days we were engaged. No date was set but word spread quickly. I still have the dishes one El Paso matron sent me on hearing that I was engaged!

Later I would kick myself for being such a fool. Although I was twenty-four, I was about as sophisticated as a twelve-year-old. Not a twelve-year-old of today, but one in 1941, in the world of Norman Rockwell. No, I was not seduced. I was as eager to lose my virginity as he was to take it. But what kind of engagement was it, with no plans, no ring, no commitment?

We went to parties together — always the same Party people, many of whom he knew but were strangers to me. We'd walk in together but that would be the last I saw of him until he gathered me up to take me home.

Once I asked him, "Shouldn't we have some protection, do something so I don't get pregnant?"

"You don't need to worry. You're far too skinny to get pregnant."

We were high in the hills above Hollywood, making uncomfortable love in his car, on Sunday, December 7. We came home to find the family stunned by the news that the Japanese had bombed Pearl Harbor. Next day, I said to Thurman, "The war changes everything. You will probably go into the army now and I'm not sure we should get married."

"You're right," he agreed, far too eagerly. "We can't plan anything now."

The end. Not quite the end, because by January I was sure I was pregnant and I was also equally certain that I would never marry Thurman. What was I to do? I wrote my darling friend Julia in El Paso, and she wrote back, "Come. Come. I don't know how — but we'll find a way to take care of it. Just come."

And that was the letter Mama found, hidden in the bottom of my underwear drawer. After a horrible family scene in which many unspeakable names were hurled at me, Mama called Florence and it was she who arranged the abortion.

Luckily Florence did not hold my union stance against me and she not only arranged and paid for the abortion, but brought me back to her house, along with a nurse, to monitor my recovery.

I remember long languid afternoon talks while Florence knitted — just another one of her skills. Was Mama entirely to blame for my unpreparedness, I wondered. Would I have done any better?

"What should I tell my daughter about sex?" I asked, presuming that at some time I would be ready to have a daughter.

Florence didn't laugh but answered, "Things change. Mores change. Who knows what society will be like when your daughter is 20."

How right she was!

Florence treated me much like a daughter. In fact, some months after her own daughter, Miriam, died (six weeks after giving birth to a little girl) Florence arranged for me to meet Dan, her son-in-law. I found him a wimp and, sure that he was quite conservative, spent the evening talking as radically as possible. Florence never questioned me how the date went but Dan returned to Texas promptly!

The summer that her granddaughter Anne was six years old, Florence asked me to stay with them while she was busy with one movie or other. I think I took two weeks sick-leave from my job so I could do it. Anne was a bright child, quite unspoiled, and I had fun. I don't remember if I was paid but I do know I was treated as a member of the family. And as part of the arrangement I rode the train with Anne as far as El Paso and got a quick visit with my friend Julia in El Paso before returning home.

Sadly, after more than forty years, the long friendship between Mama and Florence ended. By that time I was living in San Diego; but Julie, who stayed in touch with her, told me Florence's version. Although they were no longer playing bridge so often, they stayed in close contact by telephone. At some point Florence decided that there was little reciprocity in the relationship. It was always Florence who called, never Mama. Florence decided to stop calling and see what happened. Nothing. I never heard Mama's side of the story but I know she expected to hear from Florence when Papa died in 1951 and was deeply hurt that Florence did not call. In turn, Mama did not acknowledge Will's death a few months later. Florence continued acting for a few more years, but died in 1954. Mama continued her career in the movies and theatre past her 75th birthday, outliving Florence by more than twenty years.

———————

For Julia and me there have been no glitches. After she graduated from college, Julia stayed with us in Los Angeles for a short while before moving to New York. There she realized her dream of being a writer, of being involved with the arts, of participating in the exciting life of the metropolis.

Julia and I have seen each other intermittently, usually at family gatherings where she, an "honorary Rosenfield," was more than welcome. Three of my sisters — Jo, Teeta and Julie — made a point of seeing Julia whenever they were in New York. Jo even roomed with Julia for a time in the 1940's.

Julia and I did have a few days together when I was in Washington D.C. in the 1980's (as a part of an AARP training program), but most of our reunions have been brief.

On our way to Germany in 2007, Eric and I stopped in New York expressly so we could see Julia. The same sense of humor and intelligence that drew me to her 75 years before were undimmed!

Years ago, in discussing my sister Mary's admirable memoir, *Before They Disappear*, Julia urged me to write my own version of our El Paso years, a kind of *Rashomon*. So this is it! And it was Julia who was unhappy with my original title, "Bo-Peep at 90".

"Bo-Peep is such a passive person," she said. "That's not you."

And I think she was right.

Union Maid

There once was a union maid
Who never was afraid
Of goons and ginks and company finks
And Pinkerton's men who made the raid.
She went to the union hall
When a meeting it was called,
And when the company boys came around
She always stood her ground...

Oh, you can't scare me. I'm sticking to the union,
I'm sticking to the union, I'm sticking to the union,
Oh, you can't scare me. I'm sticking to the union,
I'm sticking to the union, until the day I die.

A version of this Union song was popularized by Woody Guthrie

Union Maid I

Joe de Silva, the tyrannical boss/president of the Retail Clerks Union Local 770, wanted me ? — Me, Nancy Rosenfield? — on the Executive Board? How remarkable!

At that time Communist Party members were assigned to either a union labor club or a neighborhood club. When I joined the Communist Party I was working at a Ralphs Market and was therefore meeting with other comrades working in the Retail Clerks Union.

In March of '42, Tony, the chair of our little group, suggested that we nominate someone for the open seat on the Retail Clerks Board. It would be futile but a worthy effort nonetheless. Elections in Local 770 were a farce, always had been, and we knew there was no chance for me — or anyone outside of Joe de Silva's tight little gang — to be elected. A member of the "old guard" — those guys, the somewhat menacing figures who were perpetually to be seen standing around the edges of the union hall — would be nominated from the floor and it was a done deal. Sure enough, when the actual Local 770 election was held, on cue the out-going officer nominated "Buzz", one of the old guard.

Immediately Tony rose, "I nominate Nancy Rosenfield. It is about time we recognize the contributions of the women members of our Union."

Another nomination? Unheard of! Not only that, but Joe was shaking his head and making a quick motion of erasing something. Joe's old guard was baffled. Nancy Rosenfield?

"Buzz withdraws? No other nominations? Nancy Rosenfield is hereby elected to the Board."

My affiliation with the Retail Clerks had begun in 1941, a few days after I was fired from my job at the bakery. "Nothing we can do about that," they said, "but we can certainly use another person on the picket line outside Thrifty." I think they paid me $2.00 an hour and paid for my streetcar fare.

Soon after that I went to work at Ralphs, just a short walk from Spaulding Drive, where we were now living. Pete, not the manager but the oldest and most knowledgeable of the guys in the produce department took me under his wing. Those were the days when the produce clerks selected, bagged and weighed the veggies and fruits for each customer. "A pound of string beans?" I became so expert that I could come within a single bean of tipping the scale at a pound. It was fun, and the informal spirit in the department was a world away from my unhappy memories of clerking in a department store at Christmas time. And I was having a great time talking politics and unionism over lunch and in the lulls between customers.

But as had always been my habit, I often timed in late. "You're late one more time and you're terminated," warned the manager. The next morning I was greeted by my co-workers at the time clock. Jane grabbed my coat, Ellie wrapped the green produce department smock around me, and Andy handed me my timecard, poised above the time clock. Each morning it was the same routine and I stayed on by a thread.

Then came Pearl Harbor and we were at war. There was a sudden rush at the army recruiting stations. Many of our friends volunteered. But Monday morning there was another aspect, at Ralphs. Within hours, customers pulled every can of tuna off the shelves. Loaded shopping carts literally rolled over my feet, piled high with sugar, butter, flour, in a rush to the checkout counters. What a disgusting spectacle of greed.

When our little cadre of comrades dared to nominate someone at that union meeting in March of 1942, we did not foresee that Joe de Silva would want me on the executive board of 770. Not me, necessarily, but a new face, a new way of doing things. Because Joe deeply, sincerely, wanted to win the war against fascism and he knew that the old way of doing things wouldn't get the job done. So I was the ally he desperately needed to force the union to change its patterns.

Joe's vision was for Local 770 to lead the labor movement in all-out support of the war effort. His first idea was to hold a massive dance and get every member of the union, their wives or husbands, uncles and aunts, to pay $5.00 a head, every penny to go to the USO. He was sure he could get a top-notch orchestra to waive their fee. At the first meeting I attended Joe laid the plan before the Board.

"Not union business," said one of the old-timers. "Let's stick to union business."

"Hitler has made it our business," Joe replied.

"It's a chance for Local 770 to show its leadership," I added.

But then the real roadblock: "You mean you want everyone invited? Every member?"

"Do you want even janitors?" (No black clerks in those days. And maybe a few Mexicans, but no white janitors.) "You want _them_ to come to our dance?" This from the vice-president of the union.

"You're damned right," said Joe. "Not only are they invited, I will dance with the janitor's wife. And my wife will dance with the janitor!"

And so the dance was held. And union after union followed with similar fundraisers. Today it may seem ridiculous to have been such an issue; but believe me, it was significant. Even though the attendance was token, the Retail Clerks held an interracial dance in 1942!

The dance and subsequent meetings also broke down one of the barriers which had made it possible for the old union leadership to maintain control. Local 770 had always held separate meetings for each division. "You can vote this down but the other divisions have already voted for it," was a mantra we had often heard. After the dance, Local 770 abandoned separate division meetings and met as one.

My role was tiny but I was there to second Joe's initiatives and as a spokesperson for women and the young. No one on the Board could challenge me in those areas. And Ralphs would have to think twice about firing me!

Joe Hill Song

I dreamed I saw Joe Hill last night,
alive as you and me.
Says I, "But Joe, you're ten years dead."
"I never died," said he,
"I never died," said he.

...

And standing there as big as life
and smiling with his eyes.
Says Joe, "What they can never kill
went on to organize,
went on to organize."

Another song popular at Union gatherings,
written by Earl Robinson and Alfred Hayes

Union Maid II

The winter of '43. Each morning's news brought us word that Stalingrad still stood, under the relentless Nazi attack. For me winning the war against fascism was of the utmost urgency, and working at a supermarket wasn't even close. So I hied me down to the Manpower Procurement Offices and took some tests. The first tests evaluated manual skills needed for assembly-line work. No talent there, but a few days later I took another series of tests: "Which one of these six drawings is different; complete this drawing by adding one line; what is wrong with this drawing, etc." I passed with flying colors and was hired by Douglas Aircraft at its Vernon plant.

The war was not advanced by my becoming a draftsperson, but what a wonderful break it turned out to be for me. We trainees — thirteen young women and one older man — got a crash course in drafting. Doc, our teacher, taught us some advanced math: logarithms, trigonometry and the use of the calculator (more of an adding machine than anything like today's calculators). We learned something about metallurgy, the effect of heat and cold on metals, and a lot about welding. And we were taught the rudiments of drafting, how to read blueprints, orthographic projection, and the fine art of pencil sharpening. The last four hours of our shift were spent "on the board", utilizing our new skills. After six weeks we were cut loose in the drafting room we shared with the experienced draftsmen.

Our drafting room was on the 2nd floor, above the huge machines — the reamers, the welding and cutting tools — that created the enormous jigs which the Vernon plant turned out for the Santa Monica plant where the DC 7's were built.

There were lots of opportunities to talk and naturally between the chatter about the latest movie and our bowling scores (what else is there to do when you work from three in the afternoon to 12 at night?) I talked union. My fellow trainees were not interested in joining the United Auto Workers, the union which was recruiting members in the shop. But they were as pissed as I when our promised raise, after three months, didn't come through. When our checks for the 15th were unchanged I announced that I was going to talk to the office. No one offered to go with me but I made the point that I wouldn't be just speaking for myself. I came back assured that (no thanks to me!) our next checks would reflect the raise and the back-pay owed us.

"Oh, yeah," they said. But sure enough the raise was there on the 1st of the month, and my credibility and that of the union grew.

A few weeks later I was asked by the UAW to testify in a court case before the NLRB (National Labor Relations Board). Douglas maintained that the Vernon plant was a division of the Santa Monica plant and was therefore ineligible to have its own NLRB election. Along with men from the plant who testified that our ID badges were "Vernon" and we would need a pass to enter the Santa Monica plant, I was able to show that our blueprints were labeled "Vernon", not "Santa Monica". The UAW won our case and the NRLB election that followed. My department did not "go union" but they would be covered by the contract nevertheless. Soon after I was offered a job with the union in their organizing drive in Santa Monica.

———————

The UAW had called a strike against North American Aircraft in June 1941. Although there were plenty of grievances, it was an "unauthorized strike" called by local union leaders against the national union's "No strike" pledge. Naturally the strike was labeled as Communist inspired and led. President Roosevelt ordered the army in and 2900 soldiers occupied the plant for three months.

Because I had not been "awakened" at the time, the rallying cry of "Remember North American" had meant little to me but I was to learn that it was a bitter experience that the local UAW — and the Communists — were determined not to repeat.

Since 1935, labor in the U.S. had been deeply divided between the conservative American Federation of Labor (AF of L) and the more militant Congress of Industrial Unions (CIO). The AF of L was dominated by the old-time skilled crafts (Carpenters, Machinists, Painters, Plumbers, etc.) and had never been interested in representing the "unwashed." But now the CIO — of which the auto workers (UAW) were a part — was moving into the shipyards and aircraft plants, where there were some craft jobs but many thousands of new, unskilled workers. The CIO not only threatened the prestige of the AF of L but its pocketbook as well. The AF of L galvanized the Machinists (IAM) to challenge the CIO wherever and whenever they started to organize.

Though there was little love lost between Slim Connally (Chair of the Los Angeles CIO Labor Council) and the Reuther brothers (the big honchos of the UAW in Detroit), the tenor of the times had changed. Red-baiting still existed within the CIO but it had lost much of its sting. The Communists in their ranks were good organizers, had rank-and-file support, and their skills were needed. The UAW was determined that unionizing the Douglas Aircraft plant at Santa Monica would wipe out the blot from the North American strike; the reds were needed for their success.

I was much too naïve to realize that my being hired was part of this whole scenario. I was given the title of "the UAW's first woman organizer on the West Coast." The fact that I didn't get the salary that the male organizers got (in fact I was paid as a secretary!), and didn't have a car and all the perks the men got, was completely irrelevant to me.

———————————

I was greeted with open arms by the UAW organizing group at Santa Monica. It was a wonderful mix of communists and non-politicos all equally committed to the union. Celia and Jean, Larry and George were comrades who had been working in the plant for a couple of years. But there were many others — strong unionists — who also made me feel welcome. Besides me, there were a number of field representatives (i.e. paid union organizers) from Detroit who had been assigned to Santa Monica. The pejorative cognomen "pie-cards" fit most of them. They had years of experience but were already getting fat and comfortable. Moreover, they felt that their role was strategy, not the day-to-day job of convincing workers to sign a CIO pledge card. My arrival signaled to the Santa Monicans that the union was serious about winning the NLRB election.

Celia was a welder and Jean an inspector and they had been able to find a house just a few blocks from the plant. "You should be living in Santa Monica, too," they said. I agreed. Although my family was now living in a large very comfortable flat near La Brea and Wilshire, I was more than ready to move.

When Teeta had finally gotten a full-time teaching assignment in Trona (300 miles from L.A.) it had been hard for Papa to accept an unmarried daughter moving away from home. But while there had been no possibility of her commuting to her job, Papa saw no reason for me not to do so. I argued that being dependent on snagging a ride every day from one of the field reps of the UAW was difficult and that I would be much more effective if I were in Santa Monica to meet all three shifts.

So after a few months I rented a room in a house across the street from the plant and a few blocks from the UAW office. I used to say I slept with my clothes on, would roll out of bed before the second whistle blew and before I opened my eyes I could be at Gate 27 with my leaflets in hand, greeting the shifts coming off work. (Many were justifiably leery about bringing Union stuff into the plant.)

Now we were able to keep the union office open all day and most of the night. There were always volunteers about and with their help I reorganized the card files, flagged the names of those who had shown special interest, cross-filed by department so we could see where we were weak and would need to concentrate. I kept the office swept and saw to it that there were always doughnuts and coffee on hand. And I became adept at running the mimeograph machine, asking the main office to try to find colored paper for our leaflets.

There was just one problem. Not only did most of the comrades want to meet every shift with a leaflet, they all thought they could write! I begged them to keep it simple.

"Nobody's going to read an editorial from the *People's World*. They're dog-tired after eight hours of work, and half-blind from those lights. We've got to get the message across in the five seconds between the time you hand them the leaflet and they drop it on the pavement." It was a battle, but I won, becoming the official leaflet writer. And I got them to agree to keep it down to one leaflet a week!

We gave prizes for the most pledge cards turned in each week. I made a big chart for the office wall "GETTING ANY LATELY?" Everyone giggled at the double entendre.

"Talk to the women," I urged.

"Not the men?" someone asked.

"Oh, the men are so easy. All we gals need to do is smile at a man and he'll grab for a pen, but you have to convince the women. You have to give a woman a reason why our union will help her. If we get the women behind us we'll win!"

If I wasn't at the Union office, I was at a Party meeting. I was living on excitement, the flush of doing what I loved and felt to be important, surrounded by interesting, exciting people. It was about that time that a returned soldier, Zane, joined the union. He told us he had been hospitalized, not for any wounds but because he had been unable to speak for months. He was cured by psychoanalysis and was an enthusiastic supporter of this new (to us) branch of medicine. Celia and Jean and I were enthralled with the idea that through a few sessions with a psychoanalyst we could overcome our health problems, our bad habits, our insecurities.

They decided that I was a likely candidate. Not only was I again having skin problems but they thought I was hung up about sex. "Our Jewish puritan," they called me. True, I didn't jump into bed as easily as some. (They didn't know about my rendezvous with Dave, one of the soldiers who were assigned to patrol the plant. He had started dropping into the Union office during my late nights there. Dave took me up to his sentry hut where we made love and ate bacon sandwiches. After a few exciting weeks he had been shipped out.)

So I made an appointment with Zane's doctor. I didn't know that the Party was adamantly opposed to psychoanalysis — not just because of "security" but because they regarded it as poor medicine. As soon as the Party heard I had visited a psychoanalyst, I was advised to drop the sessions and go see Dr. ____. She asked what I was eating these days. Not much. Coffee and doughnuts, mostly. "Won't do," she said, "you've got to have at least one square meal a day."

Though they had a perfectly adequate kitchen, neither Celia nor Jean was interested in cooking. They were using their ration books at a little diner nearby and it was costing them a fair amount.

"So how about I cook dinner for the three of us?" I suggested. They were delighted and before I asked them, volunteered to do the washing up. A few weeks later my landlord and I had a disagreement and Celia and Jean decided I could move in with them, sharing Jean's double bed. They had just one rule — no boyfriends in the house. Not a problem.

Since I was now living in the house, I proposed that I prepare three meals a day (available but not compulsory). Breakfast was taken on the run — dry cereal, coffee, milk. A bag lunch for each of us, a sandwich, an apple or orange and cookies (from the nearby bakery). Dinner was a real sit-down affair — meat, potatoes, a vegetable, and pudding or jello. And coffee was always on the stove.

To pay for all this I invented a "point system." Breakfast was one point, lunch was two and dinner was three points. Was a point worth 25 cents? Whatever — we started the first week with enough money — and our ration books — in the pot for me to do the shopping. Thereafter we paid up according to the meals we had eaten. We were so determined not to exploit one another that at the end of the month there were always enough left over for us to treat ourselves to a fancy meal "out." Another comrade, Leota, often ate dinner with us, putting her money in the pot and peeling off a few ration coupons.

Saturday nights there was usually a party at somebody's house. There were a few married couples but most of us were single. A lot of casual matings, plenty of music and liquor and the ever-present cigarettes. Our Saturday nights presented a good opportunity for getting to know good Union people and possibly recruiting them into the Party.

Oscar was a likely prospect so I asked him why he wasn't in the Party.

"I don't smoke," he said. It wasn't that smoke bothered him either. (At the time I was toying with the habit but soon dropped it.) Oscar said he could identify the Party members at a union meeting — they were the smokers. He seemed to think that smoking was as central to our organization as our belief in a classless society.

I signed him up but he didn't turn out to be much of a member.

Speaking of identifying Party members, there was a joke we used to tell on ourselves. One of the pie-cards from Detroit, who had been chastened about red-baiting, said, "You can always tell the Commies because they're the ones who stand up to talk about something that isn't on the agenda." Our tag line was, "Oh, but it is on _the_ agenda!"

The UAW had long since met the criteria for a NLRB election at the Santa Monica plant, but there was one delay after another. At last we were given a date. My cooking and shopping were forgotten as we got closer to the fateful event. Though we had done all the work to qualify for the election, there would be three names on the ballot: UAW-CIO, IAM-AFL, or No Union. The tension in the office was unbearable. We had worked so hard, we hadn't made any mistakes, we had done everything right — and yet ... The night before the election I suggested that we prepare two leaflets: one thanking everybody for our victory and the other saying

WE ARE STILL HERE!!
YOUR GRIEVANCES ARE OUR GRIEVANCES
WHEN YOU NEED US, WE WILL ANSWER

The pie-cards were scornful. Why was I being such a defeatist?

Me, the Bo-Peep, a defeatist? "No" I insisted, "I'm just as sure as you are that we'll win. But do you think you're going to drown every time you get on a boat? No — but you sure as hell see that there are life-savers aboard!" The second leaflet was cut.

And we did get the most votes but not by the required 50% plus 1. It was something like 41% for the UAW, 34% for No Union and 25% for the IAM. The run-off would be between us and "No Union". The second stencil was ready.

It was another six weeks of round-the-clock campaigning. Before the first-round election, it had not occurred to us that "No Union" would come in second. We had thought that the race would be between us and the IAM and that we would need to woo the non-union voters. Now we turned our attention to those who had told us they were supporting the IAM. Then Jean brought back word from her department that the IAM was circulating a card "10 reasons to vote No-Union." We could hardly believe it. It must be from Douglas. Certainly, it could not be an official labor position, however bitterly the IAM hated the UAW. But it was.

We campaigned many times harder. We worded our leaflets carefully. But to no avail. "No Union" won by 50.5%.

We were all in tears when Tenny, one of the non-Party stalwarts came into the office, "Why're you so sad, guys? Look how many votes we picked up — next time we win!"

Alas, no next time. Again we ran off the second stencil. "We're still here."

———————

We did win one election — that of Roosevelt for an unprecedented fourth term as U.S. President. The Union had a big drive to register voters and our UAW people fanned out into the community, hoping to get close to a 100% turnout. However, the campaign was not free of red-baiting, and union-baiting, with overtones of anti-Semitism.

But the U.S. Communist Party shrugged off these "aberrations." We were in the heyday of the "Browder Period." For a short period (1944-47) the Party felt we could operate like any other political group. Earl Browder, at that time chair of the U.S. Communist Party, believed that the outcome of the 1944 election and the ongoing alliance with the Soviet Union in World War II proved that the US Communist Party policies were accepted by the majority of Americans. We were, according to that interpretation, a part of the mainstream.

———————

I had been going with Mike for a while. I had rescued him from the clutches of a weepy, clingy girl at one of our parties and we had hit it off. He had come to work at Douglas as part of the union-organizing drive, but was now back in his regular profession in the building trades. Ours was an easy-going relationship, based on comfortable sex, our allegiance to the Party, and mutual respect. I had no expectations that we would get married or even that it was a long-term affiliation but was surprised when he gave me the reasons for breaking up.

"You're going places in the Party and I'm not."

"But why should that make any difference?"

"Don't you see — you're a good speaker, a good organizer, there's a future for you in the Party."

"So? I'll make speeches. So what?"

"And I'll set up the chairs?"

"You don't want to set up chairs? Then don't!"

"You'll be tired of me before we get to the chairs."

Mike was the kind of good, dependable guy that we — the Union as well as the Party — depended on. Had I belittled him, somehow? Hurt his feelings, unconsciously? I couldn't recall any instance and decided he was the one who was tired of the relationship and found this way of getting out of it.

But there may have been another factor. I wonder if it was a coincidence that it was Mike who brought me word about the "Duclos letter" which I had not yet seen. Duclos was a French Communist who challenged Browder's theories as anti-Marxist and fallacious. His article, printed in 1943 in France, was only then (1945) being circulated in the U.S. The Duclos letter would launch many soul-searching debates within the Party. Did Mike see me as having a future in a very different Party than the one we were in at present? (Incidentally, as far as I know, Mike did not leave the Party in the big exodus that followed the McCarthy period.)

Mike's departure from my life didn't break my heart but left a hole at the time.

⸻

After the UAW drive in Santa Monica ended, I looked for another job, and I was already at work at Hughes Aircraft in Culver City by the time of the '44 Presidential election. I wanted to stay in Santa Monica and have my own place, so I jumped at the chance to rent the apartment being vacated by two UAW comrades who were returning to Detroit. My new address said Ocean View, but I had to stand on my dining room table in order to get a glimpse of the sea. Built above a garage, it was one big room, with beaded board and whitewashed walls. The bed was at one end, the dining table and two chairs at the other, under the window. A tiny kitchen and bathroom were off to the right. My own digs! I loved it.

At Hughes I was working a ten-hour day and had to leave the house at 5:15 in those cold, misty winter mornings. And since I was partying or going to meetings every night, I discovered the blessings of a hot bowl of oatmeal before going to bed and again in the morning, kept hot in a double-boiler. My sisters could hardly believe that I — who had always hated the sight of a bowl of cereal — was voluntarily eating oatmeal twice a day. "Don't ever tell Mama," I begged them.

International Carpenters was the union at Hughes. Unlike most craft unions, it had organized the whole plant on an industrial basis. It seemed like a good place for me to be. I was hired as a draftsperson to work in the "loft," which meant I was usually up on my knees, crawling over the huge plates that were the jigs for airplane bulkheads. The plates were covered by a plastic coat of some kind and they needed to be lettered in ink, using a variety of stencils.

"I can freehand anything you need me to write," I said, but after a few failed attempts I agreed to use the stencils. It hardly needed any drafting ability but I was able to pick up the technique and enjoyed the camaraderie of the department.

Hughes' "spruce goose" — an enormous wooden cargo plane that would carry a payload greater than the C-47 — never fulfilled its role, or even a creditable one-time flight. But Hughes had another plane on the drawing board and we (a few Party members and our allies) pressed the company to hasten its production for use in the war in the Pacific. The Union meetings were rather hum-drum and after I spoke up — why were we doing so little to win the war? — I was elected to the Board.

The local union had an office in the Administrative building at Hughes, and there was one full-time employee, Joe. He had some title — not President, maybe Field Rep? No one seemed to know how he had promoted himself into the job. Joe was a big rawboned fellow, always dressed in a black suit. The poop about him was that he had been in prison in Arkansas or Oklahoma, had got religion and been pardoned. He was barely literate, but had a powerful speaking voice and a great baritone. I would have cast him as a backwoods preacher.

As far as we could see, Joe never did anything except walk around and try to schedule meetings with management, meetings which never materialized. We activists couldn't figure out how to get rid of him and finally decided that the best we could do was hire me as Secretary. So I resigned from my job with Hughes and went to work for the Carpenters Local. My job would be to write leaflets and put out a newsletter. And keep an eye on Joe. I was more than a little scared of him. I didn't feel that he was truly religious or had any devotion to the union. I must confess he never made a move toward me and never did anything to merit my fears, but being around him was a trial, nonetheless.

My dislike for him crystallized in April of 1945 when we got news of Roosevelt's death. The loudspeaker had just made the announcement and the flags around the plant were being lowered when he came into the office. He looked at my tears and sneered, "I suppose we're expected to lower our flag, too. If you think I'm going to be wearing a black armband, you've got another think comin'."

But then he volunteered to lead the prayer at the impromptu meeting we called at the end of the day. What a hypocrite!

He cemented my dislike in August of 1945 when the U.S. dropped the first atomic bomb on Japan. He was the one who told me about Hiroshima, gloating that our one bomb had killed over a hundred thousand Japanese, and showed the Russians what we could do.

"At least that means there will be no more wars," I said. "We can thank God for that." Ever the Bo-Peep! Which goes to show how little I anticipated the Cold War, and what lay ahead.

———————

Though I think I did good work in the union at Hughes, it was nothing like the excitement, the intensity of my time at Santa Monica. We — a corps of comrades and equally devoted union activists — had been bound up in a mission that had nothing to do with egos and everything to do with making workers' lives better. For many months we had been buoyed with hope, sharing all the high moments, all the laughter; and then in our ultimate disappointment, we shared our real tears.

San Diego

My friends Celia and Jean told me, "They're going to ask you to take the job of Secretary of the Party in San Diego."

How did they know? Because they had been asked and had turned the offer down. Jean was pregnant and though her lover had no intention of marrying her, she was going to keep the baby; and Celia was headed back to Ontario, where she had roots. "But it's right for you," they said.

So I was the third choice, or maybe the tenth. No matter, I jumped at the chance. It was September 1945. The war was over and change was in the air. When I told my family that I was going to San Diego to take the job, my kid brother scoffed.

"You sure make great career moves. In one year you've quit your job at Hughes where you made $40 bucks a week, to go to work for the union at $30, and now you take a job for the Party at $20." (The dollar amounts may be wrong, but you get the idea.)

Of course, I had to be approved by the San Diego comrades but it was *pro forma*. Recommended by the Party, what were they to do? True, my union background was a plus. I had been a Party member for almost four years, had attended Workers School, and above all I was eager and enthusiastic.

At the first meeting in San Diego, I met members of the Executive Committee. George Lohr, a tall, dour Austrian, was the Chair. Two couples, Lil and Harry and Dave and Lucia, as well as Enos and Laura were there. Lil was the most experienced and I

FBI Files for: Nancy Rosenfield, Nancy Rosenfield Lund, Nancy Lund

I was able to access the FBI files under those names through the Freedom of Information Act. Getting one's records is a lengthy but not an insurmountable task. It took me several months to get my box of almost 400 pages, neatly arranged chronologically. There were also thirty sheets that were completely blacked out but seemed to be records of who the

DECLASSIFICATION AUTHORITY DERIVED FROM
FBI AUTOMATIC DECLASSIFICATION GUIDE
DATE 05-12-2009

FEDERAL BUREAU OF INVESTIGATION

Form No. 1
THIS CASE ORIGINATED AT SAN DIEGO, CALIFORNIA   FILE NO. 100-6708

REPORT MADE AT	DATE WHEN MADE	PERIOD FOR WHICH MADE	REPORT MADE BY
SAN DIEGO	12/7/45	9/28;10/27/45	ADRIAN L. WILBUR dmb

TITLE	CHARACTER OF CASE
NANCY ROSENFIELD	INTERNAL SECURITY - C

SYNOPSIS OF FACTS: Subject became executive secretary of San Diego County
Communist Party 9/28/45 and has been taking leading part
in Communist organization since that time. Activities
to date set out.

-P-

REFERENCE: Report of Special Agent EARL P. STATEN, Los Angeles, California, May 27, 1943

DETAILS: According to Confidential Informant[   ]GEORGE LOHR stated
that NANCY ROSENFIELD, new secretary for the Communist Party
in San Diego, would arrive in San Diego September 28, 1945 to
take over her duties. According to [   ]subject arrived in San Diego and
took up residence at the home of LAURA STEVENSON,2927 National Avenue in San
Diego, where she has been living ever since.

On October 4, 1945, according to[   ]GEORGE LOHR, President
of the local Communist Party, spent a great deal of time explaining to subject
the nature of her duties and the local setup of the Communist Party. GEORGE
LOHR told her that the local group needed someone who was "conscious of the
party" and would see that the party had "functioning leadership". He said
that every Monday he and subject would sit down together and discuss problems
that came up in connection with the local group and the operation of the
headquarters office.

According to[   ]and[   ]subject has taken an extremely

COPIES DESTROYED 6-18-55

APPROVED AND
FORWARDED

COPIES OF THIS REPORT
5 - Bureau
1 - DIO 11th ND
1 - SID, Los Angeles
3 - San Diego

100-208196-6

INDEXED

EX-11

DEC 29 1945

"reliable sources" were and to whom they were reporting. Under the Act the first 100 pages are free, after that it is 10 cents a page.

I have included here and in following chapters just a sample of the FBI records over the twenty six years that I was "a person of interest." What was surprising to me was the number of "reliable reporters" they were able to get for such a minor player as me! Some of the reports were fairly accurate – such as my attendance at a People's World fundraiser or meeting – but others were wildly exaggerated or downright false.

SD 100-6708

active leading part in the affairs of the local organization since coming to San Diego. She has made arrangements for meeting places and has given speeches at Executive Committee meetings.

On October 17, 1945 Confidential Informant[   ]reported that ENOS-BAKER talked with subject and expressed his great pleasure that she was now in San Diego acting as Executive Secretary.

On October 22, 1945, according to[   ]LILLIAN HUNT contacted subject at the Communist Party Office in San Diego and asked if anyone had been assigned to take LUCIA BATT's place as speaker at the meeting of the East San Diego Club that night, whereupon NANCY replied that she was substituting for BATT. Subject told LILLIAN HUNT that TERESA VIDAL could come to the meeting of the East San Diego branch but it would be better if she would stay with the Spanish speaking branch since she could do more for that group. Subject said that the various clubs were very flexible and they wanted members to go to the club where they could do the most good.

On October 23, 1945, according to[   ]subject told ALBERTA FOUTS that the local group was starting a seminar based on five classes sent out by the state so they wanted full attendance of the County Committee and also the people responsible for leading the educational program of the different clubs.

On the same date subject and JOSEPH LANGER separated the membership list of the local CP into groups for the various clubs so that every member would be assigned to a particular club. Subject has had an extremely active part in the formulating of the boundaries of the various clubs and designating the local CP members who are to be assigned to each club.

At the Executive Committee meeting, October 25, 1945 subject told the group that registration of members is a critical job and terrific problem and claimed no work has been done in the Linda Vista and Logan Heights areas for the past two months. She said that "flying squadrons" would be formed to go from one club to another. She said that each club would have a membership director, which director would confer with subject and GEORGE LOHR, the general membership director, particularly regarding registration.

She told the Executive Committee that the County Council is to be an advisory body to assist the various clubs.

GEORGE LOHR, according to the same informant, told this meeting of the Executive Committee that since subject had come to San Diego "things were straightening out" and he did not think it would be necessary to continue to hold Executive Committee meetings every Thursday night.

UNDEVELOPED LEADS

At San Diego, California, will continue to report the activities of subject through the medium of confidential informants.

learned she was the one everyone looked up to. Laura was a tiny red-haired woman who offered me a room at her house. They all seemed congenial and I agreed to move to San Diego on October 15th, the day after my 28th birthday.

For the move Mama gave me one of the family trunks. I was embarrassed by its old-fashioned look — three wood straps over the curved top, a fabric-covered tray inside. (Silly girl, what I wouldn't give to have it now!) My few possessions rattled around inside it.

Laura's house was in Logan Heights, primarily a black neighborhood with a sprinkling of older homes owned by whites. The trunk was carried upstairs and I settled in. Did I chip in on the utilities? I don't remember. But I did chip in on the groceries. Since Laura worked the early shift (waitressing at the Grant Hotel) she would have dinner ready most evenings when I got home. Ungrateful me, I would complain about the overcooked vegetables. Got my comeback the night I commented that the soup wasn't even hot.

"Since you want your vegetables half-raw I figured you wouldn't want hot soup!"

I'm not clear just why Laura's two kids — Janet and Jimmy — weren't living with her at the time. Truancy or other teenage problems? Whatever, they grew up to be good progressive people who would make Laura proud.

Though she probably wasn't much older than me, Laura had lived the equivalent of twenty lives to my one. As a youngster she had gone to work in the fields with her sharecropper family. She escaped from that, thinking waitress work would be easier, only to see how badly people were treated there. So she organized the cooks and waitresses! A good Communist and strong unionist, she was low-key, never strident. We became good friends — a friendship that lasted long past my San Diego days.

My first day at the Party office, Enos came in. At first I thought he might be old (middle-aged was "old" to me) because he was bald and his hands were gnarled. Cement work is hard on the hands, I learned later.

"I got four kids," he said. "But that last boy, he's got blue eyes and there's nobody in my family that is anything but black. So

Elizabeth and me, we split up. But I'm keeping the kids because she's no kind of a mother." Then he went on to tell me about growing up in the Chicago west side and not realizing that there was a white Chicago until he was in his teens. He hadn't been in the service because his job in construction had been an essential one. He had an interest in San Diego's Cotton Club and had brought some of the top entertainers to town, splitting the proceeds with the Party.

I didn't say very much, my impressions of him changing as he told funny stories in which he was not so much the hero as the easy mark. And as he talked he looked at me in a way that made me melt. At Laura's a few days later, I climbed the stairs with him for the first real love-making I had ever had. Sex I had had. But this was different. This was love and suddenly — excuse the cliché — I felt complete. Here was a man with whom I could share everything. He was bright and funny and — as Mama would say — physical. Above all, he was as much a political animal as I was. I believed that we could become a team that would change the world.

And we tried!

So much happened that year. This was the end of the "Browder" period though it took a while for us to realize it. We were still under the illusion that because the Soviet Union had been our valued ally in World War II, the U.S. Communist Party could and should act like the Democrats and Republicans (only better of course!). In San Diego, as throughout cities in the U.S., there was a Party office in the downtown area. We announced our meetings in the paper, solicited membership and sent Party cards through the mail. George Lohr (Party chair in San Diego) and I met with our Congressman at a local hotel to discuss the issues we hoped would be on his agenda, such as employment and housing.

I have a lot of reasons to remember New Year's Eve that year, not the least being that it was the night I met Dick. But it was far from an auspicious beginning. Laura and I had met downtown to do our weekend shopping. It was drizzling by the time we got on the streetcar to Logan Heights, both of us loaded with paper sacks. One of the bags burst just as we walked down the aisle and Laura and I scrambled on our hands and knees picking up the oranges and apples that rolled under passengers' seats and between their feet. More spilled out of the remaining bags that we had set on the floor, rolling down the aisle. Everyone on the streetcar howled and we laughed until our sides hurt.

Once we got home everything conspired to keep us laughing. So we were in high spirits, not drunk, when Enos picked us up and we continued to laugh and giggle once we arrived at the party. There was quite a crowd, as many non-Party people as members, in a nice home in a new subdivision. When a couple arrived with a sleepy baby, we made a ring of coats on the big bed in the master bedroom and put him down in the middle.

It was after midnight, naturally, when we got ready to leave. Where was the baby?

Buried under the coats. Luckily he was fine. But why were the coats in such a jumble and where were our purses? That's when someone noticed the open window and we realized that with all the noise and excitement it had been an easy job for someone to pry open the window and make off with a dozen purses. I had Enos's paycheck in my purse, along with half a dozen checks and cash people had given me for their dues. Ouch.

We never retrieved any of the purses or their contents, but because there were no repercussions we doubted that they ended up in the FBI's hands. We surmised that it had been a neighborhood kid who found the noisy New Year's party too good an opportunity to pass by.

As for first impressions: Dick was sure that the new Party Secretary was a lush and highly irresponsible (shouldn't the Party dues have been kept secure and separate?). And I, in Enos arms, had little thought of this returned veteran. He was good looking enough but at 30 plus, still living with his mother? Not my type!

Enos and I had many Party meetings but very few nights together. He was sure that his car was marked, so he parked a long way away and walked to Laura's on the few times he came. Then in

February Laura's kids moved back with her, and I found a room to rent nearer the streetcar line. It offered no privacy and Enos was so uneasy there that I usually hurried out to meet him. But we talked about marriage and even drove up to Santa Monica so I could introduce him to my friends.

It was about February when the State Party reassigned George to L.A. and we were told that there was not enough money to keep the office open and to pay my salary (little as it was). No reason I couldn't get a job and open the office on some evenings and Saturday. I applied for a job at Safeway, but was not surprised that I wasn't hired. When the personnel man underlined my last name, "Rosenfield," in ink, I got a whiff of anti-Semitism. But within a week I was hired by the Jewish Agency of San Diego, filing and stuffing envelopes in their fundraising drive.

The Party hierarchy thought San Diego could go without a Chair for a period. Rather than take full responsibility I asked Enos and Dave to join me in a triumvirate (a term I remembered from my Latin class).

It must have been early in March when Enos suggested that the Party launch a campaign for jobs for Negroes in Logan Heights: "Don't shop where you can't work." Dave and I enthusiastically agreed. It was an issue that would reach outside the Party, uniting all the disparate groups in the community.

Enos and I drafted a very polite letter to the main Logan Heights businesses: Safeway, the 5 and 10, and the movie house, the Victory Theater. We pointed out that their clientele was Negro but none of their employees were. Safeway and the 5 &10 agreed to interview and hire from the neighborhood when the next opening occurred, but the Victory Theater's Mr. Hamecher said he would not be dictated to by an "outside group." (Laura and I, as well as Enos, lived in Logan Heights, but no matter.)

The editor of the black newspaper not only carried our story but offered to print our picket signs "Black and White Unite for Jobs."

THE SAN DIEGO UNION: MARCH 11, 1946

S. D. Communist Secretary Leads Racial Protest

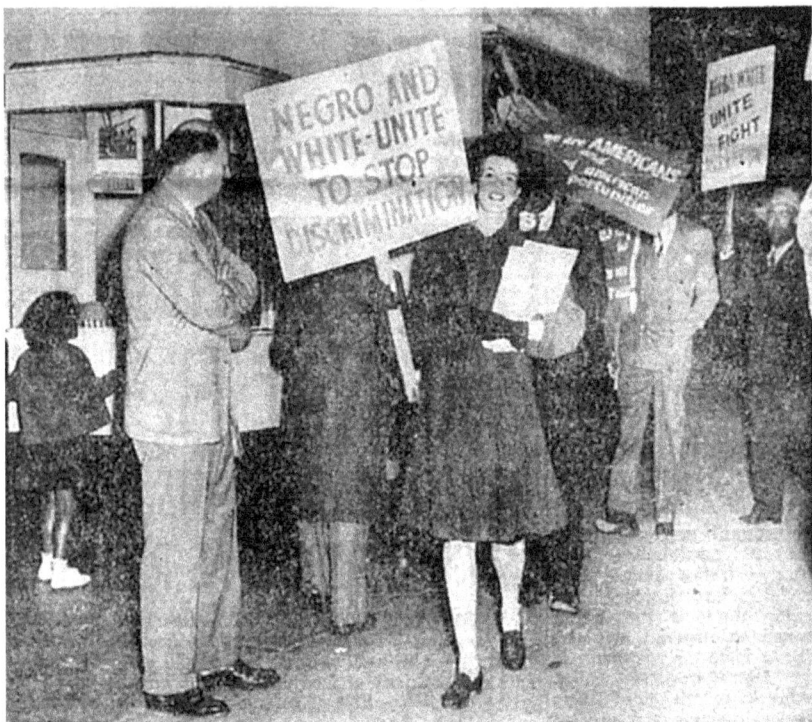

Nancy Rosenfield, county secretary of the Communist party, appeared at the Victory theater last night to lead the Negro picket line stumping for more jobs for Negro workers. At the left is Leo A. Hamecher, proprietor of the theater, whose refusal to hire additional Negro help led to the picket line.

Victory Theater picket line. See Appendix (1946) for the newspaper story that accompanied this photo.

Our picket line was wildly successful. We had no trouble getting people to walk with us. It was a cheerful, buoyant crowd. I think only one man ever crossed our line and we suspected he was paid to do so. A few days after the picket line formed outside the Victory Theater, J. F. Smith, the most prosperous — and therefore prominent — black man in Logan Heights, who had never had a white person in his home, invited me to tea! After the first stiff moments, Mrs. Smith and I found we shared a love of reading and the afternoon went well.

As for my job, the much-embarrassed head of the Jewish Agency explained, "Everyone agrees that it is wrong for Negroes to be denied jobs, but our funds depend on us staying out of politics. And having your name in the paper puts us in a difficult position, you understand."

I understood.

Mr. Hamecher sued us. Not only the Communist Party, but the NAACP and the YMCA which had supported the campaign. The judge, a long-time member of San Diego's bar, at the time composed of only white members, looked at the list of defendants and announced to everyone's surprise,

"As a member of the NAACP, I must recuse myself!" Ah, victory!

No other judge would take the case and so we won. Somewhat of a pyrrhic victory because Hamecher boarded up the theater and it was some years before Logan Heights had a movie house. But the community had rallied around us and I could hardly walk down the street without people running up to me and pumping my hand. "So glad you did it!" "It was high time!" "You and Enos — what are you going to do next?"

I believe that our San Diego fight for jobs for Negroes was the first of its kind on the West Coast, following World War II. But it certainly wasn't the last. Soon similar campaigns were successfully launched all over California and Oregon.

Our next big effort was to promote a Citizen's Committee in support of the striking workers at Consolidated Aircraft, still a major employer. San Diego was a Navy town and full of relatively young men who were able to retire after 20 years service. Comfortable with their small pensions, some of these men were willing to work for lower wages than the union was fighting for. The town was tense.

In our call to create a Citizen's Committee we were able to attract well-respected people from the University, a minister or two, community people as well as labor leaders. We hoped to spread the idea that the whole community had a stake in a favorable outcome for the strikers. But the political scene was changing – the Taft Hartley Act (an anti-labor law that sought, among other things. to oust "Reds" from the unions) had passed and Winston Churchill's famous "Iron Curtain" speech signaled the beginning of the Cold War. The "Browder Period" was dead and buried. So, in the Consolidated effort we acted as individuals, keeping the name of the Party out of it.

So what exactly happened between Enos and me? I had heard the stories about previous Party Secretaries who had all slept with Enos. In fact he told me about them. It didn't bother me. I was different and it wasn't just sex for me, as it had been with these other lightweight secretaries. Nor was I disturbed when friends pointed out that Enos was spending a lot of time with Y, a young mother who was trying to get away from an abusive husband. That seemed typical of him and didn't threaten me. We were two busy, dedicated people and things would work out.

Then, sometime in the summer of that year, Enos and I were at a Party event where there was music and though I was never much of a dancer he pulled me from my chair. I fitted myself into his arms, and he pulled me close. It felt very good.

"Miss me?" he asked.

"Some."

"What you been doing, besides meetings?"

"Not much." And then as we chatted I found myself saying, "I really had trouble getting out of the shower tonight. I just love hot water, can't get enough of it."

"Me too."

"I always turn it up, a little hotter, just before I turn on the cold water and get out."

He gave a short laugh. "Are you telling me it's all over?"

"Am I? I don't know."

But it was.

Dick

I was always walking. One of the young men on the Victory Theater picket line joked, "I could make a living just re-soling Nancy's shoes." It was some weeks after my name had been in the paper that I got a job with a bookkeeping firm. I was assigned to several small businesses, counting their daily receipts and depositing them. If I was late, as I often was, I would take a taxi to the first job. But then I would walk to the next place, and the one after that. It wasn't a full-time job, so I was able to walk to the Party office a couple of afternoons a week and every Saturday. I couldn't have afforded a car even if I had been able to drive, and San Diego's mild climate made walking the natural thing to do.

One October night the Shore Patrol raided the apartment building where I was living, hammering on everyone's doors, looking for AWOL sailors. I thought it funny and urged them to look under my bed. But the next day when I told the comrades about it, Lil was alarmed.

"That's a bad place for you. They could set you up and you'd have no way to prove your innocence. Get out of there and stay with us until you find a place of your own."

I ran an ad in the paper — "Single woman, non-smoker, no pets" — while I stayed in East San Diego with Lil and Harry and their two boys. The second week I struck gold! It was a "studio apartment" — meaning a living room with a pull-down bed, kitchenette and bath — on Date Street, within easy walking distance of the office in downtown San Diego.

I paid the first and last month's rent and was ready to move. Unfortunately, Harry, who had moved me and my trunk to their house, was working that day. No matter. Lil was sure that Joe, one of the older comrades who lived close by, would be happy to oblige her. The boys came back — no luck. Joe wasn't home.

"Well," said Lil, "go over to Dick Lund's and see if he's home."

"Wait a minute. I'd rather not ask him. He's ... he just isn't my type."

Lil hooted. "My God. I'm not asking you to date him. He'll do it as a favor to me. Nothing to do with you, personally."

Within minutes Dick came back with the boys. He hoisted the trunk onto the back of his little Chevy and we rode silently to Date Street, my few attempts at conversation dying on the vine. I showed him around the apartment then asked him, "Do you think it smells?"

"Probably been shut up too long. How about I open the windows?"

Two big south-facing windows, the sunshine poured in.

"Thanks a lot for bringing me."

"Think nothing of it. I'd do anything for Lil." And he was gone.

———

A month later I was striding up Date Street on a Saturday afternoon, a few blocks from the Party office, when I bumped into Dick and two friends, on their way to study at the Law Library.

"Hey, Nancy," he said, "how's that little apartment?"

In a poor imitation of Mae West, I replied, "Whyn't you come up and see me some time?"

Unexpectedly, Dick said a quick goodbye to his fellow students and wheeled around to walk up the steep street alongside me. Just as we got to the door of the apartment, I remembered the disaster I had left behind.

"Oops, sorry. You can't come in."

"I like that! Why not?"

"The toilet overflowed just as I was leaving — had to open the office at 10 — and I had no time to clean it up. I just threw newspapers all over the floor. It's an awful mess."

"Not to worry. I used to work for a plumber."

My panic had been uncalled-for. Only clear water had overflowed and not too much of that. But Dick cheerfully bent to the task of de-clogging the toilet. (I don't know where he found the tools. Did he go back to town to pick up his car? I don't remember.) I do remember noticing how neatly he folded up his shirtsleeves, and how he worked with an economy of movement.

When it was done he said, "There's a concert at Russ Auditorium tonight. Would you like to go?"

"Sure, if you can get tickets."

"Good. Then I'll pick you up at a quarter to eight."

The concert was dual pianists. It had been a long, long time since I had enjoyed a whole evening of classical music and I relaxed, letting the music wash over me. Occasionally I glanced over at Dick's handsome profile, grateful that he had invited me and happy to know that he, too, enjoyed music.

When the concert was over, we walked into the cool November night, arms linked. It was unspoken that he would spend the night. Keeping the mood light, as I emerged from the bathroom, I remarked, "Experience tells me that we may want a towel."

The next morning he said, "With your experience and my enthusiasm we should go far!"

I had the grace to blush, wishing I had been more subtle. But, yes. Perhaps this relationship might go some place. He was an ardent as well as an enthusiastic lover.

"I'm sorry about breakfast," I said. "I don't usually have any. But I can make toast and coffee."

"Fine."

Making toast under the broiler was an art that I never quite mastered. If I didn't burn the top, I inevitably burnt the other side turning it over. Nor was my perked coffee anything to brag about. I did have butter and an unopened jar of marmalade but no milk for his coffee. No problem, he said, buttering the only slightly charred toast.

He left shortly, but was back in the early afternoon bearing a large box.

"Oatmeal," he announced unpacking a small Quaker Oats cylinder. "Milk, jam, peanut butter, apples, bananas, raisins. Breakfast is a very important meal. And I brought along an apron, to save your clothes. And a box of chocolates."

I was amazed at his thoroughness, his thoughtfulness. Wordlessly, we fitted into a comfortable life together. Dick was a full-time student, studying law under the G.I. Bill with the aim of becoming a labor lawyer; and I was working at the bookkeeping job, keeping the Party Office open, and attending meetings almost every night of the week.

Walking during the day was fine, but at night I was dependent on one of the comrades — Bob, or Dave, or Enos — to pick me up for a meeting. Then one or the other would drop me off at the apartment by 10:30 or11:00 p.m. Dick — he the lark, me the owl — would be in bed. There would be a small lamp burning near the stove where a cup of cocoa would be waiting for me. I would undress, dropping my clothes where I stood, and crawl into the warm bed and his welcoming arms.

Sometimes we talked late into the night. He had not been entirely unwilling to pick me up from Lil's that day. His initial impression of me — that New Years Eve Party — had changed when he read about the Victory Theater fight.

"I was in the courtroom that day," he told me. "I wanted to speak to you, tell you how great I thought you were, but there were too many people around." After that he went to any meeting where I might be speaking, but always left as soon as it was over.

Unlike me (in so many ways), Dick had always been "a non-Party Bolshevik" — someone who believed in the Party's goals but never formally signed up. As a kid he had been impressed with the leaflets put out by the Party and would offer to distribute them. He would volunteer to tack meeting notices on telephone poles. In high school his best friend was a Communist and another friend was the son of a labor leader. While posted to England (489th Air Bomber Group) he arranged for the *People's World* to be mailed to him. Amazingly, his politics never became an issue. Something about his straightforwardness, Nordic good looks, and athleticism was so far from the stereotypical "red" that he was never harassed. That came later, through me!

Dick was shocked the morning I called a taxi to go to work.

"A taxi to go to a penny-ante job? I can't believe it. I never saw a taxi in my neighborhood, never — not even when a woman was about to have a baby."

Years later, Dick would joke, "My wife has a taxi-cab personality. Somebody is always going to rescue her." And to our friends, "Nancy married me because she couldn't afford the taxi."

My Bo-Peep approach to life and Dick's practical one bewildered our friends, but we didn't find them incompatible. Not only was he the lark and I the night owl, but he was a born athlete while I was the klutz. In school I would be one of the last chosen for a team and it was not unusual for one of the captains to say, "You take her!"

Looking at Dick's long slender body, with nary a bulging muscle, I could hardly believe that he had been a four-letter man in High School (baseball, basketball, football and track). In fact he would have probably become a professional baseball player except that he had to wear glasses. A botched operation to correct crossed eyes at the age of six had left him with only partial sight in his left eye, and in those days wearing glasses was unacceptable for an athlete.

A week or two after Dick moved in, I said, "You know I've never met your mother. What are you telling her?"

"Nothing. She's fine. I go by almost every day. She never asks about my girlfriends unless I get serious."

"Good. We're not serious. Just enjoying a good thing while it lasts."

I went back to L.A. for a few days at Christmas. I told the family I had a new boyfriend, nothing serious. I'm not sure they were even curious, just pleased that I seemed happier than I had been in a while.

For New Years Eve I had scraped together $10 for a new dress. Very becoming and daring! The bodice was black crepe, backless, with the high front secured by a ribbon at the neck. The skirt was taffeta, a print of tiny black and white checks.

As he watched me getting dressed, Dick kept saying, "If you wear that, I may not be able to keep my hands off you. Why do we have to go, anyway?"

I told him it was important because Lucia had persuaded the B___'s, Party "sympathizers", to host our New Years Eve party at their house. They lived in San Diego's posh Mission Hills. Good people sticking their neck out to show support at a time when so many people were dropping away. We had to go.

The B's friends circulated with our members, everyone — especially me — behaving a little more decorously than the year before. After a few dances, Dick and I sat by the French doors, enjoying the lights of the city below. Before long Enos came over with drinks for the three of us. I'd be lying if I told you I remember what we talked about. I'm sure it was political. But it was casual and easy and it came to me how much had changed in a year. I felt that I was the luckiest — and maybe even the prettiest — woman there.

———————

Shortly after New Years, Dick moved back home for the few days Julie would be visiting me. Dick arranged a date for Julie for Saturday night and then announced that his mother wanted to fix dinner for the four of us. Meeting his mother for the first time I found her to be a tall, handsome white-haired woman with a slight Norwegian lilt to her speech. It was a delicious dinner but I was uncomfortable that Mrs. Lund refused any offers of help from Julie and me. She served us as though we were at a restaurant, and she was the staff. Quite a contrast to our own mother, who expected to be waited on — and always was!

The next morning Dick picked Julie and me up to go to Lil and Harry's where we had agreed to meet Lucia and Dave. Unfortunately Lil and Harry didn't expect us and had gone for the day. As we debated what to do or where to go, Julie remarked, "I'm leaving this afternoon and you haven't done anything to make my visit exciting — why don't you and Dick get married?"

Lucia and Dave were enthusiastic. "Let's go to Tijuana and for a couple of bucks you two can get married!" (That was about as much money as we had — and no credit cards in those days!)

We swore Lil's kids, Richie and Bobbie, to secrecy and the five of us piled into Dick's car. In Tijuana, Dick bought a couple of inexpensive silver rings. Meanwhile Dave, who spoke better Spanish than the rest of us, was trying to negotiate a price for the marriage ceremony. At each place the man would look at the very pregnant Lucia and the price would go up. "Not us, the other couple," Dave would explain but could not get them to name a price.

Haggle. Haggle. We looked at our watches — Julie had to catch a train by 5:00 — and so we left Tijuana, unmarried.

"It's just as well," I told Julie as she got on the train. "Don't say anything to the family, anyway."

That evening there was a gathering at Lil and Harry's.

"Congratulations!" everyone shouted as Dick and I came in.

"I didn't tell, I didn't tell," said Richie.

"Oh, yeah. Then who did?"

"All I said was, 'I know a secret about Dick and Nancy and I won't tell where they went this afternoon.'"

"Aha!" we said. "We didn't get married after all, so there! But we'll know better than to tell you a secret next time."

It was not more than a week later when Lil came over to our apartment.

"I'm sorry you guys didn't get married in Tijuana. I'm not sure that those marriages would stand up in court but it would be better than nothing. The Party is very uncomfortable with Nancy's situation. They tell me that the police could haul Nancy in for "resorting" — I guess that's a fancy word for prostitution. It would be ugly for Nancy but very bad publicity for the Party, especially now. Dick, you've got to move out."

That was the moment I turned to him and said, "You wouldn't marry me, would you?"

To which he replied, "I don't know why not!"

"The sooner the better," says Lil.

So I immediately went to the phone and called Mary. "Dick and I want to get married and I wonder if you could get Judge Mosk to do it!"

"Married? That's a surprise! Julie told us she'd met Dick but she said, 'You know Nan, she's not serious.'"

"Well I am serious. And we'd like it to be as soon as possible."

(One of the unexpected benefits of our quick marriage was that Dick's mother didn't have time to build up a case against me, as she had with all his previous girlfriends. She had liked Julie and me, as she always did when first introduced to Dick's dates, and then – pouf! It was a fait accompli. Over the years I worked – and I am sure she did as well – to establish common ground. If I did nothing else for her, she gained Eric, her adored grandchild.)

On January 25, 1947, (as a favor to Mary, with whom he had worked on the Fair Housing campaign in Los Angeles) Judge Stanley Mosk performed the brief civil marriage ceremony at his home in Westwood, with my mother and father as witnesses. After the ceremony we went to Florence and Will's house in the Hollywood Hills where Julie and the rest of the family joined us. There was champagne and Papa toasted us with a few loving words. The setting, the champagne, being surrounded by my loving family, it was like a fairy tale ending.

Nancy and Dick Lund on their wedding day (1947)

Was it the magic of that official paper that made all the difference — that made our marriage (almost 60 years long) so unique, so complete? How, from an inauspicious beginning did it grow into one of so much love, such unwavering faithfulness? No, it was not, it could not have been, a piece of paper and a few mumbled words that made ours a true marriage.

Dick and I, without planning or willing it, crossed a threshold from non-commitment to commitment, from casual but very enjoyable sex to a wholly new dimension, from singleness to union.

Motherhood and All That Jazz

My dear friend Lucia told me about San Diego's prenatal and well-baby clinic so I enrolled. When was my last period, they asked. Hmmm — not quite sure. November? December? Then the baby would be due in August or September '47. So what if it were less than nine months from our wedding date in late January? No problem, first babies are often eager to arrive.

I was interviewed by a volunteer, a handsome very well dressed woman right off the pages of Vanity Fair.

"Didn't I see your picture in the paper last year?"

(Oh. Oh. Here comes trouble, I thought.)

"I just wondered how it would work."

"What do you mean, how would what work?"

"Communism."

"Well there would be jobs just like now. Only the workers would get a fairer share."

"Yes. I get that. But what would happen to horse racing?"

I didn't laugh. I said, "I guess we'd have to think about it."

Being pregnant felt wonderful! My eczema cleared up, my face was smooth and rosy, my hair glossy, even my fingernails grew. Unlike Lucia, who had suffered months of morning sickness with Bonnie, her first-born, my only symptom was a sudden distaste for coffee. I had boundless energy, out-walked my comrades when we covered a precinct with free distributions of the *People's World* on Sunday mornings. When I came up to L.A. for a Party meeting,

Nancy and baby Eric (1947)

Party Chairman Dorothy Healey glared at me. "Damn you — how come you don't even get sick like the rest of us? You actually look like you're enjoying it!"

I did. There was one surprising development, however. We were out of the apartment on Date Street — actually asked our obnoxious landlady to evict us to hasten our chances of getting into veterans housing — and stayed at Lil and Harry's while they were out of town. Carmen, a former farm-worker and doughty old comrade was there, too. One evening at dinner I asked Dick to pass the milk. Busy talking to the little boys about baseball, he casually replied, "Your arm broken?"

To everyone's astonishment I burst into tears, great wrenching sobs as though my dearest friend has just died.

Carmen said, "Nature is making great changes in Nancy." And to Dick, with scorn, "She hasn't done a thing for you!"

Dick was duly contrite and paid a great deal more attention to my sudden sunshine-to-rain barometer.

While waiting to get into veterans housing we found two rooms to rent from the Foxes — mother, daughter and grandson. Sharing kitchen privileges and the bathroom with the family was do-able, as long as I kept our meals quick and simple. Once I forgot to move the Silex coffee pot off the electric stove. I had just walked out of the kitchen when I heard a loud explosion. I returned to find the empty glass top of the Silex sitting on the burner. The bottom had completely vaporized, and the coffee grounds (surely I had put them in?) were nowhere to be found.

The Foxes never seemed curious about our unusual habits. I was gone many evenings, seldom came home with the same person who had waited outside for me earlier. When Ida Rothstein, from the State Party, came to San Diego for a few weeks we invited her for breakfast a few times, but otherwise we did not have friends over. Dick was going to school most nights but if he was able to pick me up after a meeting we smooched in the car before making a dash for our rooms. We were good tenants but surely they must have heard the nightly collapse of our bed, followed by our even louder bursts of laughter.

For years the memory of the collapsing bed at Mrs. Fox's would send Dick and me into gales of laughter. The bed wasn't broken. It was just collapsible. We braced it up, put books and blocks in all the strategic places, to no avail. Just when we thought we had solved the problem, just as things were getting their most exciting, the bed collapsed. Laughter and love for us went hand in hand, complementary not antithetical.

———————

That summer Dick was offered a job by Hansen, a Party sympathizer who owned a small tuna fishing boat. He was sure Dick would catch on to the routine quickly, which of course he did. They sailed out of Point Loma into Mexican waters where they fished for albacore, tuna and yellowtail. Since it was a small boat (3 tons?) they were never out for very long. Though Dick's fishing career was a limited one — five or six trips in all — it was enough for him to be able to hold his own thereafter whenever commercial fishing became the topic of conversation.

One day Hansen drove by to say he had to cancel their next trip because Annie, his housekeeper, had left town, and he had nobody to care for his two kids. He told us Andy was five, Becky three and a half, the result of an unlikely alliance with a belly dancer who had left him soon after Becky was born.

I volunteered to fill in until Hansen found someone else and suggested he bring them in to meet me. I was struck by the beauty of the two children — fairytale kids, complete with golden hair, wide blue eyes and a sprinkle of freckles across their noses. "We'll do fine," I told Hansen.

It was about five a.m. when Dick dropped me off at the house in Point Loma. I was a little daunted by the cob-webby front door and the half-rotten stoop but thought we wouldn't spend much time in the house, but would take lovely walks along the beach. The kids were still asleep. Fine, I thought, that gives me time to make a quick coffee cake, a nice surprise for them when they get up.

I opened the oven door in order to light it and released a torrent of cockroaches. They swarmed over the counter and across the floor and then completely disappeared. I slammed the oven door shut, the impact releasing another wave of cockroaches from around the burners. I gritted my teeth, struck a match and lit all four burners. Breakfast would be oatmeal.

When I sat the kids down for breakfast, Becky's eyes opened wide. "Milk and oatmeal? Annie gives us milk or oatmeal."

We got through the day, the kids following whatever suggestion I made. I made bologna sandwiches for lunch and opened a can of Campbell's stew for supper. I put the kids to bed around nine o'clock, wondering if I dared to sleep at all, imagining all the horrors when the lights were off. I made and remade the day bed in the living room, shaking the sheet and thin blanket again and again. No cockroaches or bedbugs. None that I could see. I sat at the kitchen table, reading until ten o'clock. Decided to keep my clothes on and laid down, leaving the light on. And woke from a dreamless sleep at six the next morning.

Carl, Dick's old friend — the one who had brought him to that first New Years Eve Party — came by the next morning just as I was getting the kids ready to walk to the nearby store. I don't know if Dick had asked him to check on me or whether he was just curious about this new arrangement.

I introduced the kids to him and said how very good they were. Carl put his thumb against Andy's cheek, pulling down his lower eyelid. "Anemic," he pronounced. "Doesn't have the energy to act up."

Luckily the fishing trip was a short one and I had only one more night at Point Loma before Dick got back. I told Hansen that Annie must have been pocketing the food money, because the kids were badly undernourished. I figured he knew about the cockroaches. And I said I wouldn't be back, much as I liked the kids.

"That's okay," Hansen said. "I knew that was just temporary, you expecting and all. I've decided to take them up to their grandmother's. Sheila's mother told me she'd take them, for the summer, anyway."

Mama had suggested that the next time Dick was out fishing that she and Papa would drive down the coast and I could stay at a motel with them. So a few weeks after the Hansen incident Dick dropped me off in Del Rey, just a few miles north of Pt. Loma. Papa, Mama and I had a nice day together. That evening we sat outside after dinner and, as the proprietor had promised, we watched a family of skunks — father, mother and five little ones — saunter across the patio and disappear in the woods beyond the pool.

Sitting there, enjoying the balmy July evening, I felt a weird sensation. I clutched my abdomen. "Oh, my goodness, Mama, something's happening!"

"The quickening," she said. "So that means you're about four and a half months along."

I couldn't wait for Dick to get home and share the wonderful sensation of the baby's kicking. He, in turn, felt that he had missed a special moment and told Hansen he wouldn't be going out again. I was more than happy to have him home, especially when Hansen described the storm that they had weathered that last trip.

"Poor Dick. He didn't know enough to be scared. But there were times when I wasn't sure we'd make it!"

———————

September — school would be starting for Dick so he suggested we drive to Mt. Wilson and rent a cabin over the Labor Day weekend. Some of our friends were leaving San Diego in a few days, and we stopped by to say goodbye.

Ben was getting ready to drive back east to college. We told him our plan to rent a cabin at Mt. Wilson. "Over Labor Day? Have you a reservation? No? Then maybe you better prepare to sleep out. I haven't room for this bedroll, whyn't you take it?"

We stopped at Betty's, who was leaving for Chicago. She insisted we take a flashlight and a frying pan. Lil and Harry had some junky old silverware and a knife we might use. We stopped at a market on the way and bought a tall can of tomato juice, bacon and eggs, coffee, milk and a can of baked beans. A roll of paper towels and two tin cups.

With no further provisions, and very pregnant, I went on my first camping trip. And fell in love with the experience. We didn't even have a can opener! Mt. Wilson had several camps and we drove around until we found an open site on the edge of big meadow. Picnic table, fire pit with a grill and a nice level spot for our bedroll! We gathered firewood and with the help of the newspaper, made a big fire. Dick opened the tomato juice can with the knife. After we drank the tomato juice, I rinsed out the can and it became our coffee pot. (I was over my distaste for coffee.) I did have my camera and somewhere there is a picture of that jaggedly opened tomato juice can sitting on the grate above the fire. The baked beans would never again be as wonderful as they were that night.

We rolled out the bedroll and not needing any cover, fell asleep under the stars. We were awakened by the most brilliant full moon, shining directly into our faces. We put on our shoes and took a moonlight hike. The meadows were filled with daisies and long grasses which shone like silver. It was absolutely still and magical. We could not have been more intoxicated if we had drunk champagne! We returned to the bedroll, crawled inside and slept till late.

The next day we visited the observatory, took long walks and slept again under the stars. I could not wait to tell the family how wonderful camping is. That is when Mama said, "It took man centuries to get out of the cave. I see no benefit in returning to it voluntarily!"

———————

Still no veterans housing, so we moved into a two-room apartment in Logan Heights, across the alley from Mama Epps. Mrs. Epps, a non-Party sympathizer who always attended our social gatherings, was a long-time friend of Lucia's and for some reason had decided to adopt me as her special project. The apartment had a toilet and sink but no bath; previous tenants had used the landlord's bath on the second floor. Mama Epps said that I was more than welcome to shower and nap at her house whenever I wished.

The apartments at Date Street and Mrs. Fox's had been furnished so now we needed a bed, a table and at least two chairs. These we found at the Salvation Army. Dick rounded up some apple boxes, which we set on end (covered with cotton dish towels that had started out as flour sacks), and we had a neat row of cupboards. I dyed the flour sacks red of course. More flour sacks at the window, and voila! We were set.

From the alley you went down three steps into the larger room, the only place for the bed. Mama's trunk with a bright Navajo rug thrown over it sat against the far wall, the row of apple boxes were against the wall as you came in. Our bed, a mattress set on bare wire springs, was under the one and only window. Which created a small problem since every time a car drove down the alley a shovelful of dirt landed on the bed. But really there was very little traffic. The second room was very small, enough room for the table and chairs and — behind a curtain and up one step — the toilet, and a drainboard which held the sink and hot plate. I never unpacked the nice china we had received as wedding presents, and took out just the few utensils and the minimum dishes we would need. Coffee, a few cans and our tooth brushes sat on a shelf above the sink. Toilet brush and soap under the sink. Milk and perishables were across the street in Mama Epp's refrigerator.

It was September and Dick was back in law school, taking night classes and working days as a laborer. Every day I went up the stairs a few minutes after 5:00 to draw Dick's bath. He would get home at 5:15 and just have time for a bath and a change of clothes to get to school by 6:00.

The second week the landlord, who was very old and extremely deaf, confronted me. "What are you doing?"

"Drawing my husband's bath."

"He had a bath yesterday."

"Yes. He has a bath every day. He works as a laborer and gets very dirty," I shouted back. "And he goes to school at night."

"Never heard of such a thing. A bath — every day? It will kill him."

It was the second week in November before we finally got word that a one-bedroom apartment in The Dells, veterans housing at the edge of Logan Heights, was available. Lucia and Dave, Celia and Harry helped us move our few possessions. The kitchen was furnished with a new stove and icebox and real cupboards. There was a short hallway to the bath — a real bathroom! — and a nice-sized bedroom. No closets but a large walk-in storage area opposite the bathroom. All the floors were black linoleum, the walls and cupboards off-white and there were big windows in the living room and bedroom. It seemed a palace to us — so clean, so bright! Still no baby, but now there was room for the bassinet my family had given us and the bathinette, a gift from the San Diego comrades.

At last, and only the second time we drove to the hospital, I went into labor. Between pains I walked the floor of the delivery room. Dick was allowed to be with me — up to a certain point. Thinking I would be there for a long time, I asked him to bring me something to read. He brought me the one-volume Complete Shakespeare. I don't think I opened it but it really impressed the nurses!

Labor was hard work but I probably was given whatever they gave mothers those days. Eric, at 8 pounds, 8 ounces, was born the following morning, November 23. I don't remember being cut but I do remember being stitched up after the birth and telling the astonished doctor, "Do a good job because I'm going to be doing this again!"

I wish I had the receipts, but it seems to me that my prenatal care, delivery and week in the hospital was around $250. And the care was excellent. I was in a ward with seven other women, none of whom wanted their breakfasts.

"Pass it down to me. I'm hungry!"

The other women looked enviously at my handsome attentive husband, who brought me a long stemmed rose in a small vase. "Today is our tenth anniversary!" I said.

"You've been married ten years and this is your first baby?"

"Oh. No. Ten months! We always celebrate the 25th."

That was the week of Elizabeth II's marriage. Naturally the radio and newspapers were full of the story, but on my bed was the latest copy of the *People's World*. Seeing it, Dr. N. (the one who none of us new mothers liked) scoffed, "The day we have socialized medicine will be the day I quit my practice."

"I think you should," I retorted. "There's always room for a Fuller Brush man."

My roommates loved it.

Dick was now working nights as a counselor at San Diego's Juvenile Hall, a job he had held before the war. I was — let's face it — completely unprepared to be alone with a new baby in a new place where I knew no one, so Dick had arranged for us to stay with his long-time buddy, Tracy, and his wife, May. I scarcely knew them and felt it was a terrible imposition, so after a few days I insisted that he take me back to the Dells and ask Mama Epps to sit with me.

And of course Eric cried all that night! When I gave up trying to sleep, I got up and we drank hot cocoa and talked till Dick came home.

Eric was a colicky baby and I was an over-anxious mother. Dick joked to our friends that I had a lab in the back room where I analyzed every diaper under a microscope. Bonnie was now nine months old so Lucia was eager to share all her hard won knowledge with me. The best way to fold diapers, the best way to fix formula, the best nipples. (She had given up on nursing as I had.) Unfortunately the first book she brought me was the Yale study on newborns. It sent me into agonies of measuring Eric against what a "normal" baby should be doing at birth and every few days thereafter.

When I told the visiting nurse all my concerns, she shook her head.

"He's going to grow up — so it might as well be with your help instead of in spite of it!"

Then — bless her — Lucia brought me Dr. Spock's *Well Baby Book* and I was able to relax, knowing that love would guide me over the rough spots. Eric blossomed, and when I took him to my six-week postnatal checkup, the nurses and volunteer women greeted me.

"Well, you finally made it — eleven months pregnant."

"You know what," I told them, "Eric wasn't over-term. He had no fingernails and no eyelashes when he was born. I wasn't even pregnant when I started coming to the clinic! I checked you out and decided you were okay. Then I went home and took care of it."

After those first weeks, I found that motherhood suited me, as had pregnancy. We settled into a routine. Baths and naps and afternoon walks. I had time to get to know my neighbors. Jo and Richard who lived right next door to us became good friends. Jo's four boys (aged nine to four) were the sons of her first husband, a pilot who was shot down early in the war. But she had energy enough to add Eric to her troupe.

We ran easily into each other's apartments, borrowing a cup of sugar or a tablespoon of baking powder. We didn't talk politics but I am sure she knew who I was.

Though Jo would take Eric at the drop of a hat, I wanted him with me, comfy in his blankets and buggy. He accompanied Dick and me to Sunday morning *People's World* distributions and to meetings. Nate, an old-time comrade from New York, acted surprised that I was busy checking to see if Eric had kicked off his "blanky."

"What did you think? That I was incapable of being a mother?"

"No. I just thought you were so hard-driving that you'd put him on a shelf and forget him."

Had I really been like that?

Lucia reassured me, "You were a bit hard on some of the comrades — but Nate is just lazy."

Am I Un-American?

The Korean War was more controversial than its current coverage would have you believe. It was the first salvo of the Cold War, aimed at letting the Soviet Union know that "The West" would use military force to stop any threat of Communist expansion anywhere. But the "red menace" did not scare everybody into calls for war. Many people felt that with the defeat of fascism, and the creation of the United Nations, there was now an alternative to war.

Opposition to the Korean War catapulted former Vice President Henry Wallace out of the Democratic Party and into the 1948 Presidential race as the candidate of the Independent Progressive Party (IPP).

Third parties had a long and honorable history in the U.S. The labor movement, woman's suffrage, and peace groups had run candidates for president such as Eugene Debs, Lucy Cady Stanton, Upton Sinclair, and Norman Thomas; and they had garnered hundreds of thousands of votes in the early 1900's. Now in 1948 the IPP hoped to coalesce labor and the left-leaning groups, plus the disenfranchised blacks, into a viable third party.

In San Diego the Communist Party responded with enthusiasm — and with characteristic unrealistic expectations. The IPP in San Diego looked good on paper and enough prominent community people lent their names, but the bulk of the actual work would fall on our Party members and a small corps of non-Party adherents. ("Fellow travelers" was the pejorative term.)

About this time, the State Party assigned Bernadette Doyle to San Diego. Smart, funny, warm, Bernadette was just the kind of leader we needed. Besides, she had worlds of experience in coalition building. We were on a roll!

The first order of business was a massive registration drive to get the new party on the ballot in every state. In San Diego our plan was to have IPP literature distributors on three corners of a busy downtown intersection and the registrar — who of course had to register everyone in the party of their choice — on the fourth corner. Dick, who had been a volunteer registrar for many years, was the champion registrar. He was constantly telling the IPP people to keep their distance but they seemed to gravitate to whatever corner he set up his card table. So there he was, trying to get Millie — not the brightest of our Party members — to move away, when his boss at the San Diego Juvenile Hall walked up. She frowned in disapproval and that evening Dick was fired for "inappropriate behavior" for a county employee.

Not only that, but a few days later he was called to appear before the governing board of the California Bar. Dick had excellent grades in the law classes he had been able to take, but he was a long way away from graduation. Why was he being called now when only law students who were ready to take the bar exam were asked to appear before the Board? Dick drove up to L.A. and conferred with Leo Gallagher, a well-known labor lawyer.

"Unheard of," said Leo. "You can fight it, but I don't think you have a chance. They have your number now, plus being married to Nancy. They will see to it that you never pass the bar."

Dick gave up his hope of becoming a labor lawyer and enrolled at San Diego State as a Sociology major. He had dropped out of college in the spring of his first year when he learned that a football injury would cost him four of his front teeth. Now, 17 years later, Dick would again be a freshman, this time with a string of "incompletes" to haunt him.

But we took this change in our stride. We believed that we were doing the right thing and our enthusiasm for the IPP was undimmed.

She said that according to MARX all minorities are not nations, and she cited as an example the Jews who were not a nation but who are now beginning to form their own nation in Palestine. She said that elsewhere the Jewish working classes are melted into the working classes and the Jewish capitalists are melted into the rest of the capitalist class, but with regard to the negro, the business and professional man must do his business with the negro people, however, negro workers go to the white capitalists and work with the whites.

Source B advised that ROSENFIELD also stated that prior to the Russian Revolution, the country of Russia was a "prison of nations" in which fifty-two minor nations were ruled by White Russia who put in White Russian schools all over the country. The Soviet Union gave all of these minorities the right of self-determination and most of them decided to stay within the USSR but to establish their own school system, cultures, and economies. As a result, the Soviet Union benefited because when these people were given what they wanted, they made enormous strides.

ROSENFIELD continued that the same would hold true of the negro nation in the South under Socialism because it would free that area and it would no longer be dominated by Wall Street. She continued that many negroes are leaving the South and that this will ultimately create a labor shortage there and force a raise in wages so the capitalists could then no longer pay negro laborers only $400 a year.

[blank] advised that on August 18, 1946, the Communist Party of Los Angeles held a special conference on the National Communist Party Concentration Program for the coming months. This meeting was held at the Park Manor Hotel, 2200 block on West Seventh Street, Los Angeles, and the San Diego Communist group was asked to send delegates. According to the informant, the subject attended and was accompanied by MARGARET GARTZ and LILLIAN and HARRY HUNT. According to the informant, GARTZ and the HUNTS stayed at the home of NANCY ROSENFIELD in Los Angeles over night while they attended this meeting. Upon her return to San Diego, according to the informant, MARGARET GARTZ related that the ROSENFIELD home is palatial, richly furnished and well staffed with servants. GARTZ stated that the subject's parents are wealthy and that her father made his money in El Paso, Texas, where he lived prior to 1939 when the family moved to Los Angeles. GARTZ continued, according to the informant, that the subject and her sister are Communist Party members, but that the subject's parents, although somewhat sympathetic to the movement, will not allow Communist meetings in the home and are otherwise apathetic toward Communism. GARTZ stated that NANCY has a brother who is attending college.

CONFIDENT

According to [blank] GARTZ exclaimed particularly over the fact that NANCY's bedroom in her parents house was equipped with a "whole room-sized bath" with adjoining dressing room, and that there were some forty different kinds of expensive perfumes on the dressing table. GARTZ

The FBI reports (1946) on this page and top of the next page are by one Margaret Gartz. I cannot remember any such person and since in all other reports the name of the informant is blacked out, I must assume that we knew her by another, an assumed name. As to Gartz' report of my family's "palatial home" — "well staffed with servants." Really! It was a rented duplex with three bedrooms and two baths and they had a part-time house worker. But I am glad to know that I was "willing to work in the dirtiest of places."

continued that she had never been in such a place before and that she was still nervous. According to [   ] the local Communist Party members estimation of the subject has been greatly increased due to the fact that although she has her parents' home at her disposal, she is willing to live in poor surroundings in San Diego and work in the dirtiest of places on any assignment. [   ] advises that the subject is now considered an old and trusted Party member by local Party leaders. Although she is considered to be a hard worker, according to the same informant, the subject is not inclined to be careful and has often been criticized as being erratic.

Source B advised that on September 12, 1946, the subject had an extended conversation with GEORGE LOHR, President of the local Communist Party group, concerning her relationship with ENOS BAKER, negro Vice President of the local Communist Party. According to the informant, LOHR was attempting to influence NANCY to break off with ENOS BAKER, however, the informant stated that NANCY expressed a desire to marry ENOS, but said that they had not made any definite arrangements so far. According to the informant, NANCY stated that ENOS was very particular and desired a feminine sort of wife who would stay at home and get his meals and pamper him. She said that apparently she had lost out in life and was just going to have what was here which is good enough for her. According to the informant, NANCY admitted that she does not trust ENOS and that ENOS tells one lie after another, although he might not do it deliberately. The subject stated that she used to be very scornful of any girl who went with negroes, but she was now in that very position although she could not give any reason for being there.

- P E N D I N G -

The second paragraph on this page is a completely false report of a supposed discussion between me and George Lohr. While some of the Communist Party leadership were unhappy with my relationship with Enos, George had been quite supportive. Furthermore, by September of '46 George had been gone from San Diego for many months. And by that date Enos and I were no longer even going together!

The report of my comments that I "used to be very scornful of any girl who went with negroes, but [I] was now in that very position..." is a complete fabrication.

Late that summer Bernadette came to the Dells to tell me that the Party thought it would be wise if I hid out for a while — I was about to be called before the Tenney Committee, or as we called it "the Little Dies Committee." State Senator Jack Tenney was making a name for himself as a red-hunter, with tactics modeled after the U.S. Congressional Committee chaired by Martin Dies. This was a forerunner of HUAC (House Un-American Committee). Their method was to smear through "guilt by association." Citing me along with the officers of the IPP would effectively discredit the new third party.

Eric and I left that night. At first we stayed with my sister Adele's in-laws, sleeping in their living room. Unfortunately I became very ill that first week. My mouth was full of painful sores and I ached all over. Since my sister Julie was married to a physician, she was able to get me in to see him. "Some sort of a virus that has knocked out your white blood cells," he pronounced. Whatever he gave me — an injection and some pills — worked and I improved rapidly.

A few days later Dick joined us in L.A. and we needed to find a place where the three of us could stay. Mary had friends in the Silverlake area who generously offered their place, with the one stipulation that we not disturb their many book shelves. No problem.

Eric, now 10 months old, had skipped crawling and had become a very competent walker. No sooner had we told him that the books were a "No! No!" than he zeroed in on them. With an angelic expression on his face he would back up to the book shelves; one arm would bend to his back and — Plop! — a book would land on the floor. "Why were we looking at him?" he seemed to say. "Books are always falling off shelves!"

I was a mother who was never going to spank her child but believe me I was tempted! So for the rest of our stay, Dick took Eric outside every moment that he was not sleeping or eating. Bernadette sent word that it looked like the Tenney Committee had bigger fish to fry and might not be coming to San Diego after all. The day after we returned home six members of the Organizing Committee of the IPP and I were served with subpoenas!

When the newspapers printed our names in the paper I asked my good neighbor Jo, "Will you contribute to the 'Nancy Lund Defense Committee'?"

"No," she replied, "but I'll take care of Eric Lund."

A team of lawyers from the ACLU came to San Diego to coach us on how best to answer questions we would be asked. I'd written my own speech and they had no improvements to suggest:

"Of course I am a member of the Communist Party. I am a woman and a Jew and I do not believe that either the Democratic or Republican Party has a place for me. The Independent Progressive Party opposes the Korean War. I oppose the Korean War. The Independent Progressive Party opposes the Taft-Hartley Act. I oppose the Taft-Hartley Act. I have been registered to vote as 'Decline to State'. But since I thought it important to have a choice, I have re-registered in the IPP to help put it on the ballot. I decline to answer any further questions."

We had been prepared for some defections; so when Lloyd Hamlin and Red W. declined to meet with our lawyers, we smelled a rat. That Lloyd Hamlin would be a "friendly witness" was not much of a surprise. He had been touted as one of the Party's best recruits, having been a member for only a few months. He was just out of the Navy, on 100% disability on account of severe arthritis. He had volunteered for every assignment, never missing a meeting. He told us his hobby was photography; he was just learning and the photos he showed us were not too well focused. Later, Bernadette and we understood — he gave the good copies to Navy Intelligence!

But when Red took the stand we were shocked. Red and his wife, Melissa, had been in the Party since they were kids. Unlike Lloyd, they never volunteered for anything, but paid their dues and led quiet hard-working lives. What motivated him to turn against his old friends, like Laura who had babysat their kids and taken care of Melissa when she was sick, we never knew.

There were a few good moments. It was hard not to applaud when Lois, the beautiful soft-spoken woman who had agreed to Chair the IPP, replied to the threat, "Unfortunately, I do have contempt for what your Committee is trying to do — silencing the legitimate effort of citizens to express their opinions."

Before the proceedings started, one of Dick's buddies, Bill R., insisted on sitting next to me in the courtroom.

"This is not good for your career," I told him. "Don't act like you know me."

"But I do know you and I've known Dick forever. And I intend to get to know Eric."

Luckily the San Diego newspapers didn't mention who was sitting next to me but they had a story on the front page: "Communist Party Secretary Nancy Rosenfield Lund waited to testify, holding her blue-eyed ten-month-old son."

"Blue-eyed!" I scoffed, "they can't even get the color of a baby's eyes correct!"

As I was leaving the courtroom, a newspaper reporter, Jeff Blum, asked for an interview. "Not today," I told him, "my ride is waiting for me."

He said he'd be happy to come out to where I lived. How about tomorrow at 11 a.m.?

"That's the time I give Eric his bath, but that's okay, I can talk to you while I'm bathing him and getting ready to put him down for his nap."

I had the bathinette set up in the kitchen and was just lowering Eric into the nice warm water when Jeff arrived. He asked me some questions, why had I become a Communist, when, etc. His article did not misquote me, but I found it quite remarkable that he wrote, "Nancy Lund *was acting like a mother* while we spoke."

Following the hearings, none of us were cited for contempt but the Committee must have felt that it had done its work.

In 1948 the IPP was on the ballot in most states, but hardly made a dent in the national elections. One of my good friends, who had walked precincts for the IPP with me, confessed afterwards that when she got into the voting booth, the specter of Thomas Dewey in the White House made her shudder, and she pulled the lever for Truman. It was very close. In fact Dewey was announced the winner on radio, but the next morning Truman's reelection was secure.

Red-baiting was an effective tool. Not only did it affect the IPP, it defeated Helen Gahagan Douglas, a middle-of the-road Democrat, and countless others. Our third-party hopes dwindled, and the Korean War dragged on. Four years later (1952) I voted for Eisenhower, convinced that he was a better man to end the war than the Democratic candidate, Adlai Stevenson.

The Dells

We had been in the Dells only a short while when Dick had asked for permission to put up a clothesline on the empty space next to our unit. The project's buildings were single story, with four units to a building. Built for veterans and low-income families there must have been close to 80 families. Soon after our clothesline was erected, clothes poles and lines dotted the project. We hadn't had much luck getting new readers for the *People's World* in the Dells but we were making progress on other fronts.

When Dick asked for paint to spruce up our apartment, the manager said, "No way. We give you paint and everyone else will want the same — just like you and your clothesline." Dick pointed to the FHA regulations outlining the rights of tenants.

"Tenants' Council?" laughed the manager, "go ahead, but I don't have to meet with you." But of course he did. And the Tenants' Council had more than paint on its agenda. "Why were all the black families on one side of the project?" we wanted to know. "Why weren't there street lights in that part of the project? Why didn't the school bus pick up the kids from the Dells? Who decided that the bus which ran past our project couldn't stop to pick up passengers?"

Under the watchful eye of the Council, new tenants landed in whichever unit was available and the lines of segregation blurred a bit. We found out that there had always been street lights in the "black" section, they just hadn't been hooked up! The school bus started picking up kids in the Dells but the bus that ran by the project was an Express, so our people still had to walk a half a mile to catch it.

CONFIDENTIAL

part in the affairs of the Dells Tenant Council then existing in the Dells Housing Project. [T-6] stated that the Subject and her husband distributed what, in his opinion, was Communist literature in the housing area at this same time. [T-6] pointed out that about half of the tenants in this project were negroes and the other half white. [T-6] advised that the Subject's husband, who is a COMMUNIST PARTY member, according to T-1, did not himself seek office in the Tenant Council, but seemed to guide and influence persons who did seek those offices.

[San Diego T-6] advised that in November 1948 the Subject and her husband attempted to organize an "Allied Tenants Council" which would represent tenants in all of the seventeen public housing authority projects in the San Diego area. Further, that at a meeting held at the Community Hall, in the Dells project, one CHARLES H. BECK, whom the Subject and her husband seemed to control and influence, gave a "fiery speech" stating that if the Allied Tenants Council were formed they would represent 17000 families and would then "demand" that Federal Housing not be disposed of and "demand that their rights be protected". [San Diego T-6] advised that one of the Housing Authority officers thereafter advised those present that this method of action was not, in his opinion, in line with Democratic principles, and as a result thereof the Subject's efforts to establish this organization were discontinued.

[T-6] related that the Subject and her husband were responsible for a number of leaflets distributed in the Dells Housing Area during January and February 1949. These leaflets advocated that public housing be retained by the Government and that more be built. One of the leaflets also advertised the "Negro History Week" meeting at the Dells Community House. [T-1] has advised that the "Negro History Week" is a vehicle used each year by the CP to appeal to the negro people.

[On September 22, 1949, San Diego T-8] of known reliability, advised that the Subject was then a subscriber to the Communist newspaper, the "Daily People's World". She held a yearly subscription which of that date was due to expire March 17, 1950. [T-8] advised that the Subject received this paper addressed to her as "Nancy Rosenfield, 3340 Sunnyvale Drive, care of The Dells, San Diego, California."

On December 14, 1949, San Diego T-2 of known reliability, reported that the Subject planned to attend a San Diego City Council hearing on December 15, 1949, at which a hearing would be held regarding the advisability of discontinuing rent control in San Diego. T-2 added that a number of CP members and members of the CP controlled Independent Progressive Party planned to attend this meeting and protest any measure to discontinue rent control.

On December 20, 1949, San Diego T-3, of known reliability, advised that the Subject conferred with CELIA SHERMIS that day regarding

From the FBI files (1949)

104

We had been married more than a year but Dick's mother had never asked us for dinner since that first time when Julie visited, before we were married. Nor had she visited us at the Dells or any of our earlier abodes. Dick and I, together and separately, had been inviting her to dinner each time we dropped in at her house but she always had some excuse. Then suddenly, in April, as my second pregnancy was well along, she announced, "Next Sunday will be fine."

I planned the meal carefully and sent Dick out to buy lamb chops, baking potatoes, fresh peas, an angel-food cake and ice cream. I unpacked one of Mama's linen tablecloths and put a single rose in a cut-glass vase in the center of the table, three chairs and three place settings. The silver, unwrapped and polished, looked very elegant. The peas were ready, chops were in the broiler, the potatoes already baked when Dick went to pick up his mother. And there she was, dressed to the nines, along with her long-time friend Mrs. Notter.

"I'm sorry," Dick murmured after he had introduced her to me, "but what could I do?"

A fourth place setting and a fourth chair were not a problem, but what about a fourth chop? (Not only had the three strained our budget but it was late Sunday afternoon, the market was clear across town and might not be open.)

"It's okay," I motioned to Dick. To our guests I said, "Excuse me for a minute, I just have to run next door to Jo's."

It was the first, but not the last, time Jo would come to my rescue. "Darn it, I don't have a chop, but let's cut the end of this roast to look like a chop. Need a potato? I've got boiled potatoes I was going to use for hash-browns. You can just stick one in the oven and pull it out along with the baked ones. You're the only one who'll know. And you're more than welcome to these parker house rolls. I just bought them, but certainly don't need them for our dinner."

I came back from Jo's with a tea towel covered tray and even Dick could not figure out how the missing chop and potato appeared. The rolls, split and buttered and run under the broiler, were that extra touch which my budget hadn't allowed.

Mrs. Notter was a dear and her presence seemed to make the conversation flow. "You're more than welcome, any time we can get Mama Lund to come," I told her, and meant it!

After that there was a truce of sorts between Dick's mother and me. She would suddenly appear at our door, though it meant taking two streetcars and a long walk from the end of the line. "I just thought I'd iron Richard's pajamas! I know you don't have time."

Pajamas? I would have to find them, stuffed in a drawer somewhere, since we slept in the nude. On her way into our house she would pick up Eric, who was happy in his playpen just outside the kitchen door. "That much sun can't be good for him. Look how dark he is!"

I was hugely pregnant by June of '49 when Dick's mother announced that the Jondalls — Uncle Fred, Aunts Hannah and Min, and niece Betty Ann — were driving out from Iowa.

"I told them you use margarine and so they're bringing their own butter. You won't be offended, I hope."

Of course not. It was unseasonably hot; they had packed the butter in jars, but had run out of ice halfway through the trip. During their weeklong visit the margarine was preferred to rancid butter, but was never mentioned. I have pictures of all the Jondalls enjoying Eric's antics. I was sorry to see them go; their visit had been a treat.

When I called Mama, I told her how much I liked Dick's aunts and uncle and how easy they were to please, in contrast to his mother. I always felt she was judging me and no way could I measure up to her cooking, or her standard of housekeeping.

"Just remember that Richard is her only child." (His mother never called him Dick.) "She has devoted herself to him for 32 years and it must be hard for her to share him with you."

"True," I had to admit. "In fact she has let us know that since Dick was a perfect child, and Eric is almost as perfect, she can't understand why we should want another child. But she did make me two beautiful maternity dresses. Just in time; the ones I had for Eric were completely worn out."

"Well, you have to be grateful that she's taken to Eric."

"I am. But can you believe that now she's upset because I am not going to Mercy Hospital to have the baby? She said that being born in the County Hospital will be a mark against him or her when they grow up. I told her that every application I have ever seen has a line for the city of your birth, not the precise spot in the city! When Dick and I try to talk to her about politics she turns a deaf ear. Her authorities are always 'the lady on the bus' or 'the man at the market.'"

Benjamin was born June 29. It was an easy birth and after five days in the hospital (the protocol at the time) I was anxious to get home. Jo had volunteered to take care of Eric so Dick could work and go to school. One day, in our absence, Grandma Lund had climbed through a window, cleaned the apartment from floor to ceiling, washed and ironed all Dick's and Eric's clothes and left the icebox filled with her home-baked goodies. I called to thank her and invite her for dinner. As before, she brought a friend but this time I was prepared.

As are most mothers, I was much more relaxed with this second child and settled into as much of a routine as Ben would allow. Fortunately he was not colicky but one of those babies who thinks sleep is a waste of time and prefers to be in the midst of things. "He'll be a handful to raise," the visiting nurse told me, "but he'll be worth it." How right she was!

When Ben was about a year old, a two-bedroom unit became available at the Dells and so we moved down the hill. I missed Jo but she and Richard were also moving — this time to a house of their own. As before, our apartment was at the end of the building, but instead of Jo we had a neighbor who was never home and whose apartment was overrun with cockroaches. Ugh! Our apartment was the scene of the story I wrote in "Land of the Shoes."

By the summer of 1950 the post-war building boom was over in San Diego and Dick was out of work most of the time. As a good member of the Laborers Union, Dick hit all the labor halls and finally found a job in Los Angeles. My sister Adele and her husband, Gene, offered him a place to stay and he was able to drive home most weekends. That was when my friend Celia announced she was coming once a week to give me a break. Celia didn't drive and living in La Mesa meant that she had to catch two buses and walk the half mile to the Dells. Much as I appreciated it, I protested that it was unnecessary.

She was adamant. "This is what a comrade did for me in New York when my boys were little. Motherhood is all very well but being stuck in the house day after day, night after night with two babies will warp your brain. You've got to get out — even if it's just to walk around town."

The third time Celia came, Eric and Ben set up a howl the minute they saw her. Their unhappy voices rang in my ears as I walked away and continued to haunt me for the hour I spent in disconsolate window shopping. I barely had enough cash for the bus and although a cup of coffee would have been most welcome I couldn't rationalize spending twenty-five cents in town when I had coffee at home.

I practiced the little speech I was going to make the minute I got home: "I really appreciate what you're doing, Celia, but this is absolutely the last time. I just spent the most miserable two hours of my life, the boys are miserable and it can't be any fun for you listening to them cry."

But before I was well into the door Celia told me, "We've had a wonderful time. The minute you were out of sight Eric said to Ben, 'We not cry, Benny. Gimme cookie.' And they've played like angels ever since." A milestone had been reached.

———

September 4, 1950 was my father's 70th birthday, and since Dick was already in Los Angeles I persuaded Grandma Lund to come with me and the two little boys on the train. Dick joined us at my folks' and we all slept in the big room upstairs where Mary, Jo and I had slept eight years before.

All the years we were growing up none of us bothered Papa when he was reading the morning newspaper. So I was a little apprehensive when Eric pushed the paper to one side and said, "Read me."

Papa smiled, reached down and pulled Eric up to his side, "I don't read the funnies. But your Dad and I like the sport page so let's see what the Dodgers are doing today."

Papa's 70th was quite an occasion — seven of us together for a few days, only Teeta missing. Adele, of course, with Gene and their two kids. Julie's husband, Walt, seemed to avoid the family events, but she was there, briefly, with Greg, who was a few months younger than Ben. Jo and Tip came from Florida and Dave got leave from the Navy. (I think he spent his four-year hitch playing baseball.) Leon and Bobbie were there, and Mary, looking a little peaked after a tonsillectomy, made it complete.

———

It was a few months later when Dick and I decided that we should move to L.A.; his commute and our separation made no sense. Little by little, the core of the Party of San Diego had moved north, where we would never again be as influential. Our friends Lil and Harry had moved to L.A. before us. When they left San Diego she hadn't told anyone she was pregnant and so I was surprised to learn that their third boy had been born in '49. Lucia and Dave were already living in the Valley and Celia and her husband, Harry, followed a few years later.

If Dick and I faced some hard times, they were nothing to compare with the problems Dave and Lucia had to grapple with. In the height of our fight against the Taft-Hartley Act, Dave had been the sacrificial lamb. Passed in the midst of the McCarthy era, Taft-Hartley stipulated that if the unions did not rid themselves of reds they would face sanctions, including loss of work on any government contracts. President Truman, elected in '48, was strongly anti-union and he not only signed the law but saw that it was immediately implemented.

San Diego's Labor Council had the reputation of being "pink." The state Communist Party let us know that if any group could weather the storm, it would be us. At our Party Board meetings in San Diego we debated what we could — what we should — do. What if one of our members came out openly as a

Communist? Born and raised right here in San Diego, Dave was not only a former President of the Painters Union, he was an excellent craftsman and immensely popular as well. Who could do a better job of dispelling the image of a "pawn of Moscow" than dear old Dave? He would be able to dispel all the canards about the Party. Enos and I, along with Dave, thought it worth a try. But afterwards I felt that since I was the most insistent and had pooh-poohed the difference between being "open" and "suspected", most of the responsibility should be laid at my door.

Of course, Dave was immediately expelled from the union, stripped from his post in the San Diego Labor Council and unable ever again to find work as a painter. We had counted on Harry, who was a member of the Painters and held an office in the Labor Council, to speak up. But he was absent — out of town — just when he was most needed. Probably Harry acted wisely for his own career but Dave never forgave him. Dick and I remained good friends with both families, but were always closer to Dave and Lucia. Neither of them ever mentioned my role in their plight but it was something I could never forget.

The Juggling Act

Read 'Community' instead of 'Party' and it is the juggling act that all working mothers face and will be pretty much my story as I recount the next few years. But I was far more fortunate than most women — I had a full partner in Dick.

———————

We moved to Los Angeles before Thanksgiving of '50. Papa was ill and though they suspected something about his heart, he seemed anxious to go back to work. It was mid-January when Mary called me to say that Papa was in the hospital. I stopped on my way to the hospital to buy him a gift — something silly, I thought, would cheer him up. As I walked down the long hospital corridor toward the room I had been directed to, I saw a familiar figure — Bert Givens, the son of Papa's employer and an old El Paso friend.

"Nancy," he said. "Everybody's gone. Your family...I'm sorry... You don't know..."

I looked blankly at him.

"Your father died an hour ago. But he's still here. Do you want to see him?"

So I had a last look at my beloved Papa — one that haunted me for a long time, his gaunt grey face intruding when I tried to remember happier times.

———————

The first place Dick and I rented in L.A. was on 47th Street, one of three tiny cottages at the rear of a big house. There were lots of kids next door, cared for by their grandfather. He whacked them soundly every time they went through the hedge that separated the two lots. "Sorry," I told him, "I don't punish my kids that way, but I do tell them they're hurting the bushes by running through them."

On the day I noticed a lot of red bumps on Eric's chest, I hurried next door to tell the grandfather that I thought my son had chicken pox and I was afraid he had exposed all of the children.

"Oh," he said. "Those red bumps? Don't worry about it — all the kids have been having them for a long time!"

Dick got a job at a big warehouse and we were eligible for health care. Kaiser Health Care was a good plan, plus my sister Julie's friend, Dr. Gordon, was practicing in the area. Eric had never run a temperature with the chicken pox but poor little Ben became very ill. Dr. Gordon (doctors made house calls in those days) warned me that Ben would have to be hospitalized if I couldn't get him to drink more water. Between bits of ice and fruit juice, we managed to get his temperature down, with no further complications.

The house on 47th Street was so damp that the wallpaper on the walls wouldn't stick. The first time a piece rolled up, it sounded like an explosion and scared me out of my wits. After that, piece after piece of the horrid gray paper rolled up without alarming me. I simply detached them from where they clung and threw them away. No wonder I had bronchitis much of that winter. After the family in the front house moved away, I noticed a lot of animals running in and out of the coal cellar. When I pointed them out to Mary, a Party member who came to pick me up for a meeting, she shuddered in horror. Dumb me — I didn't know rats could be that big and different colors. Obviously it was time to get out of there.

The next place we moved to was 59th Place. There were Party members, with twins Eric's age, living in the other half of the duplex. When they moved out, another couple, also Party members with a little girl, moved in. The landlord was alleged to be a Party member but left much to be desired, in both roles. The mother of two little girls across the street was also in the Party. Lots of kids on that block, lots of visiting back and forth.

Ben and Eric (1952)

Although Ben and Eric were usually good companions, there were days when they had to be separated. So I would walk Ben across the street to play with tiny, quiet Lorraine. They would take turns one riding his tricycle, with the other standing on the bar behind. Round and round her yard they went, perfectly happy for hours on end and not a squeak from either one.

At other times all the kids came to our side of the street where there were sidewalks around the entire block. One day Eric asked for a rope to tie his tricycle to the wagon we had given the boys for Christmas. Kids piled in and around the wagon; round and round the entire block they went, a mini parade. When the merriment reached a new pitch I decided to investigate. Here came Eric, peddling like mad, the wagon obscured by the crowd of screaming kids around it. And then I saw Ben, sitting buck naked on a chair in the middle of the wagon, flinging the last of his clothes into the bushes.

———————

Once settled in L.A., it was time for me to go to work. But what about childcare? Though Mrs. S. was highly recommended, when she told me she believed in and practiced corporal punishment, I looked elsewhere. We found Mrs. B. just a few blocks away — a nice quiet stay-at-home mom who would take the boys, Ben not yet two and Eric a little over three.

When Dick moved his mother to L.A., she became our babysitter. It was not a comfortable arrangement; keeping the boys and the house clean were her priorities so they were never outside. When Grandma Lund got a job downtown, at the soda fountain at Woolworth's, we were both much happier. Next we tried Day Care run by the school system. But I found that the boys would come home in the afternoon damp with sweat, never having taken off their jackets the whole day. The solution was to send them to school without jackets!

———— — ——

What kind of work was I looking for — clerking at a market or — if I could get one — a job as a draftsperson? I would certainly make more money as a draftsperson.

"But you'll never get a drafting job through the state Unemployment Office," my friends in the Party told me. "Your best bet would be to go to a Tech Employment Office. True you'll have to pay half of your first month's salary if it's a permanent job or twenty percent if it's a temporary job. But you don't need to pay up-front and nothing if you don't get a job."

So I signed up with a tech agency and was hired by the first employer they sent me to,

K C & W, a big architectural/engineering firm. It would be a long commute by streetcar and bus to West Los Angeles, making for a very long day but I was pleased to have a job.

It looked like a very temporary set-up, a series of Quonset huts on a big empty lot. I told the interviewer I had experience working with ink, at Hughes Aircraft. I didn't elaborate that working with stencils on the metal loft plates was not the same as freehand drawing and lettering on linen sheets, confident that I could make the transition.

I was one of a half dozen young women who were hired as "tracers." The job was a huge government building in Alaska.

Naturally it was in a rush. As the architectural drawings were being completed the engineers were busy with their side of the project.

We tracers were given small sheets labeled with a Detail Number and told to trace them on a designated sheet. Odd, I thought. Nothing but these dashed lines and balls. Never seen anything like that.

"What are we tracing?" I asked Millie, whose desk was next to mine.

"No idea. I just do what I'm told to do."

"Well, I can't. It makes no sense that Section 23 looks just like Section 24."

So I took the sketches for #23 and #24 to the engineer who had dropped them on my desk. "What are these that I'm supposed to trace?"

"Just do it. We're way behind as it is."

"Sorry. I can't do something I don't understand. What are these dashed lines and balls?"

"Dashes and balls?" he laughed. "Well, my curious little one, this is a big concrete structure we're designing. The walls are reinforced concrete. These are sections cut through the walls to show the reinforcing rods. Vertical rods are indicated by heavy dashed lines and horizontal bars are shown on end — like balls, if you like."

"Then there's a mistake in one of these sketches. If you're cutting a section one way the dashes are on the outside and the balls are on the inside and if you cut the wall the other way the dashes can't be on the outside, they should be inside and the balls on the outside."

"Oh, my God! You're right. Section #24 is wrong. I'm going to have to check the other sections, as well. That was a good catch. Thank you. M-m-m, dashes and balls!"

No, I didn't get a raise. What's more, when the job was over I found out that two of the tracers had been referred by the State Employment Office. Ouch! The job lasted three months and I was stuck with paying half of my first month's wages.

Back to the State Employment Office I went, and again was hired by K C & W, this time in their Structural Department in their main offices downtown. In the post-war housing boom there was a great demand for new schools and the firm seemed to have a corner on the market. There were drawers full of drawings, sepias of earlier jobs, which with minor changes and a new name in the title block completed the job. Others were more elaborate. I remember all the concrete that went into the covered walkways for Grant High School in Sherman Oaks — you would have thought they were building a freeway overpass! I was grateful to be working with pencil and eraser on vellum, rather than with unforgiving ink on linen as on the Alaska job.

———————

About this time Mama Lund made two outfits for me — dirndl skirts and matching short-sleeve "bolero" jackets. They entailed much ironing but I was grateful to have their addition to my skimpy wardrobe. One day as I walked to the coffee urn at the back of our long drafting room, an older man whose desk was on the aisle, motioned me over.

"Get out of this job! Get out before it's too late!"

I looked at him in astonishment — was he mad? What could he possibly mean?

"You have such pretty elbows! Get out of this job before they look like mine." And he showed me his inflamed lumpy elbows.

I tried not to grimace. They did look awful, as well as painful. "I don't think I lean on them much. But thanks, anyway."

Another incident occurred at lunchtime. Most of the Department went out for lunch but I couldn't afford to, so ate my lunch at my desk. Across the hall was the Design Department and one of the designers also ate his lunch at his desk. We were never introduced but we nodded to each other across the hall.

One day he came over as far as the door and said, "I've been watching you now for weeks and you eat the same thing every day, day after day. I figure it must be one of three things. Either you're on a special diet, it's your religion, or you lost a bet. You don't look like you need a special diet, I don't know any religion that is so restrictive, so I think you lost a bet."

116

"Wrong. It's much simpler. We have two little kids and I have to get them up and dressed and breakfasted before my husband and I leave in the morning. I don't have time to think about fixing lunch so every Saturday when we go to the market I buy five small cartons of cottage cheese and enough bananas for the week. That way I don't need to wonder what's for lunch." (I think Dick took an apple from home and bought milk from the lunch wagon at his job.)

———————

When that job was over I scanned the want ads as well as needling the unemployment office. Soule Steel had been running an ad for a long while. "Draftsman, experienced re-bar steel detailer wanted." Then, "Draftsman, some re-bar steel detailing." When the ad read, "Re-bar steel detailer wanted, will train," I applied. I was told that there was a probationary period of sixty days, after which I would be permanent with a fifteen-cent-per-hour raise.

A re-bar steel detailer is the essential link between the engineer and the workers on a reinforced concrete job of any size. The engineer's drawings show the size of the steel bars, their spacing per inch and where they are to be placed in the concrete. From the engineer's prints the re-bar detailer makes out a placing sheet — figuring out how many bars of each size and into what shape the bars must be bent for each phase of the building: foundation, walls, columns, etc. These placing sheets go to the shop where the bars are cut and bent accordingly. When the steel is delivered to the job site, the re-bar worker follows the instructions on the detailer's sheet. Voila! Ready for concrete to be poured.

What had been nothing but dashes and balls a year before were now my everyday meat. These were big jobs — highway bridges, big storm-drain tunnels, high-rise buildings. The detailers at Soule were helpful and I caught on quickly. Pay days were the 15th and 30th of each month. I went to work in the middle of November, had Thursday and Friday off for Thanksgiving and got a half a month's wages. Hallelujah! Christmas was a big deal with a Christmas Eve party and gifts for all the children of employees. It was a great job.

At noon on paydays we all trooped down to the Controller's office and picked up our respective checks. It was the middle of February and I couldn't wait to see if I had received my raise.

I tore open the envelope. "Damn it. They didn't give me the raise I was promised."

Ernie, right behind me on the stairs, laughed. "Don't be naïve. They promise everyone a raise but they never give it. I've been here a year and I have yet to get a raise."

"They will me. I'm going back down to the office and see about it."

Bill, our Department head, said, "Go for it, Nancy. I'll back you up."

Ernie was furious. "If they give her a raise and don't give me one, I'm quitting."

"Well, Nancy's worth it."

At the Controller's office I stood while he looked up the records, checked with Bill, tore up the check and wrote a new one. (Ernie did quit and was hardly missed.)

It was April when the founder of the company, Mr. Soule from San Francisco, made his annual visit to the Los Angeles plant. I saw him, through the glass windows of Bill's office, but he didn't come in to our big drafting room. When he left, Bill came over to my desk.

"I feel awful about this, Nancy, but I've got to let you go. You saw Mr. Soule was here. The minute he saw you he asked me, 'What's a woman doing in the drafting room?' I said you were doing a great job. I told him we never had anybody pick up the work so quickly but he said it didn't matter. 'You can give her the highest recommendation you want but get her out of the drafting room right now.'"

"You can pick up your check on your way out."

I thanked Bill and told him I knew that there was a new Fair Employment Law and I was going to see about it right away.

"Can't do a thing for you," the man at the Employment Office told me. "The law is about race discrimination, nothing about women. If they fired you because you were black we could go after them."

"Well, there is one thing you can do for me...take my name out of Drafts*woman* and put my card in the Drafts*man* file. You know as well as me that no one will ever call for a draftswoman."

It never happened. But each week when I went to get my unemployment check I insisted that the clerk (usually a woman) show me the men's file. Aha — Arch Rib Truss was listed as looking for a draftsman. "Call them," I insisted. "See if the job is still open and if at least they'll interview me." She was very reluctant but — surprise, surprise — the Truss Company said the job was still open and yes, they'd be happy to interview me.

I checked what buses would take me to Inglewood and set out. My readers today will probably not get the picture if I describe Mr. W. (the owner of the company who interviewed me) as right out of an Arrow Shirt ad. Suffice it to say he was young, handsome, deeply tanned and immaculately dressed. And nice! It was a small operation: a shop and three men in the drafting room, all designers.

They gave me a desk and I studied the sheet before me. I was stumped. My aircraft and reinforcing steel experience had not provided me with this new vocabulary. A stud? A rafter? A purlin? I put a vertical line on the sheet. Nope — it was probably a horizontal member. I erased the line and started over.

At lunch time one of the designers came over to my desk and looked at the blank sheet in front of me. "Got a problem?"

"Yes. I don't know any of these terms. I've worked in aircraft and reinforced concrete buildings but studs, rafters? If you tell me what they do, I'll know which way they go."

He gave me a brief lesson in wood construction and I had no further difficulties. But that job did not last very long — another company was suing them for encroachment of their patent and until it was settled Arch Rib closed the shop.

———————

Whatever daytime job Dick had, he was always taking night classes, trying to erase the "Incompletes" he had against his name from seventeen years before. He was taking a course in biology again and as usual was anxious to share his enthusiasm with us as we ate dinner.

"Nature is so wonderful. She really cares about protecting the young of each kind of creature. And the higher you go on the scale the more care she takes, being sure that the young are safe. Now a female fish lays thousands of eggs because neither she nor the male fish stay around to hatch them. A lot of them may never survive, but there's so many that some are sure to make it. A mother bird sits on her eggs and she and the male bird feed the young after they're hatched. And they stay with the young till they're able to live on their own. Higher up on the scale are mammals. Cats and dogs, elephants, and monkeys and people, too, are mammals. Mammal babies aren't hatched; they grow inside the mother, a very safe place, until they are strong enough to live outside. And to be sure that it gets inside that safe place the daddy has a special organ, the penis, that he puts inside the mother so the baby can grow in that safe place."

I look across the table at three-year-old Ben. His eyes are growing bigger and bigger, his mouth tighter and tighter. Then suddenly he smiles, "Oh. I get it. You mean in the old days!"

The FBI never let us feel that they had forgotten us. We had not been in L.A. very long when Eric came in to ask me, "How did that man know Dick Lund is my Daddy?"

I didn't say, "It was really brilliant of him, seeing as how you're the only white kid on the block." Instead I shrugged and reminded him that we don't talk to strangers. By the time I walked outside the man was gone. My kids remember that whenever we moved, sooner or later there would be a car parked across the street with an unconcerned man sitting for hours, reading the newspaper.

I was assigned to a neighborhood Party Club and Dick was in a trade union one. Our main activity was selling the *People's World*, the California counterpart of the *Daily Worker*. A couple of us would take a busy corner (Western or Vermont at Florence or Jefferson) on a Saturday morning with free samples of the paper. Often there would be Jehovah Witnesses at the same corner. For lack of anyone else to talk to, we would exchange a few words. We said that we were trying to help our fellow man — here on earth. I always said I admired them for acting on their convictions, but neither of us changed our minds.

Gladys and Earl, who often shared our *People's World* assignments, became friends soon after we moved to L.A. "Lettuce and Oil" (Eric's name for them) had a son, Tony, studying to be a psychiatrist. One day they asked if he could interview Eric, age five, for one of his classes.

On the way home after his session, Eric remarked, "Tony sure hates his father!"

"What makes you say that?"

"Well, Tony had these three dolls I was supposed to play with — a Mommy doll, a Daddy doll and a boy doll. And every time the boy doll had to talk to the Daddy doll, Tony would ask me if the boy hated the Daddy. At first I just said "No". But he kept saying how prob'ly the boy hated the Daddy so much and it was okay to say he hates him. And so I figured out that Tony really hates his Daddy. So then I told him "Yes" so he wouldn't feel bad about it."

Small wonder that Freudian theory was so pervasive for so many years!

Even with Dick's help I had to juggle a myriad of balls: seeing that the kids were dressed, fed, bathed and read a story at bed-time; ironing, shopping, cooking; to say nothing of getting to and from a forty-hour work week by streetcars (no taxis now); and Saturday mornings spent selling the *People's World* plus weekly Party meetings.

Much of the Party meetings were spent detecting and correcting "non-Party errors." These were usually around the race question — issues of insensitivity, old habits of language, etc. The issue would be raised at the Club level, then at a Section meeting with "higher level" Party members. Correction was supposed to be the goal but if the person fought the accusation it could result in expulsion. Couples would often split up when one or the other was under charges. All of this turmoil resulted in more people leaving the Party and fewer people joining.

As for equality for women, male chauvinism was so endemic among Party leaders that it was an empty tenet. When I think of all the strong women in the Party it is hard to believe what we tolerated. Remember, these were the '50's and Black Power and Women's Lib were not yet on the scene. Those movements accomplished what we had failed to do.

The Rosenberg case was one in which all elements of the Party were unified and where we were not without allies — just on a humanitarian basis. Julius and Ethel Rosenberg were indicted as atomic spies in 1952 and their trial was front-page news until their execution on June 19, 1953.

Even today the case against them is controversial and nothing in the Soviet records implicates Ethel. None of the other "atomic spies" were executed. Ethel's brother David Greenglass, Morton Sobell and Harry Gold all got prison sentences. Gold was the courier to Klaus Fuchs who supplied much more detailed atomic (but hardly definitive) information to the Soviets. But it was Julius and Ethel who went to their deaths.

It was clear that the U.S. was determined to make the Rosenbergs pay, no matter how flimsy the evidence. We in the Party and our allies mounted letter-writing campaigns and went out with petitions to save them from execution. All day and night we held vigils outside the Federal Building, hoping against hope that at least Ethel would be reprieved.

The execution of the Rosenbergs was an act of vengeance, not justice, designed to placate the most rabid anti-democratic, McCarthy-ite forces in the U.S. It made me ashamed of my country.

More Family

I had often said I wanted more kids. Not eight, but a family of five children seemed about right. (I settled for three, as you will see at the end of this chapter.) Rachel was conceived the night we heard that Lil's youngest child had drowned. "If we're going to have another baby," I told Dick, "let's not wait."

It was August of 1953; Lil and family were vacationing at a farm when his teenage brothers had taken five-year-old Jimmy down to a nearby pond. Logical or not, I thought the age difference between the boys explained the tragedy. Jimmy had drowned because Richie and Bobby were not old enough to be responsible but too old to be watched by their parents. What a tragedy for Lil and Harry, but even more for the brothers, forever haunted by an unanswerable "What if...?"

There was a good mix of black and white families living around 59th Place (Broadway and Slauson), but further east, around Manchester, black families were encountering hostility. Adele's husband, Gene, and Dick, as members of CORE (Congress of Racial Equality), sat guard many nights in the households of black families who had bought homes in the area. When we moved to 89th Place in 1953, there was one black family on the block. When we left six years later, there was hardly a white family anywhere around.

I remember Ben, at the age of eight, asking, "Why do they call black people a minority?" And I had to explain that our part of Los Angeles was not what the rest of the country looked like.

Nancy holding baby Rachel, with Ben and Eric (1954)

As we settled in at 89th Place I became a stay-at-home Mom. Work was scarce; I had enough earnings to draw unemployment and I was happy to get involved in the PTA. Harriet, a comrade who had a son Eric's age, clued me in as to what was happening at South Park, the school where Eric would be going. It was a crucial time in this and other schools as the community changed.

White women, who had been running the PTA for years, were dropping off the Board rather than accept black women as officers in "their organization". Harriet was one of the few white women still serving as an officer when I joined. The PTA Board at South Park was large, composed of seven elected officers and eight committee chairs, so there were many vacancies.

My experience in the Communist Party and the labor movement had taught me the rudiments of running a meeting, minute taking, and Roberts Rules of Order, etc; but the training I got through my years in the PTA would prove equally useful. The PTA was a "lab" in which I — and many women — learned the value and role of committees and how to keep accurate, detailed books. In addition, the PTA taught me several things that the Party ignored: certain people are best for certain jobs, and the importance of rewarding people for their efforts.

Rosa Lee was the first black woman to sit on the South Park PTA Board. She had felt the hostility but was determined to have her say in the school where her son, Louie, went. I was full of admiration for her and she soon became a valued friend as well as ally. As we got to know one another, I felt she respected my leftist opinions while I respected her allegiance to her church. Together we forged a strong PTA, filling the vacancies with Latinas as well as black women and keeping the few white women who had stuck it out.

I count Rosa Lee among the remarkable women I have known. Born in the South, she was orphaned at an early age. Her education and socialization were so neglected that at the age of 9, when she came to live with her sister in New York, she was diagnosed as retarded. Within a short time she proved that to be false and the principal of her school deliberately "lost" her records rather than let them destroy her chances in life. Rosa Lee went on to graduate from high school with honors, and became a R.N.

I had known her for a few years when her husband died of a heart attack. Aware that he had a weak heart, Rosa Lee was prepared for his death. When the smarmy funeral parlor director pushed her to select the "mahogany casket, because it's cozy and warm," she told him, "He is cold, so a cold casket will do just fine."

After the funeral, Rosa Lee announced that she would care for children in her home and they were lucky children indeed, my kids among them. She was kind as well as wise, sensitive to each child's needs. She would listen to an excuse, no matter how lame, but that didn't mean she could be fooled by adult or child.

I was midway in my pregnancy when Rosa Lee called me to say that an errant truck driver had run his vehicle up on the sidewalk at South Park and crashed into the school's fence. Fortunately the accident had occurred at 6:30 a.m.; if it had happened an hour later many children might have been killed. There had never been crossing guards at the school because we had relied on the traffic light at the corner of Manchester and 87th. But over the years the traffic had increased and it was apparent that our kids were in danger.

We in the PTA instantly mobilized groups of women to patrol both corners of the school. We were there morning, noon and afternoon, carrying signs that demanded an overpass so that our children could cross safely. And we made sure that the newspapers carried our story – with pictures. We called on our City Councilman, Kenny Hahn, and got his support. We started registering voters to augment our strength and – we succeeded! The overpass was built.

———————

It was shortly before Rachel was born that I got a surprise call from Mr. W., the owner of Arch Rib Truss. He needed a few drawings in a hurry. When I explained that I was expecting a baby, he offered to bring the job to me. I quickly cleaned up the kitchen, clearing the table in the breakfast nook, ready to roll out any plans that he might bring.

He was sitting on the seat in the nook and I was sitting on a chair at the end of the table, when Ben poked his face between us.

"This is your boss?" he asked, looking from him to me.

"Yes, Ben, I told you he was coming."

"And you like him?" his voice incredulous.

"Ben and Eric have been walking a picket line with their Dad," I hurriedly explained. And to Ben, "All bosses are not the same."

———————

Here it was 1953 and people could not believe that a liberated woman like me had never learned to drive. True, I had made several attempts to learn, going back as far as a teenager under Leon's guidance.

"Concentrate on keeping the hood ornament on the central line of the road," he had said. The trouble was that my left eye and right eye could not agree on where the hood ornament was, so I gave up.

During the war, a friend who was going into the army sold me his Model A Ford for $50. Mike, my boyfriend at the time, gave me a few driving lessons but I had not quite got the hang of it. Stopping the car on a hill at a red light, I felt the car drifting backward. Quickly I put the car in reverse.

"Why did you do that?" Mike wasn't a screamer but he was obviously upset.

"Reverse means opposite," I explained.

"This is a driving lesson, not an English lesson."

Some days later, after I had spent hours cleaning my apartment, I thought, "You need to get rid of that unsightly sack of trash and all those bottles."

I jumped into the Ford, on my way to the dump (I had applied for a license but had not yet registered the car in my name).

Still in my housework garb of bra and shorts, my hair tied back in a bandana, I drove ...directly into the rear end of a big blue Santa Monica Avenue bus!

I pulled the car to the curb and got out, as the driver of the bus leapt out, very distraught.

"Don't worry," I told him. "The driver of the car was entirely to blame."

"Will you write that down for me?"

Certainly. So I got into the bus, a little self-conscious that on a Sunday afternoon I was still in shorts and bra. "Driver of car was responsible." Dated and signed, Nancy Rosenfield.

"Thank you so much," from the driver.

I walked home, leaving the bottles and trash in the Ford, its bumper rising like a ski in front of the driver's seat. And there the car sat for days until the authorities towed it away. It was only afterwards when Mike and friends asked me what happened to my car that I realized that the bus driver assumed that the driver of the Ford had fled and I was a witness, volunteering my statement!

So here it was ten years later and I was still not driving. All my younger sisters were driving — but not I. Periodically I had scraped together $3 for a driver's learning permit and Dick had given me instructions on shifting gears, but each time I had let the permit expire.

That was before I met Stella. Stella, my friend and comrade, would not let me dither any longer. Stella had one mission in life — she was teaching every woman she knew how to drive. "It's my way of repaying all the people who had once given me rides, when I was like you," she said.

At first my excuse was that I was pregnant — I was uncomfortable behind the wheel — but after Rachel was born Stella would brook no delays. Eric still laughs at the memory of watching our lurching progress down the long driveway and down 89th Place as I struggled with the balky clutch and my own temerity.

For years I had had nightmares about driving — terrible dreams in which I was behind the wheel but could not open my eyes. Or that I was alone in a moving car, sitting in the back seat, needing to steer it, unable to reach the pedals with my feet. "Wake up," I would tell myself, "this is a stupid dream and you don't need to suffer another minute." But now, instead of waking myself up, I told myself, "This is just a dream but if you want to, you can direct it. Since you're in a car, drive it. You can learn to drive in this dream without the possibility of hurting yourself or anyone else." Along with Stella, I must credit my dreams in mastering my reluctance to drive.

At last the day came. Stella drove me to the DMV and waited. I drove smoothly, parked the car neatly at the curb. But the g....d... clutch would not shift into rear gear. Finally, the nice highway officer said, "I can see you know how to do it but I have other people waiting and I can't sit here all day. I'll sign you off but I suggest you get someone to look at that clutch."

All these months the car had sat in the driveway because Dick had a ride to work. Wouldn't you know that on the day I got my license, the guy quit and Dick would henceforth be needing the car? But I was a licensed driver at last!

In March of '53 Mama got a call from Teeta's husband, Dick Bell. "Teeta's in the hospital in New York and is asking for you." Mama flew east that day but arrived too late. Teeta had died of melanoma, leaving four little children ages ten to three, and a bereft husband.

We had known about the melanoma, diagnosed in '52 after surgery on a mole near her ear had failed to heal. Teeta had recovered sufficiently to go back to her teaching job and in the summer of '52 she and the family made the trip to California, staying for several weeks. The first thing Mama did was to take Teeta to a hair stylist. It didn't hide the scar that ran down the side of her face but minimized it.

It had been wonderful to see Teeta and to get acquainted with her kids, but I had no inkling that this would be the last time I would see her. I will always regret that I didn't make the effort to spend more time with her when I had a chance. In a recurring dream, Teeta is with our family at a beach house in California. We are all happy to be vacationing together, all except Teeta. In my dream she is very sad to be separated from her children. She misses them so much, but we all know that she must stay with us. If she goes back to New Jersey she will die.

It was early in '54. "Why are you going to the Doctor if you aren't sick?" asked Eric.

"I'm going because we're going to have a baby and the Doctor checks on me to see that the baby is fine."

"A baby!" The boys were excited at the prospect. They, along with Dick, hoped it would be a girl. They wanted to fix the room up for "her" that very day. But that was months ago and by May they were tired of the subject, barely acknowledged my departure for the actual birth.

That went fine. I spent just three days in the hospital — things having changed since Eric's birth six and half years earlier. This time I was determined to nurse my baby, having given up too easily with the boys. Rachel was such a mellow baby and I felt so good that six days after her birth I decided to mop and wax all the floors in the house. Afterwards with Rachel in my arms, the boys and I sat outside on the front steps awaiting Dick's return from work.

My well-being was short-lived. That night I came down with a severe case of bronchitis, complicated by my first and only attack of asthma. When Dr. Gordon arrived I was running a temperature of 104 and desperately trying to breathe. He gave me a shot for the asthma and put me on antibiotics. For the next two weeks I was too sick to take care of the baby, let alone nurse her. Dick took over and I have always felt that those early weeks of being the sole caregiver for Rachel formed a special bond between them.

———————

Later that summer, I heard Ben and Eric talking as "Jim" and "Jim". Whenever our boys assumed these alter-egos, Dick and I could relax. Jim and Jim never fought, never even argued. It was all business with Jim and Jim. They always had a job of some sort to do and they bent to it. This time they announced they were digging for oil and they were pretty sure they had found it right outside my window. Rachel was sleeping and I dozed off. When I awoke Jim and Jim were still at work. I went outside to look and could hardly see their little heads, so deep was the hole they had dug!

I gasped but was not going to chide them, feeling responsible for having let things go this far.

"You know what?" I said, "This is not the place for oil, after all. You know people who build houses say that houses need a lot of dirt around their foundations to make them strong. I'm pretty sure you can put all that dirt back and make the house even stronger than it was before and when Daddy comes home you can show him all the work you did." And Jim and Jim did just that.

———

In search of the cause of my recurring bronchitis, hay fever and asthma, I went through all the allergy tests. The task of desensitizing me seemed insurmountable...I had reacted to everything! In the course of all the examinations, the doctors had discovered a slight lump in my neck. Should I wait and see if it grew or changed, or should I have surgery? With Teeta's death from cancer looming large, I opted for immediate surgery. Rachel was just a year old.

Mama had insisted that I stay with her for a week following my operation. When Dick brought the kids to her house, the boys had hugged and patted me, wary of the bandage on my throat, but my adored daughter ignored me completely. Was she thinking, "You're the one who deserted me when I was a few days old, and you have left me again this past week."? I wept, but she was adamant, she would not come to me. "Remember this?" I asked, twisting the heavy silver and turquoise bracelet that I had always worn, from my arm. At last! She smiled, took it eagerly and then held out her arms to me. Oh, the warmth of her little body!

The lump turned out to be perfectly normal thyroid tissue but the disturbance to the fragile gland was enough to start the problems I would face over the years. Fortunately, none of my thyroid problems were lethal.

———

Eric was in the second grade and though I could hardly say he was eager to go to school each morning, most days he came home bubbly and full of energy. But one afternoon he moped about and wouldn't come to the table for dinner. When I finally got him to sit down and take a few bites, he lunged away and started throwing up before he could get to the bathroom.

I held his head, no temperature but he was shaking all over.

"What is it, sweetie? Did you eat something at school?"

"Teacher said I am dead. I am dead now. I can't play." He was crying now, great wrenching sobs. "I'm dead now."

"Oh, no," I comforted him. "That is just those stupid A-bomb exercises. Nobody is dead. It is like a game."

"Miz Evans said this wasn't a game. She said I'm dead 'cause I didn't get under my desk like everybody else did."

"Well it is just like a game. And I am going to talk to Miss Evans and the Principal tomorrow. She shouldn't scare you. You're my fine big boy and nothing is going to happen to you because you didn't get under the desk."

I called Harriet and Rosa Lee and we went together to the principal's office. I don't know about other schools, but South Park became one school where the A-bomb exercises were conducted like a game. No scare tactics. A reward for the room where everyone got under their desks in half a minute. And that was the last semester Miss Evans taught school.

———————

An active baby, Rachel had pulled herself to a standing position in her crib at seven months. But she didn't seem to care what position her feet were in. She toed in and sometimes stood on the outside of her feet, instead of on the soles. The well-baby clinic didn't think it was anything serious, but I was worried. Lucia told me about the Children's Hospital in midtown L.A. and I decided to take Rachel there.

"Club foot," the examining Doctor said.

"But her feet aren't misshapen, they're perfectly normal."

"Club foot refers to the position the foot is held. It's entirely curable but we must start now."

So my darling child went through an arduous process for the next five months. Her feet and legs, up to the knees, were encased in heavy plaster-of-paris casts. Every week or so, the Doctor would remove a pie-shaped wedge from the cast, right below the ankle and reseal the cast, gradually turning each foot to the outside – a la Charlie Chaplin. What a good baby she was, putting up with the heavy casts, crawling, when she was so eager to walk. Her baths couldn't have been much fun, sitting in the kitchen sink with her feet sticking straight up out of the water. And she had to put up with the long bus rides, and the waits at the hospital.

Finally, a few days before her first birthday, the casts were to come off. I was told to soak her legs in warm water and gradually peel the layers of gauze away. What a long, messy, tedious process. Fedya, a dear older comrade who had "adopted us" when we moved to 89th Place, came by to take us to the hospital. He found us both weeping; she in frustration, me at the sight of her miserable shrunken legs.

Not to worry. Within days her legs filled out to their natural shape. With the casts gone Rachel was ready to walk but the remedial work continued. She was fitted with special shoes, each one with a one-inch-wide canvas strap attached to the outside of the sole. The straps were wound around each leg and attached to a soft belt that she wore under her dress. The straps tightened if she toed in and relaxed if she toed out. At night she wore a contraption that kept her legs apart and her toes pointed out. Two years of this and she was dismissed from the Children's Hospital. But I think it was ballet lessons started when Rachel was not quite six that completed the cure.

———————

I was thirty six and a half years old when Rachel was born and the doctors told me that children of older mothers were more likely to suffer birth defects. Whether true or not, that advice led Dick and me to decide not to have any more children.

Dick's Work and Mine

When we first moved to L.A., Dick had worked as a warehouseman, starting at Bohemian Distilleries, then at Thrifty Drug. Paul, a fellow comrade, was the shop steward (a non-paid but important union position) at the Thrifty warehouse. He assumed that Dick was a natural to take over for him when he moved to another job. But Dick declined. "Sam has been on the job longer than me." He didn't feel he needed to point out to Paul that Sam was also the first black man hired in the department.

Later, Dick was happy to accept being elected to serve on the contract negotiating committee. The union representatives and the company execs and their respective lawyers met daily for a week. Progress would be made one day and then fall apart the next. The atmosphere grew tenser, tempers grew short.

"Let's break for lunch."

They all rose. Outside the meeting room, Dick was shocked to see that the union lawyers and company lawyers were going to lunch together. "Did you see that?" he asked Al, the president of the union and head of their negotiating team.

"It's only natural. They went to the same school, they studied the same books, they talk the same language. They may sit opposite each other at the negotiating table but basically they're in the same boat."

Dick shook his head. He would not have been that kind of labor lawyer.

I think that experience led him to go back to construction. One of his friends suggested that he could do better as a carpenter than as a laborer. All he needed to do was apply as a returning veteran, and pay his dues at a Carpenters Union Hall where he wasn't known. He applied in Orange County and got a job in Anaheim, building Disneyland's Matterhorn. Dick didn't have the training to be a finish carpenter, but rough carpentering was right down his alley. Since he had no fear of heights he fitted well there and also on his next job, building a big warehouse that jutted out over the pier at San Pedro.

When Dick didn't have work as a carpenter, he worked for the city of Los Angeles Recreation Department. One of his mentors was Abe R., the Rec Director at Green Meadows, the playground down the street from us. With Abe's encouragement Dick set up the Little Pacific League which emphasized developing each child's skill and the importance of team work in baseball. It was an alternative to the much ballyhooed Little League with its emphasis on winning. Ben and Eric and almost every kid in the neighborhood found a place on one team or another. At Green Meadows the whole family was involved, with the fathers volunteering to coach the various teams and the mothers making cookies for the after-game get-togethers. The lack of bleachers wasn't accidental; Abe wanted the game to be of, by, and for the kids.

It was the spring of '59 and Dick was taking a couple of night classes at Pepperdine, still trying to get that elusive B.A. It was there that he met Art, a serious young man who spent his summers working for the Wilshire YMCA. Art introduced Dick to John Pastor, the Y's Director, who offered him a full-time job at the Y's summer camp, Earl Anna.

As a family we had been camping for many years, gradually adding other equipment to the tent given us by our friends Lettuce and Oil. But this would be the first time that Ben and Eric were able to spend the summer as part of an organized camp. Weekdays Rachel stayed with Rosa Lee while I worked but we managed to have a good summer. Rachel and I did get to Earl Anna for one weekend, but both Dick and her brothers were much too busy to spend time with us.

In the fall John Pastor would be moving from the Wilshire Y to the Burbank Y. He offered Dick a job there, managing existing programs and organizing new ones, a job the Y classified as

"Secretary." Strangers were a little confused when they found that in the Lund household it was the wife who was the steel detailer and the husband who was the secretary! Pastor urged us to move to Burbank and we finally did in August of 1960.

We found a two-bedroom apartment to rent on Orange Grove, just a few blocks from the Y. Not the ideal arrangement but we managed by putting Rachel to sleep in our bedroom. When I was ready to go to bed, one of us would carry her out to the couch in the living room.

The best thing about the move was Dick's transfer to Northridge State, California's new campus in the Valley. The Admissions officer knew Dick from San Diego State; they both had been students there twenty years before.

"They have really screwed you," he declared, looking at all Dick's credits. "You should have been given upper division status long ago." He paved the way for Dick's graduation in two years, major in sociology, minor in recreation.

———————

Now I need to backtrack a bit and fill in what I was doing during those years. In '55 Rachel was a year old and it was time to for me to go back to work. Later, I would take up Rosa Lee's offer to look after Rachel and the boys, but now it seemed best to hire a housekeeper. I got a job at Blue Diamond as a re-bar detailer, getting a ride with one of the women who worked in the office.

I am the only woman in the third floor drafting room but I am assured that there will be no problem. I am told that by law I must take a fifteen-minute coffee break in the morning, one that the men do not get. I take my break in the lounge on the second floor along with all the women employees, but am discouraged by the vapid talk; cannot get anyone interested in talking politics.

Blue Diamond, a giant in the steel industry, has invested in one of the first computers, Univac. It is huge — a floor-to-ceiling humming monster, occupying the whole of the fourth floor. It is so hot that fans are whirring day and night to keep it working. Science, it is thought, will make it possible to correctly estimate the labor as well as the material in every job. Detailers, shop men and re-bar placers are all expected to stay within the computer estimate. Woe to us if we go over, congrats for staying under. One day, I am called in to explain why my sheets are for 30% more steel than the computer estimate for the job — concrete storage vats for natural gas. We go over and over the plans...inexplicable. Then I turn back to the first sheet — Aha! The plot plans shows three of the enormous circular vats, not two. This time it is a data entry error, not mine.

After our sheets were handed to the shop, we would start getting calls from the field. "Where's my steel? The shop promised it would be here last week, then said for sure by this morning."

"Why did you promise the steel when you knew you couldn't get it out?" we would ask Bill, the burly head of the shop,

"So ...? What's wrong with making the guy happy for a few hours? He's going to get the steel when he's going to get it, no sooner, no later. But if my little lie makes him feel better, what's the harm?"

Later, I found out that the placers had a habit of calling for a shipment long before they were ready for it, since they were trying to beat the computer's estimate of their hours.

Around Christmas time a rash of nudie calendars appear, pinned up on the large pillars which dot the floor of the drafting room.

"Like the new decorations?" asks Steve, with a smirk.

"Okay by me, but I bet if I put up pictures of nude men all of you would think I was some kind of a pervert."

I thought that was the end of it but when I came to work after the New Year's holiday, the calendars were gone and I was greeted with outright hostility.

"What gives?"

"We know you were the one who complained to management. So the big honchos came upstairs and blew the whistle. They gave Rod (our Department head) a real hard time."

"I never," I protested in vain. "I never...In the first place it isn't that important to me. And I'd only complain if I wasn't paid the same as the rest of you."

It wasn't everybody in the department, but there were enough guys who didn't believe me to make me feel isolated and unhappy.

Jack, who had been friendly from the first, made a point of greeting me every morning and making conversation during the day. He told me he was freelancing on the side and doing quite well. If I was interested, he felt he could throw some jobs my way.

It seemed like a perfect solution. Stay home with the kids, save the expense of the ride and housekeeper.

Dick set up a drafting table in the garage and I happily started out. But the day that Rachel — such a finicky eater that she could never be persuaded even to taste a new food — reached for the bottle of correction fluid and took a swig — I abandoned the idea of working at home. Fortunately, the correction fluid turned out to be a very dilute solution of Clorox and she suffered no ill effects.

Jack told me there was probably a job opening at Meehleis Steel. He knew the guy who was head of the detailing department, "Gene's a good guy, easy going, but gets things done."

It was an altogether happier experience. A small operation, there were eight of us detailers in a new building, bright, and clean. Gene had established an atmosphere of camaraderie and while I think we turned out as much work as the detailers at Blue Diamond, the room was abuzz with talk and laughter. We went out to lunch together on paydays, the guys always making room for me, whoever was driving that day.

In contrast to the shop foreman at Blue Diamond, Meehleis' foreman was a dour pessimist, never promising that a shipment would be on time. "I'll try, but it doesn't look good for tomorrow," Louie would say.

One day I was on the phone with the head placer on a big job. He was telling me he would have to lay off his crew because Louie had just told him not to expect his next order.

"Hang on. The truck's just pulling in. Sorry I bothered you."

I called Louie, "How come you told Ben he wasn't going to get his steel when you knew it was on its way?"

In a direct opposite to Bill at Blue Diamond, he would say, "You know how bad traffic is. How can I be sure the truck will make it?"

Rachel's birthday party with Ben and Eric, cousin Jan Goodman (arm around Rachel), and neighborhood children (1957)

Although 89th Place only had two bedrooms, we were quite comfortable. By the time Rachel was two, we had moved our bed to a corner of the very large living room, disguising it somewhat with pillows and an afghan. There was a garage back of the house, where both the hot water tank and the washing machine were located and there was even a built-in barbeque at one side. The wide front lawn was all grass and it became the home of "Mr. Peepers", a big brown duck which I took as a favor to a friend when he went on vacation. The duck became "Mrs. Peepers" when we discovered that the big greenish eggs we found in the bushes weren't leftovers from our Easter egg hunt, but fresh eggs she must have laid. (What great cakes duck eggs make!) Mrs. Peepers became a family favorite and it was a sad day when we came home one afternoon to find her dead, the victim of somebody's b-b gun.

We had been renting the house on 89th Place for five years when we came home from a long weekend to find a "For Sale" sign posted on the front lawn and a realtor's box (with key) on the front porch. We were in no position to buy the house but felt we were entitled to some consideration, which we didn't get. There followed a rancorous period that ended up with the landlady suing us for the water bill. She lost. We found a small house for rent, a few blocks closer to Rosa Lee and the school. It also had only two bedrooms but we converted the tiny breakfast room into a bedroom for Rachel. We lived there until we moved to Burbank in August of '60.

———————

The moment when you realize that your child can really read may come as a surprise. For me it was the day Rachel and I were on our way to visit my mother at her apartment in a building just off one of L.A.'s busiest streets. I started to pull into a parking space, but after noticing the sign, I pulled back out.

"It's okay for you to park there, Mom — it says, "No parking Mr. Schwartz."

———————

Reading the reports from the FBI has jogged my memory as to when I dropped out of the Party.

Because I was no longer in a union, I was assigned to a neighborhood Communist Party club. In January of 1960 I was nominated for Chair of the Moranda Smith Club, in which I had been a member for six years. I refused and then launched into the reasons why it was time for me to resign from the Party.

140

LA 100-18292

At a meeting of the South Central Club, Moranda
Smith Section, SCDCP on January 6, 1960 at 824 West 74th
Street, it was announced that LUND, club chairman, had
become dissatisfied with the CP and had threatened to
quit.

LA T-2 (1/18/60)

LUND was present at a meeting of the South Central
Club, Moranda Smith Section, SCDCP, on January 12, 1960
at 824 West 74th Street, Los Angeles, California. LUND
was not at the meeting when it commenced and at that time
it was announced that she had decided to resign from the
club and the CP. Those present decided they would attempt
to persuade her to remain in the CP. After LUND arrived at
the meeting she made statement which included the following
information:

She had been a member of the CP since the early
1940s. She joined because she believed the CP was the
leader of the working class, that the capitalist society in
the United States was deteriorating and was ready to fall
apart, and because she believed that the CP would bring
about socialism in the United States in a few years. At the
time she joined the CP and in the years that followed,
many members of the CP were making all kinds of predictions
concerning CP progress, however, all these predictions failed
to materialize.

She still believes in socialism and that the
United States will eventually become a socialist country.
She believes that the CP will not bring about socialism
in the United States. She believes that the CP is falling
apart day by day; that the CP is not leading the working
class, and that it is a "boogyman" in the eyes of the average
American. She described the CP as an organization of old
people, who attend meetings and discuss matters with each
other rather than attempt to interest non-Party people in
CP matters. She stated that the CP does nothing and has
nothing to offer and that those remaining in the CP are
wasting their time and money.

From the FBI files, with its usual embroidery (1960)

"I joined the Party in 1941," I said, "but in nineteen years I can't point my finger to anything it has accomplished. I still believe in socialism and that capitalism is an evil system but I've lost confidence that the Party is the vehicle to change it. The Party is falling apart because it's mainly old people — people who are comfortable attending meetings and discussing matters with each other — so much easier than reaching out to non-Party people and getting them interested in the issues."

A number of members argued against my resignation. They said that since I still believed in socialism and the goals that had led me to join, it was more necessary than ever that I stay in the Party and get it back on track. I agreed to think over my resignation, but would not accept any Club office. (According to the FBI reports I attended Club meetings into the spring of '60.)

We moved to Burbank in August of that year. I made no attempt to get in touch with the Party in the Valley and no one made an effort to contact either Dick or me. But the FBI continued to follow us until 1967.

———————

After we had been in Burbank a while, Dick found a nice apartment for his mother, just two blocks from us. She made friends with her neighbors and seemed to enjoy being close to the kids. Occasionally we would all get dressed up and take her to church — the big Lutheran Church on 7th and Vermont. Aunt Min and Mama Lund knew the minister from their Iowa days, and he seemed enlightened if not liberal. For me the time meant an hour of peace, of sitting with my hands folded, my handsome kids all scrubbed and sitting quietly, no squabbles to settle, chores set aside. When my mother challenged my acquiescence, if not approval, of going to church, I asked, "And who in this family is going to Temple these days? Not even Leon and Bobbie go!"

———————

We lived in Burbank for three years, but it was a community in which we never felt settled. It was as though we were perched on the edge, ready to make the next jump as soon as Dick would finish school. Burbank at that time was all white; it was not safe for a black person to be on the street after dark! Burbank's school system was good and our kids did benefit from that aspect, and being included in after-school Y activities. Six-year-old Rachel became an expert swimmer. I joined the PTA as soon as school started, made cookies when asked. Most PTA meetings were in the daytime, which I couldn't attend. No one spoke to me at the one evening meeting I managed to attend. I was invited to some events for the "Y wives", but when I politely refused to wear a "Nixon" pin, I was made to feel out of step.

Soon after the '60 election, I had a valid excuse to be absent from meetings — I was working at Apex Steel, a long commute from Burbank, when my car was rear-ended as I exited the freeway. The damage to the car was negligible but I suffered a severe whiplash. For the next six weeks I did the recommended rehab at home — with my chin in a sling, I sat facing a door over which the weights were hung. When I returned to work I was really welcomed — no one had picked up the re-bar assignment in my absence!

The landlord of our flat on Orange Grove had been complaining that we were damaging his precious parquet floors. (My allergist had recommended that I live without rugs or drapes and I had explained this to him when we moved in.) Now he was being persistent, so in the fall of '62 we moved to a flat two blocks away. Though it only had two bedrooms, there was a big alcove under the stairs that led to the upstairs apartment, providing a nice spot for Rachel's bed. At last a spot for all her dolls and stuffed animals.

——— ——— ———

At about the same time, things at the Burbank Y were less than happy. When Ellen, a lovely older woman who had worked in the office for years, was summarily fired, Dick became disillusioned with John P., the charismatic director. The final straw came when a lawyer who sat on the Burbank Y Board recognized Dick from the Longshore and Warehousemen Union negotiation table. With Ellen's fate fresh in his mind, Dick wasted no time in transferring back to the Wilshire Y.

He knew the Wilshire Director from two years of summer camp. Dale, in contrast to John, was low-key, modest and a good guy to work with. Dick had his pick of assignments. He opted for the "Gra-Y" — a pioneer effort to reach grammar-school-age kids who had not been the Y's emphasis before. Dick worked with several inner-city elementary schools in after-school recreation.

In June of '62 Dick got his B.S. degree and took the civil service exam for Recreation Directors with the City of Los Angeles. He came in third of the hundred or more who took the test. My brother Leon knew the director of the department and offered to sound him out as to when Dick could expect to be hired.

Over lunch the Director told Leon, "Oh, we were lucky — the guy who was doing the job on a provisional basis came in among the top five, so we hired him."

"I understand. But it's a big department and there must be other openings coming up. When do you think my brother-in-law can expect a call?"

"Oh. ... We'll most likely schedule another exam and he can take the test when it comes up."

So much for acing a test! Dick took a job as Recreational Director at Juvenile Hall. It was not what he had had in mind, but it was a good job, with many benefits. Within a few months Dick was initiating new programs along with the obligatory ball games. Among other innovations he instituted a roller skating program as a reward for good behavior. So successful was the program, with the morale greatly increased, that the Administration agreed when Dick asked to extend the skating event to include Chapman Hall for delinquent girls. It was the first ever co-ed event at Juvenile Hall.

After about six months on the job Dick learned that there were no promotions as Rec Director; it was a dead-end position within the Probation Department. He asked to be reclassified as a Probation Officer and was assigned to one of the juvenile camps where they gave him rein to use his creativity. Among other innovations, he persuaded the administration to hire a bus to take the boys to the beach — boys from the barrios of Los Angeles who had never seen the ocean. They were scared shitless but had to put on a brave front. Later Dick arranged for a mini-Olympics, a track meet in the Coliseum — the field where the real Olympics had been held! These were kids who could run like deer but had never had a pair of track shoes on their feet until that day.

Dick made many good friends with his fellow workers and the heads of the various departments began to ask for him for special assignments. As for the kids, he knew he was loved and he chuckled when he heard that they had a nickname for him: "ole cotton head."

Nancy

Sunland-Tujunga

It was the summer of '63, and now that Dick had a relatively well-paying, as well as secure, job, it was possible for us to buy our first home. Burbank and Glendale and most places in the nearer San Fernando Valley communities were out of our price range, but Sunland-Tujunga was readily accessible. The house at 10338 Irma in Tujunga seemed to be too good to be true. It had two bedrooms with a "mother-in-law" apartment added to the back, plus a large detached garage. The nice backyard looked out on Verdugo High School's football field. I asked one of Mama's friends who had real estate expertise to meet with us and the realtor.

"What's the catch," he asked the realtor. "Why is it such a bargain?"

"There's been a rumor for years that the High School is going to buy all the houses on this side of Irma. But the School Board is really broke and it hasn't made any moves in that direction recently."

So with the aid of the Cal-Vet program (nothing down) we bought the house.

"Does Nancy know that Sunland-Tujunga was the hangout of the German-American Bund up until a few years ago and that the Ku Klux Klan is still meeting there?" asked Bert, Leon's sister-in-law and a long-time Angeleno.

Well, yes, so we had heard — but we liked the house and had fallen in love with the clear dry air. When I had been diagnosed with asthma, friends had suggested that we move to the Tujunga area, where years before they had built the Sunland-Tujunga Jewish Home for Asthmatic Children. Now I was free of asthma but I felt it would be a healthy climate for all of us. Tujunga seemed very much a working-class community with a lot of small homes, set at odd angles on the rocky soil. Tujunga was the most easterly and higher of the two communities, nestled against the western flank of the San Gabriel Mountains. It reminded me of El Paso.

The day we moved was Nov. 22, 1963 — the day Kennedy was assassinated. We were shocked — but not surprised — to note that not a single flag was lowered in town. We had been warned.

———————

1964 was a crucial presidential election — Goldwater versus Johnson. Reelecting Johnson was very important but equally vital, in my eyes, was defeating Proposition 14. It was an effort to repeal California's Fair Housing, the Rumford Act, which had been passed in '63. The campaign was overtly racist — "last chance to protect your property's value" — typical scare tactics. At the "NO on 14" office in Sunland-Tujunga, I was assigned a precinct where there were many Goldwater signs. With ten-year-old Rachel at my side I set out, my little speech memorized.

"Hello. I am Nancy Lund and I live down the street from you in Tujunga. I'm asking voters to vote No on Proposition 14 because I think Fair Housing is a good policy. Just like you I want to have good neighbors, people who will take good care of their property, regardless of the color of their skin. Of course I don't want sharecroppers to live next door — but fair housing is working well in California. It's a good law."

After the third house Rachel turned to me and asked, "Mom, what do you have against sharecroppers?"

Wow! Had I just substituted one prejudice for another? Much chastened, I finished the block without that damning sentence.

But my efforts, along with many others, were of no avail. California passed Proposition 14 by a 2-to-1 majority. The ACLU and other groups challenged its constitutionality, carrying the case all the way to the U.S. Supreme Court. While the case was pending the Feds froze $120 million worth of urban renewal monies, funds that had been earmarked for California.

In May of '67 the Supreme Court declared Proposition 14 unconstitutional. And in March of '68 — one week after the assassination of Martin Luther King — Congress passed and President Johnson signed the U.S. Fair Housing Act.

One of the doorbells that I rang, that fall of '64, was the home of Bob and Yvonne Camen. Good liberals, they welcomed me with open arms.

"Wonderful what you're doing. Why haven't we seen you at any Democratic Club meetings?" they asked.

"Didn't know there was one. Never saw anything in the paper about any meetings."

"Oh, we have a good Sunland-Tujunga Democratic Club but the paper won't print anything about Democrats. We'll take you to the next meeting."

The Sunland-Tujunga Democratic Club was a part of the California Democratic Club movement. The CDC had been founded after the Stevenson-for-President campaigns of the 1950's. It was a grassroots effort, based on the idea that the Democratic Party in California should not have to reinvent itself every four years, but should be a continuous presence in their respective communities.

The first meeting of the Club that I attended was held in a classroom at the Elementary School. The first order of business was the School Board's requirement that organizations sign a loyalty oath in order to meet on school property. As a civil liberties issue it was a matter of principle to resist signing the oath; at the same time, meeting at a school helped to establish the legitimacy of the Democratic Club in the community. It was finally decided that the Secretary would write a letter quoting the first amendment and the By-Laws of the CDC and wait and see what the response would be. This maneuver turned out to be a good delaying tactic and for the next four months the Club continued to meet at the school.

I was really impressed with the discussion: articulate, well-informed, and enthusiastic. On paper there were about 50 members of the Club, ten or twelve who attended meetings. I already knew Will, who was the president of the Club. Like Paul, Dick's coworker at the warehouse, Will had all the strengths and weaknesses of many Party members. He was hard working and dedicated but terrible at involving others. Will truly believed that if he didn't do everything himself nothing would get done, not realizing that it was his own failure to delegate an assignment.

"I don't see why the Democratic Club's meetings are never in the paper," I remarked.

"Oh, I send them in, in plenty of time," said Will, "but they won't print them."

I offered to write the next announcement and to take it in to the paper.

Dressing conservatively for the occasion, I asked to see the editor/publisher. I introduced myself to him, handed him the neatly typed sheet, and said, "Community newspapers such as the Record-Ledger are invaluable in covering local events. As a community organization we expect our Democratic Club meetings to be carried along with other such announcements!"

He eyed me from head to toe (looking for horns?) and said, "Mrs. Lund? What is a nice lady like you doing in the Democrats?"

I don't think I was able to come up with a reply, so intent was I in not guffawing! I couldn't wait to get back to the Club and share my story. But from then on our announcements were carried in the paper. Along with murders, rapes and meetings of the Ku Klux Klan, they made the front page.

I became quite active in the Club but Dick, working a swing-shift, had not met my new friends until we held a Sunday brunch.

"No wonder Nancy kept him a secret for so long — he's so handsome!" said Yvonne.

Yvonne was just kidding, of course. She and Bob, who were both working full-time, were to become beloved friends with whom we would stay close over the years. But there were others — the writer-actor Bill Scott and his wife Dorothy, Bill G., Ben P., Virginia, Bee, Kay and a whole raft of younger folks — Adrienne, Chris, Vince. And Alice Mack who deserves a paragraph for herself.

A stalwart of the Methodist Church, Alice could be found in the midst of any struggle. It was she, at the age of 75, who lay down in front of an earth-moving truck and stopped the building of a freeway in the middle of the Tujunga Wash — the last "wild river" in the Los Angeles basin.

But it was with Nettie that I found a collaborator. I appreciated that she had a wide circle of contacts — artists, writers, young people — whom she was able to involve in Democratic Club events. People were drawn to her by her intelligence and wit and undeterred by her gypsy dress and personal quirks. It was Nettie's idea for the Club to hold an annual Book Fair and/or Art Fair as fund raisers. A "Fair" was a lot more work than the traditional raffle, but was much more rewarding, reaching people outside our usual circle.

Like me, Nettie was a former Party member but her marriage to Chet was the reverse of the usual male-dominated couple. Night and day he was at her beck and call. Nettie had all sorts of theories about alternative medicine so she treated Chet's bi-polar symptoms with massive doses of Vitamin B. A former longshoreman, Chet suffered from head injuries inflicted by anti-labor thugs, so I am sure living with him would have tried the patience of a saint; but Nettie's autocratic treatment of him went beyond normal bounds.

Nettie herself was a diabetic and her self-destructive obsession with food — Chet having to make a midnight run for a quart of ice cream — drove me crazy. In the end I would always conclude that her warmth and intelligence, her many good qualities outweighed her failings.

———————

Over the next years in addition to our electoral activities, the Sunland-Tujunga Democratic Club became a real community organization. We were in the lead on the fight to save the Tujunga Wash. We were not able to stop the building of the Golden State Freeway, but it was re-routed out of the Tujunga Wash. Later, a second freeway, the Foothill, came through on the south side. The two freeways brought noise and smog, changing forever the climate of Sunland-Tujunga.

When the Los Angeles Teachers Union went on strike for better pay and conditions, our Sunland-Tujunga Democratic Club held several pancake breakfasts in support. We took our places on the picket line, as individuals and officially as a Club.

Many months after the strike was settled, Rachel's history class was discussing the limits of democracy. "That means you better be careful about criticizing the school administrator," she piped up.

"It's okay," Mr. B. said nonchalantly. "Your mother will feed me again!"

———

But I'm getting ahead of my story. When we first moved to Sunland-Tujunga we had debated whether Eric, who was really enjoying his classes in Burbank, should stay with Grandma Lund and finish high school there. But we decided that her place was really too small for two people and we had heard that Verdugo, the smallest high school in the L.A. school system, had good teachers and offered opportunities in their athletic programs.

And we began to notice that Grandma Lund, who had always been so erect and moved with such alacrity, was now quite bent over and spending more and more time in bed. Aunt Min was also concerned about her and when I reported that our Burbank doctor diagnosed her pain simply as "arthritis", Min took her to her own doctor. His comment, "She's no spring chicken," shocked us. It was my first introduction to the world of medicine for elders. (I now believe that she suffered, as Dick did many years later, with collapsed vertebrae.)

After our move I would try to get Grandma Lund to come to our house for Sunday dinner, but was rarely successful. So Dick or I would make a quick trip to Burbank on Sunday evening, bringing her the complete dinner and one or two other dishes for later in the week. Then on Wednesday evening I would stop on my way home from work to check on her. I would be distressed to see that the Sunday dinner and the other dishes were in the refrigerator, hardly if at all touched.

When we bought the house, we had thought that the attached "mother-in-law" apartment made it ideal for the time when Grandma Lund could no longer live alone. And that time had come. Eric and Ben did not mind surrendering "their" apartment for the garage; enclosing its back wall made a most suitable living space for teenage boys.

My own mother had transitioned from independent living to life at the Jewish Home for the Aged with grace and humor, but for Grandma Lund the move from her own apartment to our house was not a happy one. The main factor was her failing health; but neither Dick nor I had the skill or the training to make it easier for her. Fifteen years later, as I became immersed in aging issues, I looked back with regret at my poor role as caregiver.

More and more bedridden with back pain, Grandma Lund suffered a stomach hemorrhage in '67, probably the result of years of self-dosing with aspirin and Doan's Little Pills. She was taken by ambulance to the hospital, where the doctor removed half of her stomach and cut the vagus nerve. With both of us working full time, there was no way we could care for her at home. She spent the last few months of her life in a skilled nursing facility, where the care seemed adequate. Death came as relief in September '67, just as we were getting ready to move.

Move? Because by January of 1967, the School Board had announced that it was ready to buy all the property on the east side of Irma. Dick and I tried to get the homeowners to stick together in order to get more than the minimum we were being offered. Unfortunately most of our neighbors had signed at the first notice. Only our good friends, the Burnetts and Miss W., at the end of the block, held out for several months. Then, facing the inevitable, the Burnetts bought a house in San Bernardino County, probably nearer to his job. Miss W. and we held out until the end of the summer when we, too, accepted a slightly increased price for our property.

I remember that spring as a delayed honeymoon. I was between jobs and Dick didn't go to work till 3:00 p.m. With kids out of the house, Dick and I made leisurely love in the morning, then went house hunting. We'd get home in time for a great breakfast (always our favorite meal) before he had to go to work. Besides the newspapers, we followed leads from friends and the realtor who had found us the house on Irma. We were determined to stay in Sunland-Tujunga and I had only minimum requirements: the house must have three bedrooms, two baths and a fireplace. (See how bourgeois I had become!)

The house we settled on — 10548 Fairgrove — not only met those requirements, in addition it boasted two and a half baths, the fireplace, a 15 by 30 foot family room, plus a good-sized swimming pool. A half mile north of our house on Irma, it was two blocks from the Angeles National Forest. And because the house on Irma had been taken by eminent domain, we were able to use Cal-Vet financing again. Escrow closed in September.

———————

B'nai B'rith Girls? How did I get myself into the unlikely position of being an adviser to the Sunland-Tujunga group of Jewish girls? I suppose it was Rachel's friend Carolyn Kramer. I knew Carolyn's mother through the Democratic Club. Evelyn, a lovely woman, confined to a wheelchair by multiple sclerosis, pointed out that in Jewish tradition the mother's heritage determines whether a child is Jewish. So Rachel was Jewish and eligible for membership in the group in which Carolyn was active. And they needed an adult sponsor.

The week that we spent at the beach was the crowning disenchantment for the girls and even more so for me. Only a few of the girls came, although all the fundraising through the year was dedicated to this high point of the calendar. And once at Hermosa Beach they had no idea of how to spend their time. I think they dreamed of a passel of new boys who would appear out of nowhere and not only take them to the beach but to movies and even dances. Alas, no boys came.

Much to my dismay I found that these girls (ages 12-15) were not only indifferent to world events — even what was happening in Israel didn't stir them — but they were oblivious to the dreadful smog, the accumulating trash and the obvious poverty around them. Rachel, who had been lukewarm throughout the year, agreed that I should resign. I wrote an eloquent letter, expressing my frustration and disillusionment, in the hope that I could make a difference. I never heard a word from anyone thereafter.

———————

My work history during this period was a mixed one. When we first moved to Tujunga I was still working at Apex. I decided to resign when the company was bought by an outfit that had no interest in production and seemed bent on stripping Apex of its assets and good name. On the day I gave my notice I told Bob, who was now the head of the department, "I may be a rat to be leaving you at this point, but by definition you are a sinking ship!"

Looking for jobs in the Valley, all the ads seemed to be for steel detailers. Not re-bar or miscellaneous steel (which I had picked up at Apex) but the heavy steel beams used in major construction. I was good at getting a job but not so good at hanging on to it. I would last a week or however long it took them to discover that I didn't know what I was doing. I was beginning to catch on by the time I went to work for a big Chicago company that had opened a branch in California, looking for cheaper labor costs. As usual, I was the only woman detailer and — as usual — there were helpful guys who would stop by my drawing board to help me.

One of the most helpful was Art, who became a good friend. I admired Art for the way he had overcome the serious handicap of cerebral palsy. He told me that soon after his birth, his parents were advised to place him in an institution: "He will never be able to go school, never even be able to tie his own shoe laces." That advice was rejected; Art not only went to school but graduated from high school with honors.

Art went on to college and was well on his way to a degree in engineering when he quit to get married. Art was an excellent draftsman and did beautiful work for the first few hours of each day. But by late afternoon, his hand would begin to shake and it was all he could do to sit erect on his stool. About three weeks into the job, both Art and I knew that we would be let go on Friday.

"I have worked off and on for J. Green and I'm pretty sure he's looking for someone. I'll tell him about you and give you a call."

The appearance of J. Green Enterprises was less impressive than its name. Located in North Hollywood, it was one of several small businesses housed in a low commercial building. It was basically a one-room drafting room; six drafting boards lined up one behind each other with a continuous reference table against one wall. A narrow aisle led to the back where there was a table which held a printer and a coffeemaker. Art introduced me to J. Green, who seemed a pleasant fellow. He said he would be happy to hire me, except for one problem.

"We've never had a woman and you might be uncomfortable. There's only this one restroom." I hadn't noticed the door on the right.

"As long as it has a lock on the door, I'll be fine," I told him. "As far as I'm concerned a bathroom doesn't have a sex until it's occupied."

J. Green Enterprises was a subcontractor for several small steel companies who fabricated the miscellaneous steel — the stairs and handrails, balconies and canopies — required in multistory buildings. My first day on the job Green handed me a roll of engineering and architectural drawings that was so enormous I couldn't lift it.

"Don't worry. You can do it — just remember to take one small bite at a time. And don't believe that either the engineer or the architect is infallible. We've found them in a lot of mistakes, haven't we, Bill?" (Bill was Green's right-hand man.)

I had only been there a short time when Green gave me a red pencil and told me to check Bill's drawings. I demurred. "You can do it! You'll learn a hell of a lot more by getting kicked in the backside than by sitting in the grandstand."

True! I learned by studying Bill's drawings against the plans, not looking for mistakes, but seeing how clear he made everything. Green's system, checking each other's drawings before submitting them to the shop, was an improvement over my earlier experiences where mistakes were found in the field. Later, when my own drawings came back with scarcely a red mark, it was a gratifying feeling.

I soon became one of the crew. Bill, from Oklahoma, was raising a young family. Bob was a Valley kid, not sure what he wanted to do with his life. Harry was a semi-retired history teacher who loved camping with his family. Art worked for a while until his asthma became too debilitating. Whether Green was out of the office drumming up work, or sitting in the back, the atmosphere was casual and warm. We talked about everything from sports to family to politics.

"I'm all for democracy but I don't see how it works in a family," Bill argued. "Someone has to be in charge."

"Yes. But it doesn't always have to be the same person. When I feel that Dick really cares about something, I give way. And if Dick realizes something — like going to a meeting — is important to me, he goes along even if he'd rather not."

———————

Our friend Lucia used to arrange an annual get-together of the San Diego comrades who were now living in the Los Angeles area — Celia and Verna and Bernadette. Bernadette was in poor health but she came when she could. A few times Laura and her husband came up from San Diego. More by attrition than animus we had all dropped out of the Party by this time but we enjoyed looking back on the days when it had consumed so much of our lives. It was fun to recall one event in particular that always had us in stitches.

We were beginning to be conscious of the need for "security" so we planned to have a county-wide convention of the Party out of town. Sam, an older comrade, agreed to hold the meeting at his ranch in Santee. We needed six cars to accommodate all of us and arranged to rendezvous well out of town. We made quite a caravan behind Dave who, in the lead car, was charged with sighting the sign that would show us where to turn to get to Sam's ranch. It was a very hot Sunday afternoon. Half an hour, fifty minutes and it was apparent that we had gone wrong somewhere. He pulled to one side of the dusty road and all the cars pulled up behind him.

"You got a map?" he asked me.

"No, no map. Here are Sam's directions — so many miles out of town, turn left at intersection, look for sign posted on tree."

"Well we've made a left at every intersection and it just got us back where we started."

Joe volunteered to stop at the next farmhouse we passed.

"And why would you be going to Sam's?"

"What if I say we've come for a family reunion?"

"A half black, half white family?"

"I could say we're a church group going for a picnic."

"Oh very good," piped up Dave, "Sam being a well-known atheist. OK. Everybody stay here. I'll drive back to that gas station we passed and see if they have a phone."

He came back shaking his head. "Sunday afternoon — of course they're closed."

"It's getting too late, anyway," I said. "Since we have our sandwiches and drinks, why don't we find a shady spot somewhere and plan our next move?"

A little more driving. At last a few trees. We got out. Stretched our legs. Ate the dry sandwiches, drank the lukewarm juice. "I'm sorry, guys. This was a mistake. I guess we should just take a chance and meet in town." And we settled on the Saturday of the following week.

Now, years later, we surmised that the FBI must have thought that we had deliberately led them on a wild goose chase!

———

The FBI report dated 3/31/67 at the end of this chapter is an inquiry about whether to remove me from surveillance, because FBI investigation "has failed to develop evidence of recent subversive activities ..." on my part. But my kids are sure our telephone was tapped as long as we lived in Tujunga (until August '75.) Over the years the FBI had made a number of attempts to get both Dick and me to talk to them, efforts which they recorded as being unsuccessful.

The second report, dated 4/26/67, is the recommendation that my name be removed from the list of "the Emergency Detention Program." That list, begun in early 1946, was a plan (never implemented) for the FBI to "detain" all the leading members of the Communist Party, even noting which members had children! The detention of the Japanese in America, citizens and non-citizens alike, during World War II, must have been taken as a success! (It took many years before the U.S. government admitted its violation of human rights and made some restitution to its remaining survivors.)

Younger readers may not know that in 1950 twelve leaders of the Communist Party of California, including Bernadette and Dorothy Healey, were jailed under charges of advocating the overthrow of the government. They won their freedom on appeal to the 9th Circuit Court in 1951, when the government could not prove its case.

It distresses and outrages me to know that today the U.S. government is again using "detention" and "rendition" of people suspected of links to terrorists, in violation of our own Constitution and international law.

Assistant Attorney General
Internal Security Division

March 31, 1967

Director, FBI

1 - ☐   b6
1 - ☐   b7C

EMERGENCY DETENTION PROGRAM

The name of the subject appearing below has been approved for inclusion in the Security Index by the Internal Security Division of the Department.

Name: NANCY ROSENFIELD LUND

FBI File Number: 100-208196

Department Approved: October 7, 1958

Date of Last Report: March 21, 1967

Investigation has failed to develop evidence of recent subversive activities or affiliations on the part of the subject. All pertinent information concerning the reported past subversive activities of the subject has been furnished the Records Administration Office.

It is requested that the results of the investigation be reviewed to determine whether the subject's name should continue to be included in the Security Index.

100-398030

1 - Los Angeles (100-18292)

100-208196

NOT RECORDED
199 APR 3 1967

ORIGINAL FILED IN /00...

SAC, Los Angeles (100-18292)

April 26, 1967

REC- 25
Director, FBI   (100-208196)   58

NANCY ROSENFIELD LUND
SM - C

Security Index card cancelled 1 -
4/27/67,   1 - ☐

ReBulet to the Department dated March 31, 1967, captioned "Emergency Detention Program," a copy of which was furnished your office.

By letter dated April 20, 1967, the Department advised that the subject's name should be removed from the Security Index. This action has been taken at the Bureau and similar action should be taken with respect to the cards maintained in your office.

From FBI files (1967)

The Sixties

James Baldwin's piece in the *New Yorker*, "Next Time the Fire," hit me like a slap in the face.

"You idiot. You smug, self-congratulating idiot," it seemed to say. "What in the world made you think that the Victory Theater campaign for jobs in the black community, all those years ago, changed things in any basic way? And what in the hell have you done since?"

Writing with passion, yet balance, Baldwin laid before America the awful truth that the evils of slavery persisted in the United States, that the patience which had miraculously kept the black population quiescent could not be counted on to endure forever.

I couldn't wait till Dick came home, to get him to read it. He was not as devastated as I. He saw progress, hopeful indications, the good relations developing within his department, promotions within the County.

But I felt that Baldwin had spelled out the disaster that was to come — the Watts Riots were exactly what he was predicting. He named our failures, especially in regard to the veterans of World War II. And along with everything else, it made me feel justified in leaving the Communist Party. I felt that the Party had seen the injustices, the hypocrisy of the U.S. fighting Hitler while perpetuating racism at home, but had been too much talk and too little action. Its message was a good one but it had come in a package that was unacceptable, or perhaps inaccessible, to the average American.

How far we were from establishing equity — we had only to look at the passage of Proposition 14, the initiative to wipe Fair

Housing off the law in California. True, it was finally declared unconstitutional by the U.S. Supreme Court, but the rancor and bitterness elicited by that fight certainly helped fuel the Watts riots.

Fair employment, fair housing, and voting rights had to be written into law. The tiny success of the Victory Theater needed to be replicated on a massive scale. That campaign had been 1946, now it was 1964. Changing people's minds was important, but changing their behavior was essential.

I trembled for the U.S. and I was right. In 1965 it was the fire — five horrific days in Watts and its surrounding communities, spreading to Newark, and then across the country.

During the riots, we offered our home to Adele and family, Rosa Lee Carter, and other friends who lived in or near Watts and might need a place to stay, but we had no takers. It was a tense and scary period.

Afterwards, Adele had hopes that out of the ashes some good would come of it. And some did. The UAW built a community center and eventually the Martin Luther King Hospital was opened to serve this neglected area.

I didn't get around to reading Betty Friedan's *The Feminine Mystique* when it came out in '63, but it had an immediate impact on every facet of life. Beyond "bra-burning" cartoons and snide remarks, this was serious stuff, at last.

More than Friedan, my models were Bella Abzug and Shirley Chisholm, New York Congresswomen who were shaking up the political establishment. "Establishment" — that's the word that epitomized the sixties! It encapsulated and resonated better than what we in the Party had labeled "the capitalists and their lackeys." The Establishment described the powerful people in academia as well as those in Wall Street and in Washington and Sacramento.

I loved, too, the biting humor of Gloria Steinem and the wit of the women who carried picket signs reading "Don't Iron When the Strike Is Hot!"

I had never been bashful about raising issues of equality but now I was further armed to challenge even "real nice men," in public, when they fell back on stereotypical remarks. The Sunland-Tujunga Democratic Club had just opened a campaign office and we were debating which precincts should have priority. I had a difference of opinion on which precincts we should concentrate with Bill G. (one of the really, really nice guys in the Club).

After we had gone round and round, he said in an exasperated tone, "You don't need to get so emotional about it."

"Bill," I said loudly, "would you say that to a man? Hell, no! You would say that's a poor argument – or I don't agree with you. But because I'm a woman, you can demean my opinion by calling it 'emotional'."

"Sorry," he gulped and my precinct strategy carried the day.

The turmoil of the sixties impacted everyone and our family was no exception. Hair, marijuana, the Beatles – but most of all the Vietnam War. The CDC (California Democratic Clubs, in case my readers have forgotten), was one of the first voices to oppose the war. We were early supporters of Eugene McCarthy and with difficulty broke with Governor Pat Brown who had allied himself with President Lyndon Johnson.

Our house was one place where our kids and their friends felt comfortable. We didn't hassle them about hair, or their hippy clothes, and their jeans got washed whether or not there were marijuana seeds in the pockets.

I remember the time when Dick had invited a number of his coworkers to a Sunday brunch. He gave them directions, including the admonition that "we are probably well known because of our long-haired boys and their friends." Well, as usual, the invitees had trouble finding the house but told us, "No one knew you because of the kids – they said, 'Oh, you mean those radical Democrats?' and directed us right here!" The Gene McCarthy signs had gotten their attention.

The main reason Dick and I bought an eight passenger Ford Econoline (an early version of the passenger van), was so that we could take our draft-age sons to Canada. But the boys were not about to flee. Ben never was called but Eric drew a low number in the draft lottery. He went through the physical but walked out with all his papers – which he promptly threw into the nearest trashcan. Months later the FBI caught up with him. They interviewed him in our living room (!) but that was the last he heard from them. Eric must have convinced them that he would be far more trouble than they cared to cope with.

When President Johnson came to L.A. in '67 there was a huge protest at the UCLA campus. Rachel was just getting over bronchitis, so she and I didn't go, but Dick, Eric and Ben did. Eric's sign made it to the front page of the *Los Angeles Times*: "Beware the military industrial complex. Dwight D. Eisenhower." Seeing the police in battle gear, using their night sticks right and left, punching a pregnant woman in the stomach – was my family's firsthand experience of what was happening all over the country. As a family we marched in all the peace marches thereafter but were free of harassment.

I didn't go to the CDC convention in '68, so I missed Martin Luther King's stirring speech against the war, and the growing conviction that the anti-Vietnam movement was sweeping the country. A few weeks later King was gunned down in Memphis.

It was also in March that Bobby Kennedy declared his candidacy for President. And then President Johnson stunned us with his announcement that he would not run again. But we had high hopes for McCarthy's victory in the California primary and campaigned strongly against Kennedy, naming him an opportunist and a latecomer to the peace movement. We followed the results that June night only to realize that McCarthy would not win; the momentum was for Kennedy.

Along with the whole world we watched the scene in the hotel kitchen, heard the shots, saw Kennedy falling. The fourth assassination – Jack, Martin, Malcolm X and now Bobby. My revulsion at this latest death was compounded by a feeling of guilt. Hadn't I added to the hate against Kennedy by the way we had campaigned? I resolved that from here on I would only use positive arguments in behalf of my candidate, never again would I smear the opponent or use innuendo to malign him.

Democratic Party conventions, by and large, were not anything to be proud of. In 1964 it had been the memorable fight of black delegates to be seated. Black delegates from the south for the first time in over eighty years! The compromise — seated but not voting — was truly disgraceful. But the Democratic Convention in Chicago in '68 was the all time low, both on the floor and in the streets outside. From the vacuous platform, to the jailing of protesters, to the railroading of Hubert Humphrey as the "unity candidate", it was the antithesis of all we had hoped for. Unable to support Humphrey that fall, most of us decided to concentrate on Congressional races. Although Humphrey surged the last week of the campaign, it was too late. Nixon won and the Vietnam War went on for another five years.

Eric, Rachel and Nancy

I loved having all the kids at our house. It was fun listening to their chatter, their excitement over different musical groups, their critique of movies and books. It was understood that they wouldn't smoke at our house and we had no problem with what they did elsewhere.

"Why do you think I won't get *Catch 22*?" I challenged Eric's friend, Montgomery. I had to read it. And of course I "got" it.

But I was not so happy when this same friend asked Rachel, "Why are you still wasting your time going to high school?" She was all of 14 — and fortunately stayed in school (probably because of art classes) until graduation at 17.

"Never heard of Gurdjieff?" Ben was indignant. "This will change your way of looking at everything." It was certainly changing him. Ben was at UCLA, not doing much class work but already making his mark in the Drama Dept. It was there that he met Jordan, an older fellow who introduced the kids around him to the esoteric theories of George Gurdjieff, a mystic who claimed to synthesize eastern and western philosophies.

Jordan and the group from UCLA were going to make their own movie and soon had Eric involved as well. While Eric was always the keen observer, Ben would go into things "whole hog." When younger he had outgrown model airplanes only to become enamored of slot cars. Now it was Gurdjieff that led him into embracing astrology. At great expense, he bought the huge books needed in order to plot in detail the horoscopes of everyone he knew. I had encouraged Rachel to use her collage skills to decorate the wall in her bedroom; so Ben, in turn, decided to paint his ceiling with a goddess figure and stars.

I read *Beelzebub* and *Meetings with Remarkable Men* by Gurdjieff, and I could see why his theories might attract those searching for a deeper meaning to their lives. For me, his conclusions didn't bear close scrutiny. Ben, however, was sold. Along with his conviction that we are influenced by the stars, he argued that we are endowed with unused great powers of the mind. By developing these powers, one could control others. For instance, driving down the highway he could make the car ahead of him change lanes. "See!"

"Maybe he didn't like you tail-gating him," said I.

Some of it was harmless but I was alarmed the time that two of his friends drove up to the house and announced, "We have Ben in the car."

"What do you mean — you have Ben in the car? Why isn't he here with you?"

"Well, you see — he's having a little trouble walking."

Jordan had convinced Ben that he could jump off a roof and... True, he hadn't broken his ankles, but he was hurting pretty badly.

I don't remember how long the fascination with Gurdjieff and Jordan persisted, but I do remember that Ben dropped out of school after three semesters. Rachel and I had often brought food to the room at UCLA which he shared with his friend, A. Martinez. Even to a poor housekeeper like me, the disorder was a shock. So when Ben and some of his friends moved to Santa Monica I never ventured inside their "Magic House." But Dick did, and from his description it was a typical hippy pad, complete with hammocks slung above the sleeping bags on the floor.

Dick and I worried that Ben, with his straggly beard and long hair, clad all in black including a big brimmed fedora, might be persona-non-grata at the Jewish Home for the Aged where his grandmother lived. Au contraire — he was most welcome. Perhaps to them he looked more Hasidic than scrungy.

Mama adored him as I think she did all young people. My kids always had something of interest to share with her — for Ben it was drama, for Eric poetry, and art for Rachel. They brought news of their different world while she, in turn, always managed to have a droll story about her fellow residents.

In the summer of '68 Eric hitchhiked around Europe, having worked for a year to save enough money. We got wonderful, funny letters from him such as the one following his flight to London. "I was quite tired and so accepted a cup of coffee offered by the stewardess. I had forgotten why I don't like it. It's the taste." When he returned that fall, he stayed with my sister Julie in New York for a few days. She called to tell me that obviously he hadn't been eating regularly and she would try to fatten him up a bit before his return.

Later that fall, at one of our Democratic Club meetings at our house, a member pulled me aside and asked, "Why don't you make Eric cut his hair and shave his beard? He looks scary — like Charles Manson." I shook my head.

A few moments later another member stopped me to say, "Eric is so sweet. He looks like Jesus Christ."

Wins and Losses

The Sunland-Tujunga Democratic Club had good reasons to support Tom Bradley for mayor of Los Angeles. Besides being a good liberal, Bradley had spoken up in our behalf when we had brought our fight on the Tujunga Wash to the Los Angeles City Council. Our own City Councilman, Louie Nowell, ignored our calls and petitions opposing a freeway through the last wild river in the L.A. basin. When we filled an auditorium with people protesting the freeway, he scoffed, "You don't represent the people of my District."

So we decided to go to the L.A. City Hall and fill that chamber. Nowell ignored us.

Bradley, the black City Councilman for the mostly white Crenshaw District, turned to Nowell and said, loud enough for all to hear, "Believe me, if I saw the room filled with people from my District, I would make sure that they had a place on the agenda and got to speak their piece."

And because of Bradley, we did.

In 1969 Bradley ran for mayor and we were happy to carry his material to every precinct around us. It was tough. The racism of his opponent, Sam Yorty, was palpable and it was reflected by the response we got when Dick and I went knocking on doors in Lakeview Terrace, a middle-class neighborhood. Some people were content just to slam the door in our faces, but others came outside to yell at their neighbors, "We don't want that kind in our city hall." and "Don't take any of that nigger's literature."

It was no surprise that Bradley was defeated, but support for him and disgust with Yorty encouraged him to run again in '73. Our big family room could accommodate more than fifty (borrowed) folding chairs, so we offered our house for the opening of his campaign in our District. Bradley came without the expected retinue and was among the first to arrive. As we took him through the house on the way to the family room, he noticed Rachel's collages and Ben's sparkling ceiling. To our surprise he was enthusiastic about the idea that kids could be allowed, nay encouraged, to decorate their own rooms, so it was Bradley who took new arrivals on mini-tours to see the "murals"!

Every chair was filled and there were many people standing when the meeting began. Bradley looked around the room and said with a wry smile, "It's not often that a candidate gets to thank everyone who voted for him in one room."

Happily, Bradley won that year and went on to serve five terms as mayor. His stature was such that he was offered a cabinet position by Jimmy Carter in '76 (which he turned down) and was considered as a possible Vice-Presidential candidate by Walter Mondale in '84. But his unsuccessful race for governor of California reflected the strength of racism. The "Bradley effect" was coined to explain his loss of the race. Bradley had been projected as the winner by pollsters on the basis of having people say that they would vote for a black man; but when these voters got into the booth their prejudices took over.

―――――――

The Democratic Party Convention of 1972 was the logical conclusion of all the foment of the 1960's. And I was there!

That campaign started a few minutes after midnight on January 3rd, the first moment that nominations for a presidential candidate could be filled out. Twenty people crowded around our dining room table to put George McGovern's name on the ballot. We were one of hundreds of similar gatherings throughout California, intent on electing a true progressive who would end the war and restore civil liberties in our country.

Sunland-Tujunga Residents Attend Democratic National Convention

The Sunland-Tujunga community was well represented at the Democratic National Convention held last week in Miami Beach, Florida. Serving as McGovern delegates on the California delegation were Tujunga residents Nancy Lund and Cliff Berg. Cited for their dedication and determination by delegation co-chairman Assemblyman Willie Brown, the team of Lund and Berg labored many long hours during their six-day stay in Miami Beach to make participatory democracy a reality!

Sunland resident Leon Bayer also attended the convention, serving as an alternate delegate on the McGovern California delegation.

Married for 25 years, and the mother of three grown children, Mrs. Lund has worked politically in the

Sunland-Tujunga area for more years than she cares to remember. "I first worked politically for the Rev. Jones in the school board election," Mrs. Lund said.

A member of the Sunland-Tujunga Democratic Club, she has seen the club grow over the years and become one of the largest Democratic clubs in the San Fernando Valley.

"We are very much a grass roots club that takes an interest in local community affairs as well as national campaigns and issues," Mrs. Lund said.

"The key to the entire election of Senator McGovern as the Democratic nominee," according to Mrs. Lund, "rested on the outcome of the vote on the challenge to the credentials of the California delegation. "When we landed in Miami on Sunday and learned the original 271 California McGovern

delegation had been cut to 120 delegates, of course we were disappointed and discouraged," Mrs. Lund said.

"However, my spirits were lifted when I found out I had been chosen as one of the 120 to take a seat at the opening session Monday evening and help lobby for votes for the seating of the entire original California McGovern delegation. The high point of the convention for Mrs. Lund was winning the crucial vote that evening.

"Our delegation so closely followed the reform guidelines as set down by the Democratic National Committee, that we could not believe we were being challenged," said Mrs. Lund. "The number of young people and the number of older

delegates on the delegation from the grass roots was absolutely fantastic. These delegation members were people who had raised money for McGovern at the local level and done the telephoning and precinct work for years, and for the first time they were given an opportunity to have an input into what was happening in the upper decision-making part of the Democratic Party. This time there was no control from the top from vested interests. The platform, or parts of it, had been discussed openly since last November. We didn't feel we were being handed a package. We really had something to say as to what we wanted in the package. It was our convention and we owe all that to Senator George McGovern who chaired the Democratic National Committee's Reform Commission over four years ago."

Nancy Lund . . . Delegation Leader

Nancy at Democratic National Convention (1972)

170

I decided to quit my job and spend full time on the campaign. I was made the campaign director for our Assembly District, and given a car to cover a huge area that stretched to Lancaster and Pear Blossom. After two months I turned in the car, deciding that my time was better spent in Sunland-Tujunga — where the population was — rather than hours spent driving back and forth to Lancaster to meet with a handful of people.

It was a very well-orchestrated campaign from top to bottom. Our voter lists were complete and accurate, and we keyed the talking points, the telephone calls and letters to our area. Most importantly we had a wonderful crew of local volunteers, from kids too young to vote to elders who had voted for Eugene Debs in the 1920's, and still others confined to a wheel chair but using their phones at home. All dedicated and committed.

A serendipitous addition was being brought fresh baked goodies most mornings. (Two of our supporters were mother and daughter who were writing a cookbook and asked us to be their tasters.) Twenty-odd years later, some segments of "The West Wing" on television reminded me of our campaign.

The Democratic Party Convention of '72 was operating under the new rules, largely written by McGovern after the disasters of the '64 and '68 conventions. The majority of the delegates were to be elected at local caucuses, while the party officials and office holders had fewer seats. Our Assembly District was entitled to two delegates and I was one of them, helped no doubt by Nettie's eloquent speech nominating me at our caucus. The other delegate was Cliff, a student who had worked hard on the campaign, much to the disappointment of Bill G. who had assumed he was the natural choice. Another student, Glenn, was our alternate.

Pressed for money, the campaign urged each of us to pay our own airfare and hotel expenses. That June I sent out a letter to my Christmas list, plus my doctor and dentist and the managers of our neighborhood market and gas station. I said this is a time of year we all receive graduation announcements and in a way this was my graduation, the culmination of all the years that I had worked for good causes — and I promised that I would not go on to obtain any higher degrees. Success! I raised enough money beyond my needs to help Glenn and Cliff reach their goals. And our local paper (under a different editor than the one who wanted to know what a nice woman like me was doing in the Democratic Party) sent a reporter along with us to Miami to cover the convention.

On the way to Miami (my first and only flight in a super jet) I sat between Barry Commoner, a well known liberal author and activist, and Ernie Smith, an old friend from my days on 89th Place. Marlo Thomas, Warren Beatty and other movie stars were a few seats away.

I was one of the McGovern delegates seated at the opening session of the convention, but some Party officials — led by the Speaker of the California Assembly, Jess Unruh — occupied a number of disputed seats. These office holders were challenging the new rules under which the convention was being held. Willie Brown (our hero at the time, but whom I later recognized as just another politician) made his famous plea "Give me back my delegates," and succeeded in getting most of the McGovern delegates seated.

It was a wild five days. At the Doral Hotel I shared a room with three women from the Glendale area, but I hardly slept. I attended the Women's Caucus and the Liberal Caucus as well as the California Caucus, on top of all the hours on the floor. The Women's Caucus pushed for Frances "Sissy" Farenthold, from Texas, as Vice President, but we were unsuccessful. I remember Gloria Steinem coming back to us to report, "We've been screwed. And being fucked by your friends doesn't feel one bit better than being fucked by your enemies."

It was after midnight when we finally accepted Tom Eagleton as Vice-President, an unknown to most of us. It proved to be a huge mistake. The press wasted no time in digging up the fact that Eagleton had been treated for a "mental condition" — depression — which was a no-no in those days. McGovern pooh-poohed the charges at first, backed him "1000 %", and then a few days later accepted Eagleton's resignation. Sargent Shriver became the Vice-Presidential nominee.

After the convention we in Sunland-Tujunga battled on. The Watergate story had made hardly a stir in June and was completely forgotten by November. I dismissed the newspaper and TV polls that predicted a victory for Nixon; I was so sure that our candidate, a decorated fighter pilot in World War II, would win. McGovern was such a straight talker, straight shooter, a living example of what is best in America — how could people not vote for him?

We watched the returns that night as state after state went for Dirty Dick. How could it be? The poem that I wrote a few days later expresses what I felt.

November '72

The winds have scoured the orchards
and the trees, which like our hopes
had burgeoned in the spring,
now lift their skeletal limbs
against a drear November sky.

Take heart my sons and you,
my gently weeping daughters,
this season, too, shall pass
and from these empty rows
we yet shall reap bright harvests.

Clean cradled in the dead leaf
lies the seed.

Nancy and Mama, Christmas 1974

Transitions

In 1970 Rachel was 16 and Dick and I felt that this summer should be something special. How about driving across country, all the way to Washington D.C.? From the capital, we would go on to see the historic sites in New England and thence into Canada, following the Trans-Canada Highway west to Vancouver and then home. Dick had hitchhiked over much of the country and had followed the Appalachian Trail when he was stationed in Washington D.C. but I had never been east of El Paso, so it would be as much of an adventure for me as for Rachel.

For the last couple of summers we had taken one or other of Rachel's friends with us on our camping trips. (Eric had decided, long ago, that camping was not for him and Ben was too busy with other things.) In her junior year Rachel had become close friends with two classmates, Cynthia and Maril, who happened to be enthusiastic campers. We met with their families and they were comfortable with their daughters going on the long trip with us. We soon realized that trying to do everything, see everything, in three weeks was impractical. We decided to go east only as far as Ames, Iowa, where Dick's Uncle Fred lived, and then up to Canada.

To prepare for such an extended trip I had 30-inch pipes welded to the corners of an old double-bed frame. With the van's back seat removed, the bed not only fitted perfectly into the back, but provided all that storage space beneath it. "The red box" with all our cooking gear, an ice chest and camp stove were instantly available as soon as we opened the back doors. Everything else — sleeping bags, ground cloths, lantern and duffle bags for the five of us — got stuffed in from the side door. Once we reached that day's destination, Dick and I would sleep in the van, the girls outside. When we were on the road, the bed provided ample space for the three girls to loll with their knitting or books or catnaps.

The trip turned out to be a perfect one, beyond our wildest expectations. There were fresh baked "kringlas" at the market in Ames (Norwegian biscuits almost as good as Grandma Lund's). We swam and hiked, picked wild raspberries in Minnesota, and went canoeing on the mirror-like Bow River outside of Banff. We saw a moose, and beavers, and a rainbow arching over Lake Louise. The girls were ahead of Dick, at every turn, whether building a campfire, rolling up sleeping bags, or making sandwiches for the day's lunch. They eschewed staying at a motel, even once. They washed their hair in lakes and rivers and one time under the freezing water of an old-fashioned hand pump!

Footnote: Today, October 17, 2009, Cynthia has arranged for us all to be together for the first time in 39 years — a testimony that the trip remains a unique and magical time for each of us!

The following year — and not without some trepidation — Dick and I agreed that Rachel could go with Maril and some of her friends in the "green bus" — one of the converted Volkswagen vans that were part of the hippy scene. Rachel phoned us a couple of times reporting that "since we only have good expectations, we get nothing but good 'vibes' wherever we go." Because the bus was not coming back to California, Ben and I drove our van to New Mexico to rendezvous with them and bring the girls back in time for school. It gave me a chance to visit with my sister Mary and her husband, Harold, who had moved back to Taos after their five years in California.

Earlier that spring, my friend Sophie had taken me aside after a meeting. Sophie was a nurse and I heard her concern: "You had better see a doctor about your thyroid — looks like a goiter to me."

My regular doctor, Dr. Gordon, sent me to a specialist who felt it warranted surgery. I waited until after Rachel had gone. Why spoil her summer? And I didn't tell my mother, either. Why worry her?

The diagnosis was "a cold node with a completely encapsulated cancer at its center." I was told that I would have to take thyroid medication for the rest of my life.

Six weeks after my surgery I was neither "tired and sleepy" nor "hot and jumpy" – the two questions asked by my surgeon – but I did not feel well. I was nauseated, as if I were poisoned.

The doctor finally decided on a blood test.

"Oops! Way too much thyroid now. Stay off of it for two weeks and we'll test it again and adjust the dose."

At the end of the two weeks I felt my normal, energetic self and against his advice decided that I would not take thyroid at all. I told Dr. Gordon (a good progressive), "I'm not only into woman's lib, I'm into confrontational medicine now."

"Okay with me," he said, "but I know a top endocrinologist and I'd like you to see him, just to be sure."

This specialist was so expensive you even had to pay for parking! But he was good and reassured me that my own body would tell me far more than any blood test could. As long as I felt fine, neither gained or lost weight, I would be okay.

I was used to looking for a job but after the '72 election the job found me. A contractor for whom I had done a few freelance re-bar jobs recommended me highly to Phil Weary, an engineer in Glendale. Weary needed someone to check the re-bar placing sheets for a big concrete structure for which he had done the engineering. The building, a public library in one of the beach communities, was designed by a famous architect and was quite complicated.

I went to work for the same rate I had drawn at my last regular job. Weary (I soon called him Phil) had a small office. There were three draftsmen beside me. I didn't do any drawing at first, as my time was occupied with checking the re-bar sheets against Phil's specs. When that was done I gradually took over more of the drawing. Over the next two and a half years Phil's engineering jobs shrank and I was the only employee left. I also assumed the bookkeeping duties, such as they were.

Phil, who insisted he was a die-hard Republican, was interested in my views on everything – health, religion and politics.

"I should get some kind of recognition," Phil would brag. "Here I have hired three minorities – a woman, a person over 50 and a Jew. And I've done it all without increasing my payroll." Whereupon he gave me a raise. Working for Phil turned out to be the best job I ever had.

Ben had moved to the Santa Cruz Mountains with kids we knew, the circle from Sunland-Tujunga and UCLA. He and his friends got jobs – or didn't. They moved into – or out of – various cabins, with – or without – new roommates. We weren't worried about them; they weren't in trouble. They were doing their thing. Unquote. Before long Rachel moved up there too. Eric visited them frequently, but was still living at home.

Then in the spring of '74 Rachel announced that she was getting married. Ben was less than enthusiastic about her choice, but we put it down to his obligations as "the big brother." Sean was handsome and bright. And glamorous with the aura that only a Vietnam veteran – one who came back strongly opposed to the war – could have. Dick and I thought Sean probably needed time to "de-compress" but the two were obviously in love and we felt that Rachel was mature enough to make it work. We witnessed their "al fresco" wedding under the trees, Ben officiating in his role as Universal Life minister.

Then Ben found his perfect partner, Janet. Dick and I drove up to meet her and her adorable daughter, three-year-old Becky. Janet came from a radical family, like us. She and Ben seemed ideally suited and though marriage wasn't in their plans, we couldn't have been more pleased. A few weeks later they drove down to visit us, and Becky was right behind Dick "helping Grampy" whatever he was doing.

Dick would be 60 years old in April of '75 and we had decided that it would be the year we would sell the house and retire. And we had at last found the ideal spot — Plumas County. Two coincidences led us there. Pat, a draftsman at Phil's, was surprised that I had never heard of Lake Almanor — "It's unbeatable — worth the six hour drive." And Nettie, searching for a spot in California like Lake Tahoe but at a lower elevation, had subscribed to the Feather Newspapers. She announced, "Here's your spot! Plumas County just built a community college in Quincy. They've enrolled 22,000 students and there's only 20,000 people in the whole county."

Something wrong with those figures? But up to Plumas County we went in the summer of '74. We camped at one of the public camps on the west shore of Lake Almanor. The swimming was wonderful. Everyone we talked to was enthusiastic about the area. And when we left, driving through Greenville we noticed a small store on Main Street. It boasted a large "Doughnuts" sign and below it "Health Food." Perfect! Doughnuts for Dick and health food for me! (Actually, our first choice would be Quincy, nearer to the college, but fate would lead us to Greenville.)

Spurred on by my bout with doctors and with renewed interest in diet and alternative medicine, Dick and I explored chiropractic and acupuncture and subscribed to a Health Book Club. When our good friend Bob Camen's asthma became untreatable, I lent him the book on acupuncture. Surprisingly, his doctor encouraged him to try it. Bob had amazing relief after a few treatments with a Chinese doctor. When I had a series of debilitating headaches I too tried acupuncture, with somewhat less spectacular results.

I had always loved walking but now (summer of '74) I found that regardless of which shoes I wore, my left foot was increasingly painful. So when neither chiropractic nor acupuncture helped me with the pain, I turned to Mama's long-time podiatrist, Dr. A.

"Heel spur," he said. Over many weeks he taped and wrapped my foot, turning it so I wouldn't be walking on that part of my heel. But that was a temporary measure; eventually I would need surgery. Dick was scheduled for a long-delayed hernia operation in February, so I waited till he was back on his feet before having the spur removed.

The operation was a minor one but its aftermath was not. When the doctor unrolled all the bandages and took out the stitches, I was aghast at how dry and flaky my skin looked. "No problem," he said. "You can get cortisone ointment at the drug store and rub it in."

Bad advice. The area where the stitches had been removed opened up and I had a gaping hole below the ankle, all the way to the bone. No blood, just a hole. Dr. A. was sorry, but too late. There was nothing to be done but wait for nature to do the healing process, from the inside out. No telling how long that would take. Meanwhile keep my foot elevated.

I am on crutches (which I never learn to properly manage) when Ben, Janet and our darling Becky visit us, on their way to Guatemala. Janet has a degree in anthropology and speaks Spanish. She has had this plan for a long time; they will find a village where they can live simply. She might teach, Ben will find something. They'll buy lots of wonderful Guatemalan fabric which they can sell on their return.

Here in Tujunga I must stay off my feet so Becky crawls into bed with me. We spend long hours with boxes of crayons and reams of paper, making elaborate "stained glass windows." When we are tired of that we take turns drawing "squiggles" which the other one must finish, turning it into an animal or person or maybe a flower. A week, maybe two? I am the one who spurs them to buy the tickets to Mexico for the first leg of their trip. I can't go with them to the station, but wish them a sincere bon voyage.

Ben had moved on from astrology, so I never had any confirmation on how the stars were aligned that spring, but as I write this I am amazed at the succession of things, the confluence of events, that occurred in March and April of '75.

EVENT I. Here I am on crutches when Alan, Dick's supervisor from the Probation Department, comes over to talk with us about Dick's plans.

"Plans?"

"Well, yes. Dick has earned a promotion but he has refused it. He tells us that he doesn't think it right to take a promotion when he plans to retire."

"Right."

"But you haven't sold your house — haven't even put it up for sale, am I correct?"

"Right."

"Believe me, I don't want to lose Dick, he's a great asset to the department. I just want to get an idea of your plans."

I explain, "Of course, we won't have any money to move until we sell the house. Our son and his family have been visiting, and between my foot and one thing and another, we haven't got a realtor. Yet."

"I can give you the name of my brother-in-law. Jake's a square shooter."

We take his name and phone number.

"So where are you going, once you sell the house?"

Dick says, "A place you've probably never heard of — we hadn't. Plumas County."

"As a matter of fact I do know it! My sister is married to a doctor who practiced up in Quincy until a few years ago. If you like I can give you the name of the realtor who sold their house for them. Her name's Scott. Married to a Supervisor or Fair Manager, I think."

The next day I call Jake, the realtor. He comes over that evening and I show him the architect's plans for the house. It has the square footage, materials, everything. Great! We agree on a price. (I think it was $10,000 more than we paid for the house, seven years before. We will have to pay off a big mortgage, of course.) Jake doesn't think we have to do any "prep" to show the house. (Because of my foot, we have hired someone to clean the house and it is in fairly good order.)

EVENT II. Even before he has time to run an ad or put up a yard sign, Jake has a prospective buyer. Did he raise an eyebrow at the collaged wall in Rachel's bedroom and Ben's bright ceiling of stars and goddesses? No matter, our house is sold, escrow to close by the end of May!

EVENT III. I am on crutches when Mama goes into the hospital. Now 87, she has become thin over the last year and has begun to look her age. But she has not lost her twinkle, her interest in everything that goes on around her. Our family feels that the Jewish Home in Reseda takes good care of its residents, with regular check-ups, and medications monitored. On the day that the Home arranges for their bus to take Mama to the hospital for some tests, she replies that she has a luncheon date and will have her friend drop her off after lunch. Neither she nor any of us think it can be serious.

Dick and I go to the hospital where other members of the family – Leon and Bobbie, Adele and Oneil, and grandson Don Bell and his wife Pam – are gathered. I want to tell them my news but hesitate telling Mama. Before long it spills out, "Can you believe it – we've sold the house and by summer we'll be moving to Plumas County! But it isn't that far. We'll be coming back so often you won't know we've moved."

"I'm not surprised," Mama says. "Just surprised that it isn't China."

But Mama's condition turns out to be serious. They order a liver biopsy which does not go well. Mama rejects further probing; and it is too late. She becomes jaundiced and is sinking fast. Dick and I visit her one last time. Julie has flown down from San Francisco, Mary flies in from New Mexico and David from Virginia. Mama dies that night, April 14, just three days after keeping her luncheon date.

We were all devastated, none of us prepared. Despite our widely separated lives and interests, Mama had been the lodestar, the center around which we had all rotated — forever. I wept and could not stop weeping.

Over the years Mama had gradually divested herself of her good jewelry and china. When she went into the Home she had divided what was left of her furniture and books. Everything had been neatly and equitably parceled out to her seven living children and Teeta's kids. But that did not indicate to us that she was dying; it was just that she had no room for "things."

In lieu of a funeral, the Home held a memorial with an exhibition of Mama's drawings. Though legally blind, Mama had spent her years as a resident with her pastel box open, a bright light at her table, and whatever paper was at hand. One of the "angels" (supporters) at the Home had selected a large number of her drawings to frame. On that day the long halls of the building were hung with Mama's still-life artworks — some bold, others dreamy — many of flowers and fruit which we had brought her — forever preserved. Happy as I was to see Mama's work appreciated it was all too much for me, too many memories, too many moments when I could have said more, done more.

But what was shown at the Home was just a fraction of Mama's work. I had a chest full of her drawings, taken for safekeeping over the years. Dick decided that we would have our own "Expo." He quickly constructed several large pegboard screens, perfect for pasting up Mama's unframed drawings. We invited family and friends to our big family room on a Sunday afternoon. I cried all that afternoon but then it was over. Somehow it was the "closure" I needed.

Dick thought that his last day at work would be his birthday, April 26. But the nice guy in the county's personnel office pointed out the benefits Dick would get by completing his 13th year of work for the county. The escrow on the house would be closing at the end of May, so we arranged with the new owners to stay, paying rent, till the end of July.

In May I was visited by someone from the State Disability office.

"Mrs. Lund," he said, "you had a very, very minor operation and should have been back at work in four weeks. This is going into 15 weeks."

I took off my sock and showed him the hole. He shuddered — and I continued to draw disability until September.

But I could swim! By late April, Dr. A. had advised that public pools were out but our own pool (immaculately maintained by Eric) was okay, and sunning my foot afterward would help in the healing process. Although I had launched each of my kids into becoming good swimmers, it was a skill I had never acquired. Now, with or without family, I spent long hours in the pool, gradually leaving the "friendly" shallow water and splashing my way into the "hostile" deep water. What joy!

———————

Our moving was decided. But was I ready to leave? Dick went to Bekins and brought back the large and medium-sized packing boxes that we would need; they sat in a corner of the family room, still folded, untaped, unpacked. I dillied and dallied over what to pack, what to keep. I now recognize that I was filled with misgivings. What were we jumping into? We had burned our bridges — what lay ahead?

Shifting Gears

We had a plan: we would rent a house until we found one we could afford. No need to store our furniture and then have to go back to Tujunga to get it once we found a house to buy. On July 4th weekend Dick and I made a quick trip to Plumas County. We drove up Highway 80 to Truckee and then north on Highway 89 and stopped at a little grocery store in Blairsden. *Mirabile dictum* – the local paper had an ad for a house for rent – or sale – in nearby Delleker. We hurried over and found it perfect – a two-story home, three bedrooms, two baths and space for a garden if we were interested. Plenty of room for the furniture we planned to keep.

The house was right on Highway 70 just outside of Portola. There we were met by Al and Jessie who were handling the property for their daughter and son-in-law. They were hoping to find a buyer for the entire spread — the big house, two cabins, several storage sheds and a mobile home in the back — but they were amenable to renting if we would agree to show the house to any potential buyers. We agreed with alacrity and paid a first and last month's rent.

So it was up to Delleker that we came on August 2nd. Dick drove a big U-Haul, packed "to the gunwales"; Eric and I drove our van, also heavily loaded. Dick was way ahead of us as the van struggled up the long grade on Highway 80. We crawled into a gas station near Donner Summit and I told the attendant I was afraid that the transmission had gone out. Lucky for me, he was not only capable but also honest.

"Don't ever go into a gas station and tell them what you think is wrong," he warned me. "They'll sell you a new transmission — or something else, big items that you probably don't need. You're just overheated."

It was mid-afternoon when Eric and I pulled into the driveway at Delleker. Dick was halfway through unloading, all by himself. Our plan was for Eric, who needed to get back to his job, to drive our van to Sacramento, leaving it at the airport there so he could catch his flight to L.A. When he got home he would call to tell us where he had left the van. By the following day, giving us plenty of time to unload, we would drive the U-haul to Sacramento, and drop it off after picking up our van. Like many a good plan, it fell through miserably.

It had been a blistering hot August day and Dick had finished unloading the U-Haul all by himself. "I'm beat," he said. "Don't bother with dinner. I'm just going to fall into bed."

"Oh please," I begged him, "please just get in the tub and shower off some of that dirt and sweat. I've just made the bed with lovely fresh sheets."

A few moments later, I heard a crash. Dick had fallen in the shower, breaking several ribs, I was sure. I helped him to bed, still wet and grimy.

Now, all these years later, it makes a good story but at the time I swore I would never forgive Eric. Was his pool cleaning job more important than Dick's health? Not only that, but as the evening wore on, I waited in vain for a call from L.A. So I began calling all the friends I could think of. If I didn't catch Eric, at least I could leave a message that it was urgent for him to tell us where he had left the van. In those days (at least in Plumas County), toll calls went through the operator and after the fifth fruitless call, she and I were on a first name basis.

"Nancy," she said, "who in the world are you trying to reach?"

"My son."

"And how old is he?"

"Twenty-seven."

"For-get-it," she drawled.

I had to laugh. I felt it was a perfect introduction to Plumas County!

(Yes, eventually I did hear from Eric. One of his friends had reached him and he did finally call.)

Al and Jessie — what a blessing they were, from the first — were privy to all this drama. The next day Al took Dick to Portola Hospital, where X-rays showed three broken ribs — about which they could do nothing. And the day after that we went to Sacramento, Al insisting on driving the U-Haul while I drove his truck. That trip turned out to be a comedy of errors, as well. Al was as clueless as I, so after dropping off the U-Haul we went to the tiny Sacramento Executive Airport. We drove around quite a while looking for aisle "G" before realizing that there must be another airport, a big one, somewhere on the outskirts of town.

Dick's ribs healed quickly (or he let me think so) and we settled into our new life giddy with happiness. I wrote our friends in Tujunga, "We always had a great time camping, but then came the last day when we faced going back to the traffic and the smog. Now it's as though there is a rainbow arching across the sky and under it the words 'You don't have to go back!'"

Jessie seemed surprised that Dick and I felt no need to find separate interests, divide tasks, make our own friends. "Just wait," she said. "This retirement thing can get pretty old, fast."

But everything was equally new and exciting for each of us and having someone to share our enthusiasm made it even more meaningful. Each day there was something special. If I looked out the window and saw the horses across the way, their necks crossed in a loving peaceful embrace, I would call to Dick, just as he would call me to see the mountain quail scooting under the trees.

We sat outside together. We sanded and refinished our old oak table, a job which had been waiting fifteen years for us to have time to tackle. And we planted a large vegetable garden using the plentiful manure from one of the storage sheds. Just think, our own beets and carrots and lettuce!

And we had visitors. My sister Julie was the first. As soon as she heard about Dick's fall she said, "I can get away next weekend and I'll bring a rubber mat for the bottom of the tub. In the meantime put a towel in the tub, if you must take a shower."

We took Julie to eat at one of our favorite breakfast places. We drove up to Plumas Eureka State Park, climbed to the top of the old mill race, oohed at the fresh imprint of a bear's paw. Julie was her usual witty, indefatigable self. "One thing I don't understand about Plumas County is why Beer and Worms are always on the same sign. Can I get beer without worms?"

Delleker is just an hour's drive from Reno so maybe that is why we had so many visitors. Our dear friend, Lucia, came, staying a few days. I have a picture of her in the garden holding up a freshly picked carrot. Kay from our Sunland-Tujunga Democratic Club, our old friend Rosa Lee Carter, and Sol from Dick's job, all came to visit. The weather stayed mild and we spent most of our time outdoors.

But it did snow right in time for a family Thanksgiving. Brother Leon and his wife Bobbie stayed with us. Sister Adele and her husband Oneil, niece Jan and her current boyfriend and his four kids stayed at the nearby Chalet, which offered sleds for the children. We were pleased that there was no hint of discrimination at the arrival of the two mixed-race couples.

Busy as we were with introducing family and friends to all the attractions of Plumas County, we were also house-hunting. Barbara Scott, our local realtor, lamented that there wasn't much for sale in Quincy. One house she showed us was built right on the ground — okay according to the lax standards of the time — but I felt a foundation was not an optional feature. And then there was an interesting house in Meadow Valley, with a marvelous view. But when we noticed a sign at the edge of the property "Snow not removed beyond this point," we demurred. We continued to scan the newspaper for homes for sale.

And it was in the paper that I saw a notice of a Women's Conference being held at Feather River College. Wonderful! Not only was the conference free but free transportation was being offered. I met the bus in Portola and attended the day-long conference. There was a great mix of young and older women and the discussions were lively. There was nothing "hick-townish" about it. But I did take notice when a young woman from Chester commented, "I don't drive in the winter, I just let the snow pile up on my car till spring."

And most wonderful of all, there was actually a follow-up of the cards handed out at the conference. In January, much to my surprise, I received an invitation to a women's get-together in Greenville. And it was at that meeting that I met two women who would become my dearest friends — Jane Braxton Little and Nan Degelman.

Nan Degelman, Dick and Nancy Lund (circa 1977)

But hang on, we haven't got to Greenville yet. I think it was early October when we saw the ad in the paper "105 Hillside Drive. Brown house with green trim, needs a little work." We called Barbara who knew of the house but didn't think it was a possibility for us. She told us that the house was presently rented to a young family, the R's, and because they were on welfare they couldn't be evicted. We went to see it anyway and it turned out that the couple were looking for a bigger place and would probably be moving soon.

The house sat against the hillside, facing west. It had two bedrooms, one bath and a livable attic above. Twenty by thirty feet, the whole house wasn't much bigger than the family room of our home in Tujunga, but I could immediately see the possibilities. A new coat of paint and getting rid of the green trim would be the first order of business.

The first day we looked at the house, a man sitting outside the house across the street called us over. "I built that house," he told us. "Just up from Bakersfield so I didn't know much about the climate — snow and all. I picked out the place to set it, so pretty sitting against all those trees, not realizing that it's in a double draw. So all the rain and snow drains right through the garage. You might think about that."

We took another look. The garage seemed fine. Mrs. R., who had occupied the house for several years, said that they hadn't had any problems. We put some money down and waited.

We did not have to wait very long. By Thanksgiving the papers were signed and we owned the house for $15,500. Or to be more accurate — our little nest egg having shrunk appreciably — we owned two mortgages on the house.

Al advised us to start cutting wood, as winter was fast approaching. We bought a chainsaw and His and Hers rawhide jackets (fake rawhide but nice and warm) and went to work. Our ineptness in this new world was apparent in the pitiful pile we cut but our enthusiasm was undimmed. With hot cocoa in our thermoses and generous sandwiches, each trip became a picnic. We reveled in the beauty of the forest, the soft earth underfoot and the wonderful smell of new cut wood. We filled the back of the van with whatever the day brought.

We moved to Greenville on Dec. 5th, into "the little house on the hill that gets the sun — what sun there is," as one old-timer described it. The R's had left the place in apple pie order. The yellow/brown shag carpet had been shampooed and the cotton curtains were washed and hung.

A few days after we moved, Rachel called and asked if it was okay if she came up. Of course we were delighted! She didn't say that things were not going well between her and Sean but we understood.

It was great to have her ready hands helping us set up our little wood stove. Replicating what the R's had done, Rachel and I lined the wall behind it with used aluminum sheets (available from the newspaper in Quincy). The aluminum reflected the heat so well that the wall, a few inches behind the stove, remained cool while the bookcase three feet away felt warm to the touch.

———

We were constantly being shocked by the different world we had entered. One day, shortly after we moved, I did some major shopping. My groceries were checked and bagged when I discovered that I hadn't brought my wallet.

"Just leave my bags right there," I told the young woman. "I've got to run home and get my wallet. I'll be right back."

"That's okay," she said. "You can take them and pay me tomorrow." It was my first time to shop there — she had never seen me before!

And then there was the evening when we realized there was not enough milk for breakfast. Dick and I jumped in the van and drove the three blocks to the market. The town was dark, deserted. It was not yet 9:00 p.m. and not a thing was open.

———

Soon after we moved we attended our first community meeting, held, appropriately, in the Town Hall, just a block and a half from our house. I don't remember the topic but we were impressed with the number of big rangy men standing in the back of the hall, their heavy jackets and hats unremoved. At some point one of the men spoke up,

"Sounds a little like an environmentalist talking." The venom in the way he pronounced environmentalist was palpable.

I wrote my sister Mary that I could probably stand up at a meeting in Greenville and say, "I'm a Communist" and people would shrug and say, "Well, that's odd." But if I said, "I'm a member of the Sierra Club," they'd ride me out of town on a rail!

Our first Christmas in Greenville was special. Eric came and his first words were, "Greenville is just like the Black Forest." But he was disconcerted that the living room windows looked out on the auto dismantler's yard.

"Don't worry," we said, "the snow will cover it!"

Sean came up and it seemed that Rachel and he could work things out. They talked about a move to Plumas County.

I wrote the following for our Christmas cards that year.

Snug in our simple life
contentment wraps us warm
a wood-stove time to dream —
and draw up plans that meet
no deadline.
{Our letter box bears witness
that the world is not much changed}

We call ourselves "trail blazers"
like Thoreau we would lead
city folk to nature's way
{But that's a kind word for those
who fled the struggle while the battle raged}

In local parlance we are
"refugees" — and that we'll buy.

From these peace-restoring mountains
we send our love
to you who dwell in valleys.

Settling In

It was March when Rachel and Sean moved to Delleker, renting one of the cabins from Al and Jessie. Sean got a job in Reno as a cashier, training to be a croupier. He told us that it made him sad to cash the small paychecks of so many working stiffs, people who could ill afford to gamble, sitting next to the idle rich. Rachel soon got a job in Portola. Dick and I were delighted to have her so close (54 miles!) — we had learned that closeness was relative in Plumas County.

Rachel insisted that Easter brunch should be at their place. She would make Eggs Benedict, one of her specialties. That week Mary and Harold were visiting and Adele and Oneil flew up from L.A. Rachel knocked herself out "spiffing up" the cabin, the meal was delicious, and we enjoyed all being together.

I wanted to show Mary and Adele something in Quincy, so the men drove back together to Greenville. I remember this because of the following exchange.

The men had been home well over an hour and we were not yet back. Dick was antsy, standing in the street.

"What are you worried about?" Harold asked Dick.

"They should be home by now."

"Three Rosenfield women? And you are worried about them? Any one of them could take care of an emergency — and three of them...?"

I remember that Mary and Harold toyed with the idea of moving to Greenville, but alas, did not.

Gardening in Greenville was a problem. Eric had sent a sample of our soil to a lab and the list of recommended amendments indicated that we should look elsewhere if we wanted to grow anything. As for finding a spot that was sure to get six hours of sunlight — forget it. But Dick terraced a place and we planted carrots, beets, lettuce, and potatoes. We composted our kitchen scraps directly into the soil. Dick wrestled the hose up to the garden daily. We had some success.

Soon after we moved to Greenville we got a letter from Stark's Fruit Co. Surprise — Eric was giving us 12 fruit trees. They would be delivered in early spring.

I immediately called the company, "Our son made a mistake in ordering so many trees. He thought we were buying a ranch but we bought a half-acre place that is heavily wooded. We'll take four trees and the balance in bulbs and vegetables."

"Sorry," they said. "Your trees are marked and set aside for delivery to Delleker. Can't be changed."

"Please note our new address, 105 Hillside Drive in Greenville. We are not in Delleker."

Without notifying us that they were on were on their way, the trees were mailed to our old Post Office Box in Portola. On a Friday. And we got the notice the following Monday afternoon, too late to drive to Portola. It was a very sad dehydrated bundle of trees by the time we picked them up. And some were not even those that Eric had ordered. I found homes for six of the trees and Dick planted the others. Of the lot only the two cherry trees survived.

———————

A podiatrist in Greenville? Yes, according to the *I.V. Record*, there was a monthly visit at the local doctor's office. Appointments could be made by calling ... the telephone number of the Secretary of the Greenville AARP.

I called, explaining that I was not a member.

"Oh, the appointments are open to anyone. Making the appointments is just one of the community services that the AARP does."

194

The day of my appointment, the pleasant woman at the desk not only checked my name off the list, but urged me to have a cup of coffee and take my choice from a full tray of home-baked cookies.

She also invited me to the next meeting of the AARP. "If your husband is 60 or over you can join as a couple. We have interesting speakers and it's a very friendly group."

The Chapter was just a year old and, according to JoAnn Brown, the President, it was growing rapidly. "Because there really isn't much for people to do. The old timers have their churches, but newcomers are looking for a way to meet people and get involved."

And getting involved is exactly what happened to Dick and me along with many others. There were committees galore. Community Services not only made appointments and served refreshments for the podiatrist and for the hearing aid specialist, but also for the representative from the Social Security Office. There was a group who were working to get a Senior Nutrition Program going in Greenville, and another group who were looking into transportation issues. And a Legislative Committee which got information from the AARP about both State and Federal issues.

Dick and I volunteered for the Legislative Committee. There was a Supervisorial race coming up in our District and one candidate had asked if he could speak at one of our meetings.

"Wouldn't it be better if we held a Candidate's Night and invited all the candidates to speak?" I asked.

All the members agreed but no one had any experience in chairing such a meeting. So I agreed to do it.

The meeting was held at the Town Hall and was well attended. Each candidate was given a three minute opening statement and two minutes closing. After the floor was opened for questions from the audience, each man got a chance to respond.

I thought the evening had gone quite well but I was not prepared for the ovation when it was over.

"You were terrific."

"You did us all proud!"

And more than one AARP member came up to say they wanted me to be the next president of the Chapter.

"You don't really know me," I said. "After I've been a member for five years, if you still want me then, I'll do it."

Five years later they did, and I did.

I had great expectations of the Women's Group when it convened in February as a follow-up of the Conference at the college. But there was no "program" and people who had a lot to say (like Jane and Nan and me) held back waiting for others to voice their opinions. Attendance dwindled and after a few meetings it disbanded. Some of us talked about forming a book group but that didn't pan out until twenty-eight years later!

By spring Dick and I realized that we could not live on Dick's retirement of $395 a month; and neither of us was old enough to draw Social Security. The unemployment office was sure that Dick could get a job at the prison in Susanville but that was absolutely the last thing he would consider. He got a job in the "Green Thumb", a federal program to employ older people in community improvement projects. That job, working along with local old-timers, proved to be a blessing in many ways. One of the men was a retired railroad engineer, another had retired from Fish and Game, others were Forest Service men. Their stories were marvelous and he learned much about the county. The job was at the Fairgrounds. And right across the street was the Sierra Pacific Lumber Company whose "burn pile" was stacked with perfectly good lumber available for the taking. Dick was sure that he could use the 2 X's and 4 X's in some project and the scraps for our wood stove.

As for me, I called on the only architect in town. He gave me a few sheets to copy but soon we both realized that it was not going to work — he was not used to working with anyone and was annoyed by my many questions. One day I noticed an ad in the local paper offering drafting services, including steel design. I called the number, asking if they might need any help. Larry Stahlheber laughed – the ad was supposed to bring work his way. But over time he did throw a few jobs my way.

It must have been after Easter when I noticed a scraggly group coming up our stairs. Skinny and scraggly but strangely familiar. Could the little girl in Indian clothes be Becky? She was! And the pregnant woman was Janet, and the most scraggly of all was Ben. We embraced them – anxious to feed them and hear their stories.

We knew that in February there had been a massive earthquake in Guatemala. Ben had called to say that they were okay but that Becky and Janet (who was four months pregnant) were coming home. They would stay with her folks in Connecticut until he too could return. Apparently Ben and Janet had not yet purchased the fabrics that had been part of the plan, so he was staying to do that. Had he offered to help the victims of the earthquake? We never asked, never heard.

Now they were home and would be looking for a place, probably in the Monterey area where many of their friends were. Becky was full of stories about "the Machete Man" – a scary interlude in which Ben also wielded a weapon of some sort. Janet's stories were of a more positive sort. They had brought gifts – huaraches for each of us – heavy cotton shirts in beautiful colors in traditional weaves, as well as napkins and tablecloths. The bulk of Ben's purchases were being shipped.

Janet had not yet seen a doctor but she looked beautiful and healthy. And I decided that since we were in no position to give them any financial help the least I could do was suppress my worries and keep my mouth shut. They stayed about a week, promising to keep us "in the loop" from now on.

Cypress (later renamed Jessica) was born on July 7, 1976 in Pacific Grove. Since Janet's folks were visiting them, we decided to wait until they departed. I was so happy to hold the beautiful new baby, who seemed content to be in anybody's arms.

197

Becky, Nancy with baby Cypress, Dick and Janet (July 1976)

The house and yard in Pacific Grove were, as I described them in a letter to Mary, "Chaos – petrified! Much of the problem is due to the quantities of boxes and enormous woven straw hampers overflowing with Guatemalan fabrics crowded into a small house with inadequate closet space. I discovered that the boxes had been packed and moved innumerable times, without a label or an identifying date. Every time a box was opened whatever was loose at the time got stuffed in before re-sealing. So every box was likely to contain three socks, plus all kinds of goodies that Becky and Janet could not bear to part with."

We refused their insistent offer to sleep there and stayed at a motel. While Dick worked outside, I spent my time scrubbing and arranging things. About the third day I said to Janet, "I'm assuming you're like me and don't feel resentful. Somehow I've always had a sister or friend or neighbor who came in and rescued me — and so it's only right that I be the one to offer now."

"Resentful, no. A bit guilty seeing you work so hard."

"Oh, guilt is fine — what more could a Jewish mother want!"

Saturday night we went to see the local production of Macbeth in which Ben played Banquo. Janet was greeted by their many friends, proudly displaying the new arrival labeled "BABY" since they couldn't decide on a name. Ben had received the only good notice in two local papers. Ever-critical me, I thought he was excellent. He looked stunning, invoking a sense of grandeur and mystery that no else sustained. Even his friend Marty, who was a good and intelligent actor, played down to the awful level of the others. But Ben gave his part his full intelligence and effort. I wrote Mary, "One can only imagine how he would be in a good production."

We took Becky back with us to Greenville, stopping on the way for a quick dip at the Feather River Forebay outside of Oroville. I had some plans to work on, but fortunately Becky made friends with the two little girls who lived across the street from us, which helped her pass the time. After a week, Becky and I took the Greyhound bus to San Francisco where Julie met us and Ben picked up Becky. By that time I had come down with Becky's cold, but after a day in bed at Julie's I felt well enough to take the Greyhound bus home.

———————

By the end of August Rachel had decided to move back to the Bay area. For some time I had sensed that things were not "right" between her and Sean but she obviously had not wanted to talk about it. From Dick's and my observation, the marriage had done much for Sean. He was no longer the sullen, negative fellow but his long hours in Reno meant that they had very little time together.

Now Rachel said something that touched me deeply, as it did Dick when I repeated it to him, "I want a marriage like you and Dad — where you do everything together because you want to — where your family comes first. Sean doesn't rush home."

I told her that Dick and I certainly don't do everything together. My involvement in politics and even my friends have not always coincided with his. Dick has always gone to bed three or four hours earlier than I, and he doesn't read any fiction, etc. etc. In the early years it was his devotion as a father than made these differences insignificant. Now we share more enthusiasms — the house, the garden, the incredibly beautiful place we have chosen, the serene life we have made for ourselves. I told her we have both changed, blended, in the almost thirty years of our life together and that her Dad and I stimulate each other by our very differences — which unfortunately hasn't happened with her and Sean.

I Hang Out My Own Shingle

Through 1976 I had hit and miss work with Larry Stahlheber, drawing unemployment checks or partial checks depending on the actual income for the period. But in the winter months Dick's work with Green Thumb would be fewer hours so I needed to find something steady.

It was November when I got a temporary job with the County Building Department, replacing the file clerk who was on maternity leave. It was an opportunity to learn about the County's permit system, and I was impressed that the Department Supervisor, Coy Block, was courteous and helpful to homeowners and contractors alike. The friendly atmosphere extended to me and my questions; and little as the money was, it made a difference. I became good friends with Charla who was the other clerk in the department. After the first snow I decided it was not fun driving the 24 miles to Quincy and got a ride with another County employee, Sandy, who also lived in Greenville.

Soon after Christmas, Leon called to say that Bobbie was in the hospital again. Earlier she had been diagnosed with congestive heart failure and warned that she must stop smoking. I felt that Leon could use some moral support and decided to take a few days off. Luckily I was able to get a ride with Sandy who happened to be driving all the way to L.A. It was less fortunate that the long trip was in her old-style jeep. I was not only cold and wind-whipped, but I also ended up with an aching back.

At the hospital, as Leon and I walked down the long corridor we could hear Bobbie's labored breathing. She was unresponsive, lying under an oxygen tent. Leon said she had suffered a massive stroke and the doctors gave her little chance of recovery.

"What did she want?"

"I don't know. We never talked about it."

That was my first encounter with the issue of end-of-life decisions and I have often cited it as an example of how important it is to write down your wishes and put it in the hands of a trustworthy person. Bobbie never regained consciousness, suffering needlessly for another two weeks while the costs to Leon mounted. It was a lesson Leon refused to learn.

———— ·— ·— ————

When my file clerk job ended I persuaded the County Engineering Department to hire me under CETA (California Employee Training Act) at $3.02 an hour. The irony of hiring me as a trainee was brought home when the head of the department looked at the drawing I had just completed and asked what the welding symbol meant!

Although I had flown — not ridden — home from L.A., my back had never recovered from the trip. A few weeks later, when I reached down to pick up a piece of paper, my back went into a muscle spasm. I was in agony and called the job to say I wouldn't be in that day. Being horizontal, I always found, gives one an opportunity to look at things in perspective. I realized that I had never been so frustrated on any of my jobs in the past. Even the dumbest jobs had always had some redeeming features. I resented being classified as a trainee and the pay was abysmal; plus the ride back and forth to Quincy was not doing me any good. Surely I could do as well or better if I started my own drafting service. I got up, limped to the phone and called the County.

"Sorry, but I don't think this is working for me. I won't be back."

I crawled in bed and as I turned on my side, literally felt my back snap into place!

———— ·— ·— ————

I sent Mary my drawing of the business cards that I wanted, asking if she could run them off on her "super mimeograph." Two weeks later I had 150 cards in my hands and a list of contractors who I planned to visit.

I put an ad in the paper and paid for an ad in the telephone book. We came back from a trip to Reno and there was a call. A young couple who I knew from their grocery store was ready to build their own home. We drove out to look at their parcel — a level lot on the North Valley Road. They had some ideas of what they wanted, three bedrooms, two baths, a family room, and an attached garage.

"We could put the family room above the garage. We call that a split level," I said, "and that will leave you room for a garden."

"Yes! That's exactly what we wanted but we didn't know the word."

My first job as Nancy Lund Drafting Service went swimmingly. Of course I had much to learn but Coy at the County Building Department was as helpful to me as he had been to others. A few years earlier the permit system had been so informal that plans sketched on a paper napkin were approved, but by 1972 the county had adopted the Universal Building Code and there were forms to be filled out: specifics about the type of roofing, siding, windows. How was the house to be heated? While everybody in Plumas County burned wood for their major heat source, they needed a secondary source of heat — either electric or propane — "in case they couldn't get out to chop wood."

Larry had paid me $6.50 an hour — what should my rate be? I think I charged $8 an hour for that first job. Although most architects and engineers set their rates by charging a percentage of the finished house or so much per square foot, I told my clients I didn't want to gain by making the house more expensive, or larger than their needs. I thought that basing the rate by the hour was the fairest system for both me and them. I assured them that I kept careful notes of the time I spent on each job: preliminary studies such as alternatives for floor plans, and the final drawings. I guaranteed that my plans would pass the Building Dept.'s "Plan Check", and if corrections were needed there would be no charge.

A SOLAR HOME

South Elevation
House designed for solar potential.

One room or

Your dream
home in the
Sierras...

We Can Work It Out

Nancy Lund
Drafting Service
25 Years Experience

Greenville, CA 95947
(916) 284-6423

Advertisement for Nancy's business, June 28, 1979, Feather River
Publications. See Appendix for accompanying newspaper story

204

Although I continued to advertise for a number of years, aside from that first house my work always came through referrals. After I had done several jobs for him, John Cunningham, general manager of Barlow Construction, would call me as soon as their client had selected a site. Often these were well-to-do couples who had just retired or were contemplating retirement, people who were not quite sure what they wanted. Conferences with them could be a very time-consuming process.

"Nancy, I'm counting on you to do your magic," John would say, leaving the job in my hands. That was the best compliment I could ask for!

In the summer of 1977 I had a scare when the local doctor had advised me to see a specialist about a lump on the side of my neck. My sister Julie, now a Nurse-Practitioner, knew a surgeon at Stanford Medical Center and made the arrangements. The lump proved to having nothing to do with my thyroid, and I was told that there was no reason to fear a recurrence. I had never felt ill and now was feeling more fit than ever.

As 1977 came to a close, Dick and I found ourselves in the best of all possible worlds. Greenville, and especially Hillside Drive, was proving to be even a better choice than we had expected. June, the neighbor across the street, had lived in Greenville since '47 and although she was only 9 years older than I, decided to treat me like a daughter. She was bright and witty, a wonderful font of information about the community. And the other three families on our hill were not only friendly but had kids about the age of Becky.

Dick had bought a table saw and a few basic carpenters' tools and was excited about the prospect of making toys and games for kids out of the wood he had collected. Not for sale, of course, knowing Dick, but as gifts and to share.

Our financial situation had improved, and our kids seemed to be doing well. Ben had a good job with a commercial fishing outfit, Janet and the two little girls were flourishing, Rachel was happy with her job and Eric had just written a screenplay that he hoped to submit to a studio (once his Aunt Mary had typed it into suitable form).

We drove down to Pacific Grove for Christmas. Seeing our children and all their friends was always fun.

We had no inkling of the cataclysm that 1978 would bring.

1978 - 79

To my children and grandchildren:

 This has been the most difficult chapter for me to write and may be the most painful for you to read. But in writing this story of my life how can I – trying to be honest – skip or pave over the watershed events of those years? Watershed for both me and you.

 I want you to know that through that time I never stopped loving you.

 And all the years between that time and today have healed the wounds and made our feelings for one another stronger, more loving, and more enduring.

Love,
Mom

 In 1977, Rachel and three girls from Tujunga were living in a big house outside of Salinas. Eric was about to move up there, too, taking over the garage as his "digs." when we visited them that Christmas. Dick and I did not foresee any trouble when we learned that Ben was becoming deeply involved with a Sufi Muslim group that had moved into Pacific Grove and were kind of camping outside Ben and Janet's place. We knew one of the group, Michael Sugich, from Ben's UCLA days. We had found Michael to be an earnest and thoughtful young man whom I had especially liked when he took me aside one evening in Tujunga to say, "You have done an amazing job with your kids. They are free of all the hang-ups that so many kids have." We thought that the Sufis were probably similar to the group led by Pir Vilayat, whose sessions Rachel had attended.

Eric told us that he thought Janet, who was in Connecticut with the girls, was entitled to know that Ben was contemplating joining the group.

Ben had replied, "This is not the kind of thing you can tell over the telephone."

Remembering the many brief but wildly enthusiastic enterprises that Ben had embraced — from animal studies to slot-cars, from astrology to Gurdjieffism — we were confident that this too would be short-lived.

But when we visited Pacific Grove in February, things looked different. We learned that Ben had given up his fishing job "so that he could be available to his Sufis." Just how Janet was supposed to manage, we were not told.

When the group left Pacific Grove, Ben — who had taken the name Mahmud — went with them to Tucson. Janet had rejected his offer to "come with me and be my Muslim wife." We were told that the offer, repeated three times, and refused three times was recognized as a divorce in Islam. I am sure that Ben (Mahmud) felt that Janet was rejecting not only him but the opportunity to know God as he had come to know Him.

Janet took Ben's decision as completely irrational. Like me, she was a political animal to the core; nothing in her family, her associates, her interests had led her to explore the spiritual side of things. Knowing Dick and me, Janet had no inkling that Ben could be converted to any religion, let alone one that was so restrictive to women and in many other ways alien to our culture. Janet's first marriage had been an unhappy one and she had left her husband long before Becky was born. She chose to raise Becky on her own, being a single mother at a time when it was not as common as it is today. Though she and Ben had never officially married, Janet was more deeply in love than when they first got together and she had every reason to think of their union as a permanent one. Now all that was wiped out. She and Becky were on their own again — this time with twenty-month-old Cypress.

We had no patience or sympathy towards Ben (it would be awhile before we could think of him as Mahmud). We loved Janet as a daughter; the two little girls were our precious granddaughters and we could not fathom how Ben could leave them. As unhappy as I was, I think Dick was even more deeply hurt.

"How did I fail?" he said more than once. "Wasn't I an example of what being a father means? Didn't I teach him anything about responsibility — even if there isn't love?"

I kept repeating to him and to myself what Mama had said to my father, all those years ago, when I sided with the union against their very good friends: "We brought the children up to think for themselves and now Nancy is thinking for herself."

It was not just that she said it, my parents lived it. They accepted my becoming a Communist and later when three of my sisters followed me, they did not blame me or try to change them. But that mantra didn't work for me.

I tried to rationalize that this was just another phase, that surely Ben would come to his senses. If he was unhappy with his work, was frustrated as an actor, or wanted Janet to act differently — we could understand it. But to throw everything away and go off with what we regarded as a bunch of gypsies was incomprehensible.

Rachel, too, was hurt by his desertion of Janet and the two little girls. While Dick and I could not understand Ben's conversion to Islam, she could understand the pull of the spiritual for him. When she heard that Ben had married Zulaika, one of the leaders of the sect, Rachel took it as another undeserved blow to Janet. Her loyalty was torn between her brother and feelings for Janet, Becky and above all, Cypress. It was a hard time for her.

———————

As parents of kids growing up in the 1960's we had been among the most flexible, accepting their way of living without changing our own habits. I had little respect for those who smoked pot "to be with their kids." Or blossomed out with beads and Nehru jackets. Now, as unhappy as we were, we were not about to disown Ben. We knew a family who had cut all ties with their daughter when she embraced an extreme fundamental Christian sect, and another mother who would not talk with the kid who gave up a promising career in law to become a Hare Krishna convert.

One of our friends tried to comfort me by saying, "Kids have to break away from the nest, find some way to differentiate themselves from their parents. It would be pretty hard for your kids to find anything that you couldn't tolerate, so he had to do something outrageous!"

Of course that was not the case. In later, happier days, Mahmud told us that he felt he was following in our footsteps. In Islam he had found a society in which there was no racism and no tolerance for the rampant greed that characterized capitalism as we know it.

I have the letters I wrote to Mary at the time, "I haven't been able to sleep for days and my stomach is bothering me for the first time in my life." In a later letter I wrote that Eric and Rachel had answered my long, bitter and accusatory letter with an equally long thoughtful one. (I wish I had copies of them both.) They felt that Ben's turning to Islam was not an idle whim but filled his need for something "more." And that their brother had a spiritual longing that had been unfulfilled up until now.

I can't say I bought the argument but was comforted by their reply, knowing that Rachel and Eric recognized the turmoil that prompted my letter. They were sorry for my anguish and wanted me to see that it was not as bad as I thought and that there could be a future communication between us and Ben. The biggest issue for me was the welfare of the girls and Janet. She had given up the house in Pacific Grove and had moved into the large house in Salinas where Eric and Rachel were living.

When we drove down in May — or was it June — Rachel had moved out of the house and was renting a tiny place in Monterey on the grounds where good friends Marty and Jackie lived. Rachel seemed restless to me and I was not convinced she was as happy as she claimed to be.

———————

Back home a few days later, we got terrible news from Janet. She told us that Ben had come back to Monterey for a few days — with his wife, Zulaika. There had been an impromptu party for them (Dick and I had long dubbed Ben and his friends the "Reunion Group" since every occasion became an excuse for a reunion party of sorts). Naturally she had not gone and Rachel had refused to attend. But the following morning Ben had called Rachel and asked if she wouldn't meet him at the beach so the two of them could talk. Janet didn't know what they talked about but at its conclusion, Rachel had packed her Volkswagen with a few things and driven to Tucson.

We were devastated. Rachel called when they arrived in Tucson, giving us her address and saying, "I wanted to see for myself what about the 'community' is so special." She was staying with a very nice couple. And would keep in touch.

During the next months we got letters from her which sounded as if she was becoming disillusioned with the group. "They're all very bright – doctors and psychiatrists and teachers – but they have no practical sense. They forget to pay the electric bill, so the lights get turned off. Stuff like that."

In August she wrote that she wanted to get a passport and asked us to send her birth certificate – obviously they were thinking of going back to England where a number of them, including Zulaika, came from. It took a bit of digging but we sent the birth certificate, with trepidations. Nothing in her letters convinced us that Rachel was having a good time.

My friends urged me to go and get her. "No," I said. "She's twenty-three and quite mature. She would have told me if she wanted me to come." But I did write her yet another loving letter along with a small check. "Here's bus fare, if you need it. And if you don't want to come back to us, your Aunt Julie will be happy to have you. And even though you've never met her, my long-time friend Julia, says she has a spare bedroom and would love to show you the bright lights of the Big Apple."

I didn't hear for a few days and then I got a call. "Your money came at just the right time. I'm staying. And I'm getting married and I want you to come!"

I hardly dared to ask, "Is it an arranged marriage?"

"Oh, no. They don't do that. I want to. It's my decision."

I don't know whether it was just the question of money or whether it was Dick's disgust with the whole business, but I flew alone to Tucson. And there I met the mother of the groom even before I met him. Marge and I immediately bonded, an instant liking for one another. Probably part of it was relief. We recognized each other as "normal" — whatever that is. Two nice, middle-class, literate Americans. Our kids were not marrying some exotic, strange "outsider." And Rachel's intended — born Mark McQuiston Priest but now called Abdul Jami — was a nice looking fellow, taller even than Ben and soft spoken. Marge told me he had been a member of the group for six or seven years and had never been married.

I met Zulaika, who seemed to be the one in charge. She was a beautiful tall brunette, and I was impressed by her dignity and very upper-class English accent. There was a feast that evening. We sat on the floor on comfortable cushions and were served from big platters of food, rice and lamb, curried chicken and some dishes I didn't recognize, with the men waiting on us. Zulaika had arranged places for Marge and me to sleep in the homes of members.

Rachel had taken the name Radyya (later simplified to Radia). At some point I would ask how the names were chosen, and was told that as we respect someone by calling him "Doctor" or "Professor" it is a form of honoring those whose names appear in the Koran. So from here on Rachel shall be Radia and Ben shall be Mahmud; although dear Marge never stopped referring to her son as Mark.

The wedding was held at the home where I had slept. Part of the service was in English, part of it in Arabic. Marge and I sat on cushions on the floor, again, and after the ceremony and another meal, the men went into a different room and we women were entertained by belly dancing. Apparently the dancers, who were not very good, were members or friends and there was a lot of laughter and good natured banter — mostly in English.

Marge and I flew out the next morning, she to San Francisco, and I to Reno. We promised to keep in touch with each other and agreed that things looked much better than we had dared to hope. When Dick picked me up at the airport I was not exactly sanguine about a happy ending to the saga but certainly less apprehensive.

———————

Radia did stay in touch, letting us know that she had had a miscarriage but had recovered quickly. Then she called to tell us that she was pregnant again and wanted to know how I had coped with "morning sickness." I commiserated with her but said I had been lucky — pregnancy agreed with me. Unfortunately, for her it was morning sickness that lasted all day. Then she wrote that the whole group was moving to Atlanta.

"Why Atlanta?" I asked.

"The shayk says that Atlanta is becoming a hub, the center for the communication industry. It is a good place for us to be."

From Atlanta she wrote that she and A.J. (Abdul Jami) were sharing a house with Mahmud and Zulaika. The baby was due the first week in September and she hoped I would be able to come before that and stay a little afterwards.

———————

What followed were the most difficult weeks of my life and ones I am not proud to recall. It was a combination of disapproving of the way they were living, being very angry at how Mahmud conducted himself, and — above everything else — concern for my daughter. The group had been able to find places to rent in the black section of Atlanta. It was an area that was becoming "gentrified" and they had not been able to develop good relations with any of their neighbors. In fact they had been robbed several times under the illusion that they were a bunch of rich white folks. Radia and A.J. were living on one side of a duplex, which they shared with a mother and her three small children. On the other half of the house, Mahmud and Zulaika also had a young family living with them.

I got the impression that A.J. had the only car in the group. He had been able to find work as a painter and wangled one for

Mahmud as his helper. They seemed to be the only ones who had jobs at the moment.

I found the refrigerator and cupboards bare and bought groceries only to see that each time I did so their whole community was invited to dinner.

"What would have happened if I hadn't been here and been able to buy food?" I asked Mahmud.

"Allah would have fed us," he replied.

Although that answer baffled me, it was Mahmud's treatment of Zulaika that most angered and disappointed me. How could Dick's son treat his wife as a servant, ordering her around and even demanding that she get out of a sickbed to serve us tea? She had delegated the job to the little girls who were staying with them, but that did not please Mahmud. Most appalling to me was the fact that Zulaika obediently got out of bed and served us tea.

I was in tears when I said to Zulaika, "You must hate me. You must think that this is how I raised my son. Believe me, he never saw his father act the way he does. Dick would never, never under any circumstances, order me around — nor would I have stood for it."

"Oh, Mahmud is wonderful! I have no complaints." Her reply amazed me. It might have been one that a Party member would have used to excuse her husband, but that was thirty years ago.

As soon as I arrived in Atlanta I learned that the baby would be born at home with the aid of a midwife. Knowing nothing about midwifery, I felt it was putting both Radia and the baby at risk. As the actual labor began I was unable to stay in the room with my darling daughter and I had to go walking outside. Only when A.J. came to tell me that they had a little boy was I able to go back.

Then, on the day before I left, Mahmud insisted on taking me to a wholly unnecessary fancy tea at a downtown hotel. Not only that, he took A.J.'s car, thereby jeopardizing — if not losing — the job for the two of them. My attempt to be pleasant was a failure. At least, I thought, maybe I can get through to him that what he is doing may be contrary to his interests.

"You know," I said, "in the Party we had both good and bad people. Some were just inept but there were others who were planted by the FBI or Navy Intelligence. They were agent provocateurs. These guys seemed to be the most loyal, hard-working members, but their proposals were dangerous and deliberately misleading. It wasn't easy to tell the good from the bad ideas."

He listened attentively.

"What if your shayk is leading you down the wrong path? How will you know?"

His reply shook me to the core and I abandoned any hope of further conversation.

"We have a saying that the shayk's wrong doing may be better than your own good doing."

I shook my head in disbelief. But my main anxiety was for Radia's future as a wife in this environment. I was afraid that A.J., being younger and less domineering than Mahmud, would be influenced by him. I couldn't bear the thought of Radia being treated like chattel. *Happily, my fears were unfounded.*

I stayed in Atlanta for a week. I doubt I was of any use, and I know that I was a total mess. Not since Mama died had I wept so much. I cried when I was alone in the room where I slept, but I was also in tears much of the time where I could be seen by everyone.

On my return Radia wrote and mailed us pictures of the baby. Thankfully she never mentioned what a meager support I had been. The whole group moved to San Antonio when the Zayd was a few months old. The shayk had a good reason for the move (San Antonio was the hub of the perfume industry?) but by this time I had given up hope of understanding his reasons — or the willingness of the group to follow his whims.

———

P.S. In 1981 when their second child was about to be born, I wrote Radia that I had no intention of coming. I am sure she was much relieved.

P.P.S. The next time we saw Radia and family it was altogether different. When she wrote that they were leaving San Antonio and asked if we had room for them for a few days we were delighted.

Zayd was three and Jeedie (Hamid) was one and half years old. I was relaxed and happy and Dick couldn't get enough of having his beautiful daughter under his roof, even briefly, and he adored the two little boys. But we reluctantly admitted that it was only fair that the family spend some time with Marge too. A.J.'s plans seemed fluid but when they decided that their next spot would be Spain, Marge insisted that Dick and I spend the last week with them in her home. Her house, at almost the crest of Mt. Tamalpais, was beautiful, full of art from China and her own work. Marge was the perfect host – the kind of person who anticipates your needs without seeming effort. We had a lovely few days together and sad as we were that an ocean would soon divide us, we had a great time.

—————

P.P.P.S. Janet and Ben had talked about moving to Chico, now in the fall of 1979 it was just her and the two little girls. We were happy to have them a mere two hours away rather than the six-hour drive to Salinas. Janet took substitute teaching jobs while she went to the University to get her teaching credential. Becky was in one of the new "open classrooms" and little Cypress attended a preschool on the UC campus.

We visited as often as we could and often brought the little girls back with us to Greenville. After those part-time teaching assignments Janet got a full-time job in Nord, a farming community outside of Chico. If there is such a thing as a born teacher, then Janet is one!

Nancy and Dick (1990). Part of a series by the PSA 3 (Area on Aging) to show aspects of the lives of senior leaders. See Appendix for newspaper stories about Nan's work on behalf of seniors.

Aging — Together

Before I became so involved in all things aging, I was active in the local Democratic Party. I helped at the booth at the County Fair and did some telephoning before meetings. Betty, who worked in the Planning Department, was one of those on my call list. Since I was in Quincy I decided to go up to her desk and tell her in person about the upcoming meeting.

"Guess what I'm working on," she said. "It's a development on your hill." And she showed me the plan. "The Planning Commission has approved it — sixteen lots above your house."

"That's unbelievable! Hillside Drive is so narrow two cars can't pass. And how do they think anyone can build on a hill that's so steep you can hardly climb it — to say nothing of the trees they'd have to cut? Do you mean to tell me that they can do something like that without notifying the neighbors?"

Apparently they could. I asked Betty if there was any way we could stop them.

"Yes," she said. "There's an appeal process. It can go before the Board of Supervisors, who can overrule the Planning Department, but they seldom do."

I scurried home and talked to the four families on our hill. They were all as indignant as I and pitched in for their share of the $75 appeal fee. Unfortunately the Board would not sit as the Planning Commission until the following month.

In the interim I wrote a leaflet calling for a public meeting to protest the Planning Department's arbitrary system. All homeowners could be in jeopardy unless they had a voice in what

218

happened in their neighborhood. What if I hadn't stopped by Betty's desk that day? Bulldozers and tree cutters could be on our hill right now. We wouldn't have had any warning and it would have been too late to stop them. Although my leaflet was quite amateurish, a number of people showed up at the meeting, among them Greenville's Fire Chief. He shook his head in disbelief, "No way we could get our fire engine up that hill!"

My friend Jane Braxton Little arrived a bit late. Her husband was at work so she brought her two little pajama-clad toddlers, setting them down on a blanket. Turning to the spokesperson from the Planning Dept. she asked, "What about the masses? How do they figure into your calculations?" To my delight, she had used a phrase that resonated with me, if nobody else. There was no reply to her query.

The day of the hearing before the Board, the lawyer for the developer was seated up front and given all the time in the world to state his case, while all of us from Hillside Drive were relegated to seats as observers. My attempts to speak were unrecognized until I burst out, "We are the people from Hillside Drive and we paid $75 for this appeal. When do you plan to listen to us?"

Finally I was called on and stated our case briefly. Our own District Supervisor, Russ Papenhausen, did not recognize us but acted as though we had just got off the boat, not the people he saw shopping at his store! However Della Blust, the only woman on the Board, announced, "I can't vote on something I haven't seen. I propose that we table this item until we have gone to the site and seen for ourselves if the plan is feasible."

A few days later the Board made their visit to Hillside Drive. They didn't need to go very far up the hill before it was apparent that the developer had pulled a fast one. He intended to sell lots that could never have been built on. As Della questioned Jim, the Fire Chief, on how he managed to get up such a narrow road, Russ's face grew redder and redder. He suddenly became very concerned.

"I am going to direct the Road Department to post a "Not a Through Street" sign, right here on Highway 89, so people don't think they can find a short cut. And we should stop any woodcutting above the homes before some kid gets hurt or run over by a truck!"

We had won!

The "Not a Through Street" sign was erected the next day. Over the next few months we called Russ the few times we saw a logging truck drive down Hillside Drive. Then they stopped altogether.

———————

Beyond our activities in the Greenville AARP, it was Dick who first became involved in "senior issues." One of our new friends was Jewell Standart who was a dynamo, not only in the Greenville AARP, but in her church, the local Soroptimists, and the efforts to get senior nutrition and transportation programs going in the county. She suggested to Russ that Dick be appointed to the Plumas County Senior Committee (later called the "Commission on Aging").

In the late 70's Plumas County was in a loose confederation of fourteen northernmost counties, NorCal, which was funded by various state and federal agencies to provide nutrition and transportation services for people aged 60 and over. Although there seemed to be plenty of money, NorCal was poorly organized and badly administered. When their records were turned over to the state it was impossible to reconcile the books or account for how the money had been spent.

Now there were federal regulations breaking up each state into PSAs (Planning and Service Areas). The 14 counties of NorCal were to be broken up into four PSAs. Plumas County ended up in PSA 3, with four other counties – Tehama, Butte, Colusa and Glenn.

Jewell and Dick along with Russ Papenhausen represented our county in a "Task Force" charged with recommending the best administrator for our PSA. Russ strongly pushed for each county administering its own funds and programs – which was possible by creating Joint Powers Agreements. But Dick knew that the other

220

counties did not have Boards as favorable to their seniors as Plumas and even here political winds could change. Dick wanted the administration to go to Chico State University which had already demonstrated its concern for seniors. Chico had, on its own initiative, set up a very efficient Senior Information and Assistance office with its own toll-free telephone number.

Through many meetings, over many weeks, Dick's viewpoint prevailed and the University Foundation became the administrator of our PSA's Area Agency on Aging. Dick was named on the first Advisory Council and I started attending meetings along with him and Jewell.

Russ proved to be a difficult member of the team. Although Russ and I would later become strong allies, I am sure it was he who became mellow, not I!

I think it was because of Dick's leadership that Plumas became the dominating force on the Area Agency on Aging Advisory Board, even though we were by far the least populous of the five counties. Dick declined the nomination for Chair in favor of Ed Barrett, who was from Portola (in eastern Plumas County) and the only black man on the Council. Later, Ed was followed by our good friend, Al Becker, also from Portola. As time went on I became involved in the Advisory Council but in those first years it was Dick.

———————

And in our Greenville AARP Dick made his Legislative Committee reports so interesting that it threatened to take over the monthly membership meeting. Dick was full of information gleaned from the State and National AARP, plus clippings from the *Sacramento Bee*. When he said, "Since we now have Nutrition lunches on Saturday, how many people would like to meet right after lunch to discuss this further?" ten hands flew up.

Unbelievably we had more than twenty people coming to regular Legislative Committee meetings, discussing issues, writing letters, signing petitions. When a Regional Director of AARP visited us, he was amazed. "If we could only put this show on the road!"

Over the years a Social Security representative had come to Plumas County, alternating between the various communities. Now they announced that they would no longer be coming here but would be available in Susanville — 45 miles from Greenville but more than 100 miles from Portola. We mounted a letter campaign to our Congressman, Norm Shumway. Within days a representative from the Social Security office paid Dick and me a visit. He assured us that the visits would continue, which they did until attendance had so dwindled that we could not justify them.

When P. G. & E. went before the PUC (California's Public Utilities Commission) for an electrical rate increase, the Greenville AARP mounted a protest. Many people in our area had been sold "all-electric" homes and could ill afford the current rates. We approached Assemblyman Stan Statham for support of our efforts and he responded with alacrity. The next thing we knew the local newspapers and our mailboxes were filled with information about Statham's campaign to oust the current members of the PUC for their blatant bias in favor of the large corporations. Well and good!

But then Statham took it one step further. He created his own organization (I forget the acronym) to fight the fat cats of the utility industry. All we needed to do was send $10 to become members of this righteous crusade.

It was Statham's Field Rep who answered my call. "What the h... is Stan thinking? Doesn't he know that he's on our payroll? Doesn't he know that he's being paid to represent us? Since when do we have to bribe him $10 more to get him to do his job?"

That was the end of that organization! I think that the increase went through but was lower than what P. G. & E. had asked.

It was not Dick or me, but AARP member Ross Johnstone (a conservative, retired businessman) who started the petition campaign against the new charges which Citizens Utility Co.

wanted to impose on all out-of-area telephone calls. In Greenville every call we made, outside of Chester, was an out-of area call! Soon our campaign was joined by the store owners, the Rotary and Veterans of both communities. The Public Utilities Commission was reluctant to hold a public hearing but our protests were joined by a group in Ferndale (who had a lawyer) and the Commission finally acceded to our demands. When Dick and I volunteered to go to Ferndale for the hearing, one of the store owners wanted to pay our expenses. But we refused — it would be a fun trip to an area we had never visited. Although Citizen's had a phalanx of lawyers, very impressive in their Armani suits, they did not prevail!

And I could write a whole book about Bidwell Water Company and Greenville AARP, a struggle that went on for over thirty years. AARP, joined by the whole community, fought every increase sought by Tom Jernigan, the owner of the private water company. Sometimes we succeeded but more often he got at least part of the increase he asked for.

In 1996 Jernigan mailed an anti-incumbent piece against Supervisor Robert Meacher who was running for reelection. According to the piece Robert Meacher and Nancy Lund had prevented him from making the improvements he had wanted to make. I promptly wrote a reply and it made a perfect flyer:

"YES! Robert Meacher and Nancy Lund exposed Jernigan's misuse of the fees ear-marked for those very improvements.

YES! Robert Meacher and Nancy Lund stopped Jernigan from collecting $6.50 a month for leaks that he never fixed.

YES! Robert Meacher and Nancy Lund reported that "Boil Notices" for unsafe water were not posted in a timely manner."

Jernigan had made Robert's reelection a cinch!

And what could be sweeter than that in 2001 Indian Valley Community Services District was finally able to buy the water company? And I was one of the five Directors on the District Board at the time!

Among my new friends in the AARP was Ruth Park. A teacher and writer, she not only read Harper's and the New Republic but showed me how to do the Double Acrostic. A kindred spirit! She was pleased when she got a part-time job with Chico State's Senior Information and Assistance program. I was baffled by the alphabet soup of names and acronyms that she was starting to spout so asked if I could also attend the two-day seminar to which she was going. I would pay my own way, of course.

One of the many workshops was led by Emma Gunterman who had many years of experience as an advocate for rural workers. She edited a breezy and informative newsletter that I had seen. Her newsletter carried items of interest to all low-income persons and was beginning to cover the often-overlooked needs of older people, especially women. As she described how the legislature works in California, Emma emphasized the possibility of seniors becoming effective advocates in the Capital. Her enthusiasm was contagious and I was completely sold.

Senior legislation — that was the place where I would concentrate from now on!

So Dick and I headed together into this new world of Aging. It was nonpartisan and non-racial, at least as far as Emma and people like her were concerned. It was what we had been looking for — a chance to work in the mainstream for the things we believed in. Here was a place where we could express our hopes and use our energies for a peaceful and just society. Although Greenville AARP was open for our leadership, it was too isolated. However, in the five-county Area Agency on Aging we could become effective in a much wider arena.

The California Senior Legislature was born in 1980, created and funded by the state. A "shadow legislature", the CSL had the same number of members as the regular (we called them the Junior) legislature — forty Senior Senators and eighty Senior Assemblypersons. The members were to represent and be elected (!) by those over age 60 in their respective PSAs. This decision gave a slight edge to us in rural northern California. Our fourteen counties would have four Senior Senators and four Senior Assemblypersons, where there were only two Senators and two Assemblypersons in the "Junior Legislature." Elections for the two-year term would be in the spring. Members were encouraged to write at least one proposal which would be researched and written in "legalese" by the same body that wrote the bills for the regular legislature.

The CSL would meet in October each year, in the Capital, in the same halls and committee rooms where the regular legislature met. In a four-day session they would debate, amend, and pass proposals, prioritizing those of greatest importance. (We didn't say, but thought, what an example of efficiency we would be — one unknown in Sacramento!) The CSL then needed to find elected members of the State Assembly and State Senate who would adopt CSL proposals and introduce them as bills. The CSL would be the bill's advocate through the whole legislative process, hopefully until its passage in both houses and signature by the governor.

There were only two candidates who put their names forward for CSL posts in our area. Anne King, a brisk, conservative businesswoman from Red Bluff, was our first Senior Senator and Linda B., an activist from Chico, was our first Senior Assemblyperson.

Anne was smart and a quick study. She came back from the CSL session with great enthusiasm. Sacramento had been an eye-opener for her. She no longer thought of herself as a Republican but looked at things in a nonpartisan way. By the end of that first year and after attending a number of Advisory Board meetings, Anne made a point of seeking Dick and me out. She seemed anxious to know our opinions and we were pleased that she invited us to go with her to the Nutrition Sites and retirement groups in the five counties. Anne took her role very seriously; she felt an obligation to get seniors involved in legislation. But Linda turned out to be something of a loose cannon. She had her own agenda, focused on Chico, and rejected any suggestions Anne or we made. We soon gave up trying to work with her.

After Anne's four years (two terms) as Senior Senator she was tired and insisted that I should be her successor. I thought Dick should run, but he said that his hearing was a handicap. He could manage in small settings but would miss too much in large groups. (We didn't have money to buy effective hearing aids – if such things existed.)

I filed to run and this time there was opposition. Archie McC., a well known Sociology professor at Chico State, also filed and campaigned hard. To everyone's surprise I won, due to the great turnout from Plumas County and Anne's endorsement of me. Thus began my eight years as Senior Senator – every bit as exciting and rewarding as Anne had promised.

Speaking of/for Seniors

It must have been a day in 1986 when I heard my sister Mary's voice on the radio. Our favorite station was NPR where we listened to the news from a source we could believe in. I listened in surprise as Mary expounded on the benefits of IHSS (In-Home Supportive Services) as an alternative to placement in a Nursing Home. Keeping frail elders in their homes, through help with their daily living chores — preparing meals, cleaning up — would cost the state far less than care in an institution. And the quality of life for these elders would be enormously enhanced.

I could not disagree with a word she said but I was amazed that she should be called to speak on a subject in which she had no experience, and as far as I knew, no interest.

I marched into the kitchen where Dick was washing dishes, "Who the hell does Mary think she is? Since when has *she* become an expert on Aging?"

Dick smiled. "What are you so excited about? I'm playing a recording of a tape I made of you at the last session of the CSL!"

Yes, I had spoken eloquently and emotionally on behalf of my proposal to make IHSS a state entitlement. If it were an entitlement the funds would go for each client's requirements, rather than to the current program which was managed by each county's Department of Social Services. To be frank, it was Emma Gunterman who had brought the issue to me and helped draft it. She had been trying for many years to change the way services were provided.

"In some counties the seniors are well fed but their homes are dirty; in other counties seniors' homes are tidy but they're not being fed," she had told me. "The program should be an entitlement. It should be tailored to the needs of the individual, not to the priorities of someone in the Social Services Department."

We made the proposal as an amendment to the existing law which had established In-Home Supportive Services. Once it was an entitlement, eligible seniors would get appropriate care. And the program would not run out of money before the end of the fiscal year, as so often happened in many counties.

Nancy speaking at CSL, 1990. See news stories in Appendix for details.

My proposal became one of the top ten priorities for the CSL that year and Senator Bill Green, a Democrat from Los Angeles, agreed to introduce it as his bill. We wanted the bill to have a co-sponsor in the Assembly and I had no trouble convincing Stan Statham, a Republican who represented our area, to add his name to the bill. (Those were the days when bipartisanship was considered normal!)

SB 840 passed both houses and was signed into law by Gov. Brown in 1986.

At the first session of the CSL that I attended, I could see that our fourteen rural northern counties with their total of four Senior Assembly persons and four Senior Senators were no match for the big delegations from Los Angeles and the Bay Area. After the opening dinner I suggested that the eight of us get together as a Rural Caucus.

They responded with enthusiasm and so it was easy to arrange to meet in one of our hotel rooms to discuss all the proposals, especially those originating with us. We met again before the last session and agreed to vote as a block on our list of priorities. The priority choices were weighted: your first choice got ten points, the second nine, and so forth.

Wow! We were effective. When someone suggested that we meet at least once between sessions, Ross W. offered his home. He lived outside of Redding so it was as central a location as we could get. Husbands and wives also attended so it was a large and very lively group. Getting to know each other better was one of the benefits, but more importantly we discussed which of the rural issues most needed attention and decided who would write a proposal on it.

At the session the following year we invited the members from Riverside and Imperial Counties to meet with us. And by the fourth year we were so successful that everyone in the Senior Legislature was claiming to represent a rural area!

———————

As Anne King had done, I made it a point to visit all the Nutrition Sites, and as many of the AARP and Retired Federal Employee meetings as possible. I would usually have a handout on some current issue and often a petition to go with it, one that Dick and I had put together. While the AARP and Retired Federal employees had some legislative activity, I wanted the seniors at the Nutrition Sites to be made into participants, to realize that that they could do a lot more than just voting every two or four years.

After being introduced as a Senior Senator, I felt that an explanation was due — that the CSL was a "shadow legislature" organized along the same lines as the "real legislature", and that we were recognized as the voice of seniors. "I came to listen as well as to talk. So I would welcome questions and suggestions."

On one occasion there was a woman who had been very restless as I spoke. She obviously wanted to ask a question so I called on her.

"Why don't you be honest and tell us what you really are? You're just a lobbyist!"

"Well," I answered, "there are a couple of reasons why I don't think 'lobbyist' is the right description. First of all, lobbyists are paid, and I am not paid by anyone at all. Secondly, lobbyists don't speak for themselves; they are paid to sell something, to carry a message, usually in behalf of some big corporation. And I don't think any corporation would be happy to hear what I am talking about. No, I think the right word for me is 'advocate'!"

During my four terms as Senior Senator there was a succession of Assemblypersons who represented our area. For one reason or other, none of them played much of a role until Berry Keir agreed to run for the post. Berry was in every respect a gentle giant. He had been a conscientious objector in World War II, had marched with Martin Luther King and lost his job as a minister in San Diego because of his support of Cesar Chavez. Our very dear friend Joyce Griffith — with whom we shared many beliefs — had introduced us to him when she was still living in Plumas County. Asked our opinion, we told her we highly approved of him as her partner and were happy when they moved in together in Chico, where Berry was the director of a regional Green Thumb program. Berry was an enthusiastic supporter of the CSL's campaign for a national health plan. I looked forward to working with him on it and other issues but after just one year his health had deteriorated to such an extent that he was unable to continue.

National health had been the CSL's top priority for many years. Recognizing that a complete overhaul of the health system was required, the CSL sent a delegation to British Columbia, Canada, to study their single-payer system, one that covers everyone and eliminates the for-profit health insurance industry. Learning that each province had adopted the single-payer concept over a period of years encouraged us to push for a California plan whether or not there was a national one. Then the CSL persuaded two UCLA professors to study the pros and cons of the single-payer system. Their data proved that the system would work here, covering everyone at less cost to the state than the present inefficient hodge-podge of individual, insurance and government payers. The next step was to get it on the ballot. The CSL was the prime mover for Proposition 166 in 1988. When it failed we worked with a much broader coalition, gaining wide union support and getting even the ... dare I say stodgy? ... AARP to join the campaign for a new initiative on the ballot, Proposition 186. Obviously we were not successful. Had we been, the debate over the 2010 Health Care Reform bill would not only have been unnecessary but laughable!

I had one other successful proposal, which added an amendment to the existing law that established Adult Day Health Care Centers in California. These centers provide a safe place for seniors, especially those with cognitive problems, to spend their day, allowing a family caregiver to go to work. But rural areas such as Plumas County did not have the resources or the numbers to meet the current requirements for setting up such centers. My proposal would allow "satellite centers" to operate in rural areas under the aegis of a larger licensed center. A satellite would have more flexibility as to hours and attendance and staffing but would have the benefit of guidance from the established center.

Alas, though the measure was passed and signed by the Governor, no Adult Day Health Care Centers were ever set up in rural California. I surmise that was because existing Centers were already overloaded with funding hassles and bureaucratic hoops to jump through. They had no energy to take on further headaches.

I was honored in my last year in the Senior Legislature by being asked to give the opening remarks for our assembled Senators. I wanted to be sure that our session would continue its commitment to reforming the health industry, though we had not yet achieved "a tipping point." Today we are all familiar with that concept, but in 1992 the best I could come up with was the "hundredth monkey" analogy.

So here I am on the stand, talking about the first monkey on a nameless island washing her yam in the ocean, and then the second, and a third — leading up to the point that the hundredth monkey changes the way the whole tribe and even those on another island eat their yams.

But before I get to that point I look out on that sea of faces and realize I have lost them. "What the hell is the matter with Nancy," they are thinking, "and what has her weird diet got to do with legislation?"

It's too late to make the analogy, they will never get it. I finish lamely, in a rush to leave the podium. That evening, on the bus going back to our hotel, one of my fellow Senators tells me, "Whatever your idea was, it certainly went over like a lead balloon."

———————

During my eight years as a Senior Senator, the CSL had minimal money woes. (That came later.) Our expenses to attend the annual session in Sacramento were covered — driving for some of us but airfare for many — as well as the room and food for the four days we would spend at the official hotel.

Husbands and wives were welcomed. During the session Dick, like many others, volunteered to fill in as recorder or runner for a committee. On the Sunday evening before all the hard work was to begin, the CSL held a big dinner at the hotel. There would be a keynote speech from a prominent lawmaker and then a buzz of conversation arose from all sides.

Dick was seated next to Ed, a fellow Senior Senator, and I was sitting on Dick's right. We were on the dessert course when I heard Ed ask Dick which area he represented.

"I'm not in the CSL. I'm just Nancy's luggage-carrier and I get to come along when she's down here."

"Oh. A luggage-carrier? You mean ...?"

"Well, yes, we're married."

232

"You are? You're married to Nancy?"

At this point I got into the conversation, "Why are you so surprised that Dick and I are married?"

"It's just that you both like to talk so much!"

———

Attending meetings of the Area Agency's Advisory Committee with Dick, I got to know Peg Taylor, the most devoted senior activist I had ever met. In fact Peg was so involved in every worthwhile cause that we knew the reason why she came to our meetings late and left early — how else could she fulfill all her commitments! Peg was concerned that the nursing homes were not providing their residents with the care they needed and pushed for an Ombudsman program to train seniors to be the advocates for the residents. It was a new concept, later written into the OAA (Older Americans Act).

In '82 I volunteered for the Ombudsman training. The six-week session was scheduled to start in September but was postponed again and again and finally started in mid-December. It turned out to be a very rugged winter. I was the only volunteer from Plumas County, so Dick and I drove the 90 miles to Chico once a week. Accidents on Highway 70 are not unusual but that year they were bizarre. A huge oak tree smashed into a car, killing the driver, just a few minutes before we arrived at the spot. A few weeks later a boulder the size of a Volkswagen crashed into one of the tunnels. And there were ice and snow that made driving in the canyon dangerous. Each Wednesday morning when Dick dropped me off for class I was greeted with applause.

We were taught a great deal about the laws governing nursing homes and residential homes for the elderly and also the physiology and psychology of aging. To sensitize us to the disabilities that afflict many seniors we were blindfolded, had our ears stuffed with cotton, and our fingers tied up with tape; and while handicapped given orders to eat or go to the bathroom! There were 16 men and women in the class, only a few of them went on to become active Ombudsmen.

That spring, armed with a certificate and a badge declaring

me to be an official Ombudsman, I visited all of the long-term care facilities in Plumas County. I would introduce myself to the Administrator, explaining that I felt my role to be one of liaison – to help communication between the residents, their families (if any) and the facility. I rarely had to be confrontational.

"I've got nothing for you today," I remember a woman calling out to me as I entered her room at the nursing home in Quincy.

"That's great," I replied. "I'm not looking for trouble. Right now I'm just here so we can get acquainted with each other. So if you ever do have a problem you'll know who to talk to."

The nursing home in Quincy (which was called Care West but had earned the nickname "Care Less") had 50 beds and was by far the largest of the facilities in Plumas County. Greenville had an 18 bed long-term-care wing attached to its hospital, while Chester and Portola hospitals had fewer long-term care beds. And there was a small residential home in Quincy and one in Portola. I tried to visit Greenville and Quincy once a week and the others when I could.

Dick, who often went with me, felt that the residents would enjoy some of his games, to augment what the activities director was offering. In Greenville he got a number of AARP members to join in a weekly round of games – from a large set of big-numeral dominoes which he had made, to wheelchair "fishing." We also took games to Chester, occasionally.

———

When AARP announced its Women's Initiative, I was delighted. At last there would be a mainstream organization that could get national attention to the inequities still facing women. The stature of the AARP would not only help focus on women's treatment on the job and their burdens at home, but could point out remedies.

I applied for and was accepted in the first cadre and was sent to Washington, D.C. for the one-week training. I called my dear friend Julia (best buddy from El Paso High School days) and arranged to meet her there. We shared a room at the hotel and during leisure hours she was my guide around the Capital — museums, galleries, the symphony and an evening at the restored Ford Theater.

On my return I enthusiastically sent letters to all the Soroptomist and Business and Professional Women's Clubs in Nevada and Northern California but got few responses. Aside from being asked to make a presentation at a big regional AARP conference in San Diego, I got very little support from the organization. I think the Initiative fizzled out after a few years, but I had already dropped out.

Although the AARP did pay mileage expenses, the Ombudsman program in those years did not. Nor did the CSL pay for the hundreds of miles we drove to cover the meetings and Nutrition Sites in five counties. But that was not an issue for Dick and me. We felt we were like those who tithe at church, getting a great deal of satisfaction and positive feedback from doing so.

"You amaze us," we were told, "but then — you enjoy what you're doing." As though unless it was onerous, there was no merit in our work.

The Plumas Board of Supervisors had always been responsive to senior needs so it was never a hostile atmosphere when we asked to be on their agenda. This time we in the Commission were distressed at the Board's delay in naming a director of Senior Services and because of the urgency of the issue we asked each community to get as many of their people possible to attend. So the room was full of seniors, not all of whom we knew.

Dick spoke and then I followed, mentioning that Plumas County was losing out on possible grant funding because we had no one to apply for them. This got their attention.

As we left the building we thanked everyone for attending. Then as we walked to the parking lot one man called out to me,

"What relation are you to the real Nancy Lund?"

Apparently the real Nancy Lund was the one who wrote all those brilliant columns in the paper!

So it became a private joke between Dick and me. "Am I making love to the real Nancy Lund?" Dick would ask — and be sure of the answer.

Meanwhile ...

While I was so involved with the Senior Legislature, the Women's Initiative, and the Ombudsman program and Dick was busy with his games and the Commission on Aging, much else was going on.

Well, for one thing, by the fall of '81 the long-awaited addition to our house was finally under way. It was to be a twelve foot by twenty-four foot addition, half of it would be a living room (one wall would be floor to ceiling books and records) and the other side would be a shop for Dick's tools and projects. Instead of the miserable covered entry and rickety steps there would be a new redwood porch and new sturdy steps. My plans had been approved by the Building Department and Dick and Eric were ready to start building. No longer would I have to roll out my pie dough on the dining room table; Dick would make proper counters as well as incorporating the maple cutting board Radia and A.J. had given us into a kitchen island at just the right height.

When our thirty-fifth wedding anniversary, January '82, rolled around, there were still bare studs separating the old living room from the new; but we invited all the AARP members to our housewarming anyway. (I knew it was Jewel who suggested a money tree — which we accepted with gratitude!) It took us another year before we had money to carpet the living area and get heavy drapes to pull across the picture window and front door at night. Oh, it was lovely to have the additional space and for our many books to be out of boxes at last.

It was a dream I had never dared to dream! Marge (my co-mother-in-law) proposed to take me to Europe. We would wind up in Spain where Radia and family had been for a year and a half. Dick and I didn't have money to buy gifts, so he got instantly to work making wooden toys. One of my two suitcases was packed with them, including a small Noah's ark and its many animals. The special gift for Radia was Mama's heavy silver necklace from the days in El Paso where a local jeweler had designed the piece to her order. It was far too elegant for me to have ever worn, but I figured Radia could carry it off with pizzazz.

Marge had everything worked out — she would rent a car in Brussels and we would spend two weeks leisurely seeing Europe and two weeks with the family in Granada. The night before we would be in Granada, we stopped in Seville. And in the few minutes it took for us to register at the hotel and use the facilities, someone broke into the car and stole all four of our suitcases. Of course we reported it to the policia. They looked at us askance, "You have your passports, your money and the car — what are you complaining about?"

The toys! Oh, how much we had wanted to call Dick and tell him about the joyous reception of the Noah's ark. Gone! As were all the games so lovingly planned and created, and the precious necklace.

C'est la vie! (My French deserted me until we reached Spain and then it was the Spanish words that eluded me.) Como le va!

Once in Granada we had a joyous reunion. They lived in a funny little flat high in the Albaycin, the gypsy enclave on a hill opposite the Alhambra. Zayd at three-and-a-half was now fluent in two languages and little Jeedie amused us by his, "Mama, come here aqui!" Their place was too tiny to accommodate us, so we stayed in a downtown hotel. With our suitcases gone we needed at least a change of clothes. Marge and I went shopping in the early mornings before the family was up. We came to expect that great buckets of soapy water would be sloshed and swept away in front of every store before we could enter. And that everything closed down from noon till four p.m.

We had not known that Radia had just had a miscarriage but after a day or two in bed she was able to join us. Abdul Jami led us through the glories of the Alhambra, to Cordoba, Malaga and the Mediterranean and into the forests of the Sierra Nevada. Like many visitors, Marge and I fell in love with Spain — from the flamenco dancers to the gypsies who seemed to know where we'd go next and from the quaint plazas tucked into unlikely corners to the soaring cathedrals laden with New World gold. Above all we were overwhelmed by the friendliness of the people.

I called Dick frequently and on his birthday, April 26, he told me it was snowing in Greenville — the third snow of the month. But of course it would be gone by the time I got home.

For almost a year I had not heard a word from Mahmud and I had been trying to reach him at the various numbers he had given us. Then, the last day we were in Granada, I tried once again. And he was there! He sounded well and gave us the joyous news that Zulaika was pregnant and the baby was due in a few months. There was no way we could get together now but he promised to keep in touch.

At the end of the two weeks we said regretful goodbyes and headed home. How happy I was to reunite with Dick! He had fared well enough without me but did not have the pleasures I had had to make up for the separation.

———————————

Letters and phone calls kept us in touch with both of our far-flung families. Zulaika and Mahmud's son, Jabir, was born in England in July of that year. And Radia and Shakir's third child, a daughter, was born in Spain in April of 1984. The baby, Hajar, was four months old when Radia and family returned to the States, and our newly (finally) expanded house more easily accommodated them. Dick and I moved our bed into the shop. Dick made a sandbox for the boys, Eric took them exploring to a "castle" high in the woods behind our house and I had the joy of giving my darling granddaughter sunbaths on our new front porch.

Radia and the kids stayed with us while A.J. went to San Francisco, where among other things he legally changed the family name to Massoud. Abdul Jami became Shakir and Jeedie became Hamid.

In February they were ready for their next move, this time to a newly established community of Muslims in Abiquiu New Mexico. They were able to find a house to rent and settled into life there. After a month or so, Shakir called Eric to see if he were interested in a job as gardener and swimming-pool maintenance. He was!

That June Dick and I drove to New Mexico and spent two happy weeks with them, fitting in a visit with Mary in Taos before returning home.

It was dead winter, December of '85, when Mahmud called to say that he and family were in the States and would like to visit. Since putting a bed in the unheated shop was not an option, I needed to make room for them in the attic, which had been Eric's abode. Figuring that things which were buried under heaps of current clothing were no longer of use, I carted off cartons to the local Thrift store. Later, Eric would have a hard time forgiving me for tossing out an expensive pair of shoes.

Mahmud, Zulaika and their handsome two-and-a-half-year-old son, Jabir, were with us for two weeks, their first time in Greenville. We did the few things there were to do — trips to the little museums in Taylorsville and Quincy and a dog sled race in Chester. They insisted that the next time, we should visit them in England.

Mahmud's long-time friend, A. Martinez, who was now a sit-com star, had invited the old "reunion" group to a get-together in San Francisco. We gave them a ride as far as Sacramento, where I had a meeting to attend.

We had had quite a bit of snow in December but now it started raining and it rained all the way to Sacramento. We got home a day before all the roads in and out of Greenville were washed out by the combination of snowmelt and warm rain. 1986 was labeled a hundred-year storm but ten years later we had another hundred-year storm!

240

In late March of '86 Radia called to say that they were leaving New Mexico and wanted to know if they could stay with us until they found their next community. How glad we were to have them!

It was May when Ramadan came around that year. Radia was pregnant and I was indignant that she still planned to fast. I always think of myself as flexible but in this instance I failed. I couldn't adapt to a household where breakfast was before dawn and dinner after sunset for some, while others stuck to the regular schedule. So they left. And although they have long since forgiven me, I still cringe at the memory of their first night away, freezing at a forest camp on Highway 36.

They drove from San Diego to Seattle, investigating not only the Muslim communities but housing rentals, schools and climates – and then settled on Chico just 90 miles from us! Shakir cruised around looking for houses to rent and stopped at one where painters were at work. Yes, the house would be available in a week or so. It was a wonderful house, sitting in a big yard with fruit and walnut trees around it. The one drawback – it had a swimming pool and with three small children, soon to be four, it posed a problem. Build a fence around it with a child-proof gate, we advised; which they did.

"It even has a room reserved for you and Dad whenever you want," Radia told us, "and there's a house trailer in the back of the house that would be just right for Eric."

It was a perfect arrangement all around. Eric had as much privacy as he wanted as well as being involved with the lives of three active children. As for Dick and me, ninety-mile proximity was the best of all arrangements for us to see both them and Janet and the little girls. Besides, I was on the road so frequently that we often stayed overnight both coming and going to meetings in Chico, Sacramento or Red Bluff. Before that we had often stayed at a motel – always one that had a swimming pool. Now there was "our" own with the extra pleasure of splashing around with Zayd (age seven), Hamid (five-and-a-half) and Hajar (two-and-a-half).

Shakir had a plan for Eric and himself – a gardening business in Chico. But when he broached the subject to his mother, Marge countered with an alternate: No, she would not buy him a truck; but she would buy the Chico house if he would go back to college. Done! He enrolled at Butte Community College.

Omar was born in Chico in October 1986. The midwife in attendance was alert to Radia's hemorrhaging and she was rushed to the hospital in time. She recovered quickly and the family settled into a routine. Before long she enrolled Hajar in a beginning ballet class and there met Hollis, the mother of a little girl a few months younger than Hajar. Hollis and her family became close friends of Dick and me, as well as with the Massouds. Over the years we would camp together and enjoy each other's company in a variety of ways.

For the next two years Shakir was active in the Muslim community, held a part-time job, managed to be an involved father to his growing family, while taking a full load of classes at Butte Community College In fact he did so well in achieving his AA he was offered a job in electronics. However he was more interested in using his skills in becoming a medical technician. Through some of his Saudi friends he had heard that a hospital in Saudi Arabia was looking for people with electronic skills. Instead of three more years in college he would get on-the-job training. So that is where he and Radia set their sights. Which led to the next chapter in their lives — and ours.

We had heard glowing, first-hand reports about Elderhostels, so in 1988 Dick and I enrolled in a three-week program in Britain. Airfare was included and a chance to fulfill our promise to visit Mahmud and Zulaika. We spent a week each in Scotland, the Cotswalds and London with the varied, congenial group of twenty-three people. The classes were stimulating and taught by experts, and there were tickets to theatres, trips to castles and museums. We had comfortable rooms in each of the three campuses and ate hearty food in their dining halls. I think the only money we spent was for Dick's nightly glass of ale and my glass of sherry and the souvenirs we bought for family and friends. All for what some people were paying for air flight alone!

Nancy and Dick in Scotland (1988)

One of the perks with the Elderhostel program was that you could opt to use your return trip tickets at a later date. So before we left California we arranged to stay an extra two weeks. Mahmud would pick us up in London, we'd go back with him to Norwich where we'd spend a few days and then we'd all (Mahmud, Zulaika and Jabir) go to Norway, where I had reserved a "chalet."

The ship departed from Newcastle, a half-day drive from Norwich, which gave us a taste of that part of the country. Since there were five of us, we had two cabins on the ferry that landed in Bergen, a twenty-four-hour trip. Having our own car made it seem easy to drive to where we would stay for a week. But I hadn't realized that Mahmud's British car was a right-hand drive and we had to traverse tunnels and steep, curvy, narrow roads on left-hand roads.

Our "chalet" was really a simple cottage on the side of a fjord, but it was a perfect spot. The countryside was verdant in mid-August and we took long walks as well as ferry rides to points of interest. We loved it when on one ferry a woman's voice came on the intercom, "This is your Captain speaking." We had a great time, although I think four-year-old Jabir would have just as soon skipped the whole thing.

On the return trip to Newcastle we learned how rough the North Sea can get on what seemed to us like a nice day. After a day in Norwich, we returned to London for our flight home.

Different in almost every aspect from my trip to Spain, this was immensely better in that Dick and I got to share every sight, every experience.

———————

Home in time for me to run for a seat on the Indian Valley Hospital Board. The saga of the Indian Valley Hospital, its ups and downs, its good doctors and bad ones, its Administrators and Board members, is worthy of a book in itself. Suffice it to say that many of us were disgusted at the conduct of the present Board including the ousting of two good people for spurious reasons. So on the last day to put our names on the ballot, Spence (an active member of the AARP) and I went to Quincy and signed on as candidates.

It was not a position I wanted and I had said I wanted to lose by one vote. Actually I lost by three and probably would have not done so if one of the recalled members had not put his name on the ballot at the last minute. Thanks, Russ.

———————

In 1989 Shakir was hired as a medical technician at a military hospital in Saudi Arabia. So the Massouds moved to the hospital compound in Al Hada, high in the mountains south of Jeddah. The following summer we arranged for them to join us in England. With a little financial help from us, Mahmud and Zulaika were able to rent a farmhouse outside of Norwich — plenty of room for the six adults and six children, ranging in age from Jabir's little brother, fifteen-month-old Bashir, to Zayd who would be eleven in September. We have fond memories of our time together, the prison-like castle in Norwich, a ride through The Fens in a flat-bottomed boat, and a day spent in the famous Kew Gardens. After the Massouds went back to Saudi, Dick and I stayed in a B & B in Cambridge, and retraced some of Dick's memorable spots from his time there during the war. Much had changed in the intervening 45 years!

——— ———

Back to Greenville and our usual busy schedules. Our family doctor, Dr. Natali, always described Dick as "the poster boy for aging" so it was a surprise when he discovered that Dick had suddenly developed a heart murmur. The cardiologist in Chico felt that since Dick was asymptomatic, he was a candidate for repair of the valve rather than replacing it with either a pig or titanium valve.

My ever-knowledgeable sister Julie polled her contacts in Kaiser's Cardiology Department and heard high praise for the repair procedure. So Dick spent his 77th birthday in the hospital in San Francisco recovering from open heart surgery. Dick figured he would be back to his usual self in August when Radia and family would visit us. Although the surgery had gone well, Dick couldn't tolerate the various drugs designed to keep his heart in rhythm, so a pacemaker was implanted and we headed home.

——— ———

It was several months after we left England that we learned that Zulaika and the two boys were living in Spain and that Mahmud's efforts at reconciliation were futile. Later Mahmud would bring the older boy, Jabir, back with him to England, while Bashir would stay in Spain, cared for by a Spanish couple.

As he had in the past, Mahmud traveled to various cities as part of his Islamic group's outreach and it was in the course of one of his trips to Germany that he met Na'ima. She was a talented photography student who had recently converted to Islam. Within a few months they married and moved to Dresden, shortly before Germany was reunified.

Nancy and Dick with Julie and Wally Aron (1990)
at an Elderhostel in Ashland Oregon

Surprise! "You have a new granddaughter!" It was Shakir's voice on the telephone on May 12, 1993. Just as we had not wanted Radia to worry about Dick's surgery, they had decided not to have us worry about her pregnancy. All had gone well, and Khadejah became the latest member of our growing family.

Best of all we got to see her (and the rest of them) when Shakir arranged for us to spend three months with them in Saudi Arabia. Not so simple — entrance into Saudi Arabia required prior approval before our visas could be issued. After two months of back and forth mailings and telephone calls and just two days before our scheduled departure, Dec. 18, we were notified that the visas were in Chico. "For goodness sake, don't mail them," we told the official. "We'll pick them up on our way to San Francisco."

It was late at night when Shakir met us at the Jeddah airport. He pointed out the shapes of wild camels as he drove us 40 miles through the desert. Then he pointed to lights to the right, lights which seemed to us to be in the sky. "That's where we're going — 5000 feet above where we are right now!"

Al Hada was a gated compound where only employees of the National Guard Hospital were housed. The family had a very nice fully furnished and spacious apartment, with three bedrooms and two baths. So steep was the terrain that their first-floor apartment was level with the third floor apartment across the street to the south!

It seemed an ideal spot for the family, in many ways like an old-fashioned community where you looked out for the neighbor's kids and they looked after yours. But at Al Hada you did have to be mindful of traffic.

Dick and I found that we loved waking up to the musical call for prayer at 5:00 a.m. (and could usually go back to sleep). Radia had a scarf and hijab (a long dark coat that covered me from collar to ankles) for me to wear whenever we went out — even to the nearby souk (shop). A trip to Taif, the nearest town, was an adventure, driving past the rocks where a band of baboons cavorted, ready to climb all over the car looking for treats if we stopped for even a minute. Jeddah is very metropolitan and busy since its airport is where the majority of Muslims alight on their way to Mecca. We toured a museum or two and went to the big souk with hundreds of small shops — one street for gold venders, another for silver, streets where shoemakers ply their trade, and others where fabrics are sold and a tailor will make you a gown or "harem" trousers in two days.

All nine of us piled into Shakir's station wagon whenever we went out — Radia held the baby on her lap, Omar sat on mine, and Zayd held Hajar. On one such trip we went high up in mountains which are quite verdant, blessed by the fogs that come up from the Indian Ocean.

My one attempt at camel riding was a disaster. With Hajar sitting in front of me, the camel jerkily rose from the mounting position (sitting?) to his full height. I was unprepared to be sitting on a very round hump, with nothing to hold onto except my equally frightened granddaughter. No one on the ground

recognized my panic and the smirk on the face of the camel driver, who held the very docile animal by a rope, added to my distress. Finally Radia realized that it was not going well and persuaded the camel driver to let us dismount. Again the rocking motion as the camel first bent its front legs, then its back. Ah, terra firma!

Swimming in the lukewarm waters of the Red Sea, on the other hand, was delightful. Hajar and I gathered shells and glued them atop a candy tin as a reminder of that happy day.

When it was time for us to leave, Omar started crying, "Why, why are you going?"

"Don't you remember? Yesterday I told you we'd be leaving tomorrow and today is tomorrow."

"How can today be tomorrow?" he wailed.

But it was.

Some weeks before we left, Dick had a sore throat and then a rash on his face which we thought might be an allergic reaction to an antibiotic. But when Shakir took him to the hospital, the Doctor saw at once that it was shingles. "Have your kids had chicken pox?" he asked Shakir.

"All but our six-month-old baby."

"Well she's sure to get it." And of course she did, poor baby.

I, in turn, recognized that I must have developed Bell's palsy one morning when I couldn't close my mouth on the brim of my cup of tea. It was a mild case and quickly subsided with cortisone treatment. We were both pretty well recovered by the time we left.

On our way home we had arranged to stop in Germany to spend a few days with Mahmud, Na'ima, and their three-month-old baby Kasim, who were now living in the Black Forest. In contrast to the heat of Jeddah, we were treated to a snowy,

248

Christmas-card picture. Their third-floor apartment was above a farmer's rooms and below that was the cow's stall. As we climbed the steps to our rooms the only odor was that of sweet hay.

From a hill not far from their place Mahmud pointed out that we could see France and Switzerland. We did a little sightseeing along the cobblestone streets of Stuttgart and learned that this part of the Black Forest caters to German families on vacation, not to tourists like Dick and me.

On our way back to Frankfurt we stopped in Lahr where Na'ima's family had prepared a "tea" for us — with no less than six desserts — cakes, tortes and cookies. Mahmud and Jabir had picked up a lot of German but Dick and I communicated with the extended family by smiles — they having no English and we no German.

Then home again, home for good, we thought.

The Veterans Home

Happy as we were in Greenville, why did we move to the California Veterans Home in Yountville? We learned about it through a film shown at one of our Commission on Aging meetings in late 1995. Far from being the stereotypical "old soldiers home," it depicted an idyllic life in a beautiful setting. Best of all, the Home was now admitting couples, only one of whom needed to be a wartime veteran.

So a few months later we went to Yountville and were given the tour. Everything lived up to our expectations. There was a ten-thousand volume library, a woodshop with up-to-date tools (and free materials) and a buffet-style dining hall. Couples were assigned to one of the residential halls; their rooms were large (bigger than many studio apartments) with a Men's Bath and Women's Bath at each end of the wing. The consistent medical care was one of the main attractions — Greenville was being served at the time by fly-in doctors and we were now going to Chester for care. Not only was there a full hospital on the grounds, but there was a large staff of physicians who provided scheduled checkups, with specialists coming in for regular dental and optical services — all of it included as part of the residential fees.

As a veteran, Dick's fee would be $600 per month and my fee would be proportional to our income. We would not need to sell the house and would still be able to keep up the mortgage payments. (We had refinanced the house for the addition and to pay for our trips overseas.) Eric would stay in the house, paying the utilities, and we could spend weekends and longer periods in Greenville or take trips to visit our family.

Dick was more excited than I about the prospect of making the move. I did not demur, although I had misgivings. No doubt Dick's heart surgery had made him think long and hard about what would happen to me if he died — while I was sure that we had many years ahead of us. We were told that there was a long waiting list for couples — three to five years — so we sent in our applications immediately and waited. The wait wasn't long at all. We were admitted on April 30th and assigned to a room on the ground floor of Building D. Everyone was helpful but the best part of it was the friends we made right in our building. There were three couples with whom we "clicked" instantly: Mary and George, Audrey and Myrt, and Ethel and Dwayne. Though they came from very disparate backgrounds (from each other as well as from us), we enjoyed each other's company and spent time together.

We had some wonderful times while we were there. Many of our friends and family visited us, including sisters Mary and Adele and granddaughters Becky and Jessica (who was on her way to New York).

So what went wrong? Not having our own bathroom was the biggest drawback as far as Dick was concerned. He was repulsed by the other men's sloppy habits; nobody seemed to wash their hands, toilets were left unflushed and urinals were dumped and carried back without rinsing. That was not like the women's bathroom which reminded me of home — with all my sisters gabbing and catching up with yesterday's happenings.

The dining hall was another hurdle. I remember our interview with the Home's dietician after we had been there six weeks or so. When we told her that we were pleased with the food, she smiled. "You haven't been here very long!" How true.

The Dining Hall was only open at stated times: breakfast hours were from 5:00 a.m. to 7:00 a.m., lunch from 10:30 to 12:30, dinner from 4:30 to 6:30 p.m. There was no way we could get there for all three meals. After a few months we, like almost everyone, installed a small refrigerator in our room. We could then use the stove in the utility room and take our meal back to our room. And we began eating out a lot, too, which put a strain on our budget.

I was disappointed that the only time Dick went to the woodshop was when I went too.

I drew the plans and Dick constructed a set of shelves for our room, and some small objects for gifts. Very little, considering that we spent thirteen months in Yountville.

Married couples vied for the apartments in Building L. Actually the "apartments" had been nurses' quarters – two small rooms, each with a wash basin and a toilet accessed from each side. I think it would have meant a great deal to Dick – even though he'd still have to share the shower room. We put our names on the list for an apartment, and waited.

Residents were encouraged to take jobs (at a tax-free compensation of $2.50 an hour). Dick never applied for one, but I took a job in the hospital lab. No medical expertise was required, just filing the myriad reports and delivering appointment slips to the hospital. I enjoyed getting to know some of the inner workings of the Home and it was a congenial group. My hours were usually from seven a.m. to noon. I thought Dick could meet me in the dining hall, getting under the wire for lunch. Usually he wasn't there so I would go back to our room and find Dick still in bed. Lunch in our room. Again.

From the first week we started attending our Building "D" Residents Council. The meetings were pretty toothless affairs, with a little fundraising and plans for a spaghetti dinner.

After the first meeting I talked to some of the women about the shabby appearance of the grounds around "D" compared to other residence halls. Why couldn't we put in a garden if we paid for the plants and did all the work? We found out that approval from the Administration was required, which we applied for and got. A variety of plants were selected, beds prepared and planted with six of the women participating. It really made a difference and we won kudos up and down the line. Then we found out that the wonderful garden in Building C was in jeopardy. Vic, who had created it, done all the work, used his own money, had failed to get prior permission and they were about to demolish it! Vic alerted me that the Administrator had called a meeting with him and the director of "C". I spread the word and attendance at the meeting spilled out, moving to ever bigger rooms as people from other buildings came in support of Vic. The garden stayed and Vic was admonished to go through the proper steps from now on.

Our friend George, who worked in the Admin building, clued us in on the politics of the Home. The Allied Council, for all the Home's residents, held monthly meetings. They were well attended but consisted of reports from various departments of the Administration and were of little news. Maybe people came for the refreshments and to see whose birthday was being announced.

There were two small informal groups who were trying to change the way things were done in Yountville. One group, led by a much decorated former prisoner of war, had a very ambitious goal — the elimination of all the fees currently being charged to veterans, basing their claim on the original charter of the Home. Most of the residents felt that it was unrealistic to compare the Home of today with the original one, built like a barracks in the 1870's. It had been self-supporting, with the veterans raising their own food and doing all the work.

Although George would have denied being the leader of the second group, Dick and I regarded him as its spokesman. It had less far-reaching goals; just wanting to make the Allied Council more independent of the Administration. Dick and I made friends in both groups but agreed with George that the less ambitious plan was achievable.

There were many people who agreed with us, but only ten of us met regularly. We decided that the first step was to elect a new president of the Allied Council. (There weren't a lot of people who were willing to stick their necks out!) We united around John, a well-liked long-time resident. Dick argued that electing a council president "the way we have always done it" was not acceptable. Their tradition was one in which the Executive Board would invite the candidates to the next month's Allied Council meeting. The candidates would be introduced one by one and asked a few questions by members of the Board. The candidates did not face each other and there was no audience participation.

Our group decided to follow Dick's description of how a real candidate forum should be run — with the candidates facing each other and the questions coming from the floor. We announced the date for the "Candidates Night" and there was no point in the Executive Board holding their façade.

Three candidates ran and John came in a strong second. The run-off was a farce. A box of ballots was "lost" and then mysteriously reappeared, putting the incumbent ahead! We protested — going over the heads of the Home's administration — to the Veterans Administration in Sacramento. Under the circumstances they announced that they would not recognize the results. A third election was held and our guy won, handily.

My friends urged me to accept a post on the new Executive Board but I declined. I knew that many of the women veterans felt that the non-veteran spouses were interlopers and I felt that the new Board had enough on its plate without opening that can of worms.

Dick's other initiative during our sojourn at the Home was to start a Book Club. Though he was told that previous attempts had flourished and then died out, he decided to invite a few people over to share his enthusiasm for *The River in the Center of the World* by Simon Winchester.

As word spread about the Book Club, he discovered that there were several published writers in the Home, among them Gilbert Gordon. Gil's book traced the history of Louisiana and how the provisions of the charter of 1803 had been violated. As a native Louisianan he told us of his own family in which some members were black, like himself, but others white, all recognized as relations. The next week Rita had a book on the Lewis and Clark expedition. The Book Club was off to a great start.

Then, in May of '97 we were notified that my fees would be going up. It seems that the Home had incorrectly deducted our monthly health insurance premiums when figuring our income. It would no longer do so; consequently my monthly fee would go up. That blow and the fact that we seemed no nearer to getting an apartment (after a year our name on the waiting list had only moved from twenty-third to twenty-second) tipped the scale.

Our leave-taking in mid-June was very sad, so many good friends. Dick didn't want to dwell on the shortcomings he had with the Home so we used our economic woes as the reason for leaving — we were among the few residents who had not sold their home on entering.

———————

There was irony in the fact that Dick, who had been so enthusiastic about moving to Yountville, was overjoyed to be returning home, while I, who had my doubts about the move, now felt bereft at leaving. I looked around for something to fill the gap, bought a computer and enrolled in a writing class at the Feather River College in Quincy. There were some excellent poets and writers in the group and I enjoyed our critiques of each other's works.

I wrote a piece about my Aunt Amba's cookies, her subtle way of undermining Mama's strict dietary regime. This led me to suggest to my sister Mary that we collaborate on a book of reminiscences and recipes, with each of us alternating chapters. She agreed and our little book *Let All Who Are Hungry* was the result. Mary was the typist, editor and "publisher", using her local Kinko to print and bind the small book. I think we sold — or gave away — about two hundred copies. In a way, this memoir is a continuation of that effort — reminiscences without the recipes.

Our family from Saudi Arabia visits us (1996). From left: Shakir holding Khadejah, Nancy, Omar, Hamid, Hajar, Radia, Dick
(Only Zayd is missing)

Our family from Germany spent a month with us, in time for Dick's 90th birthday (2005). From left, rear: Kasim, Na'ima, Mahmud; front: Allyia, Aisha, Ibrahim

Extra Innings

E xtra Innings – the chance to go ahead, to do what you failed to do in the allotted time. So here is how I spent my extra innings, and how they went.

Dick and I were greeted warmly on our return to Greenville and we resumed many of the roles we had played prior to our departure. Dick was again the Chair of the Plumas County Commission on Aging, which had missed his leadership; and we both were involved in Greenville's AARP.

By 1997 I had the opportunity to be active in the California State AARP, which seemed to me to have become more political and progressive. I applied for and was appointed to the SLC (State Legislative Committee.) It was an exciting group of people and I was pleased to be a contributing member. Reform of the nursing home industry was its current top priority and my experience as an ombudsman made it a subject I knew – and cared deeply about. With a broad coalition behind it, the measure we sponsored contained all of our demands: increases in staffing and enforceable fines for violations. Despite the nursing home industry's powerful lobby it passed both the California Assembly and Senate with scarcely a negative vote. Our celebration was cut short when Governor Gray Davis, a supposedly liberal Democrat, vetoed the bill. That may not be the primary reason he was recalled a year later but it was reason enough for me.

The next year the outgoing Chair of the CSL had asked me to consider running for her post but I demurred. I didn't have the ties to the "movers and shakers" that some other members had and would therefore be less effective. I also knew that it would require more and more time in Sacramento, plus the long commute was becoming a burden. However I did accept the post of AARP's Congressional District #2 Coordinator, where I had roots.

Then came the National AARP's campaign to add the "missing piece" from Medicare — i.e. prescription drugs. Dick and I organized a committee to meet with our Congressman, wrote letters, carried placards, got signatures on petitions and spoke at every nutrition site in our far-flung district. The measure that passed was deeply flawed — it subsidized the pharmaceutical industry and locked in the health insurance companies. It was no surprise to learn that when Medicare Part D passed the House (in the wee hours of the morning of December 3, 2003) there were more lobbyists on the floor than legislators.

With two full years to put the plan in effect it still created massive confusion with its proliferation of plans, all with different premiums, co-pays and different drugs covered by their formulary. Fortunately volunteers from HICAP (Health Insurance Counseling and Advocacy Program), such as Indian Valley's Lynn Herman, stepped into the breach. Things finally settled down, and in the end Part D was a help to many people.

The Greenville AARP was not alone in its dismay that our national AARP leaders had quickly bought into a plan that fell so far short of our demands. It has always been hard for me to accept compromise although I must admit that Saul Alinsky, father of community organizing, had a point. He argued that if you go into negotiations with 100% demands and come out with 30%, people will accuse you of selling out. But in fact you have gone from nothing to 30%!

Six years later the Democratic administration pushed through the National Health Reform Act of 2010. There were many who felt that at last we had an opportunity to push for a "single payer health system" (such as the one which has operated in Canada for so many years). For me — and many progressives — the fact that "single payer" was taken off the table — even before negotiations started – was like going into the battle with 60% demands instead of 100%. But that hardly means that the right-wing is correct in calling for its repeal.

———————

Beside the eight years I put in as a Senior Senator, I had one experience as an elected office holder – as a Board member of the Indian Valley Community Services District (CSD) from 2001 to 2005. Since Indian Valley (Greenville and surrounding communities) is not incorporated, the five-person CSD Board of Directors is the nearest thing we have to a City Council, managing the fire departments and some utilities within a large district. Like many official bodies in rural areas, the CSD officers are all volunteers. At the time I took office the only salaried people were the fire chief (who also managed the sewer system) and a part-time secretary.

I could have been appointed to the Board earlier than November 2000 but I proudly announced that I wanted to be elected and thus not beholden to the current Board. Ironically and disappointingly, my name did not appear on the ballot because I was unopposed (a quirk of our local election system).

One of my main reasons for wanting to get on the Board was the acquisition of the water system from the privately owned company that was so miserably managed that 80% of the water it chlorinated was lost to leaks! The CSD was finally able to purchase the system through federal loans and some grants. Now we needed a full-time secretary, a crew to manage the system as well as a certified water safety person and a business manager to oversee all this responsibility. The young man we hired as manager was bright and energetic – and the only applicant who agreed to the small salary we were able to offer.

Prior to my coming on the board of the CSD the chairman had been a benign despot. Now I tried to convince the current Chair that the days of the one-man-show were over. Unfortunately he didn't get the message and his interference in the opening of the swimming pool ("Get your fat ass down here," to an employee) got him censored; whereupon he resigned. As the Vice-Chair I succeeded him. My friend Jane Braxton Little, who had promised to serve on the Board if I did, was appointed to the vacancy.

A few months later the business manager – on his own – searched the Fire Chief's office at a time when he was out of town. The excuse was to rectify the Chief's dilatory bookkeeping. The Sheriff, notified that someone was in the Fire Department office, arrived and the business manager and his helpers fled.

Word of the "raid" spread like wildfire in the community. The local newspaper carried pictures of the up-turned drawers, and as you can imagine, all hell broke loose. The Fire Chief was well loved and there was the threat of mass resignations from the volunteer firemen. The CSD was unpopular, especially since we had recently raised water rates following the purchase of the system. In addition, the CSD secretary had offended some of the firemen and others in the community.

Fences needed to be mended – and fast – so I called a number of meetings to give people a chance to be heard. With Jane's help and cool head, the meetings succeeded in cooling things down, although some members of the Fire Department never returned.

There were two empty seats on the Board and one of the CSD's most vocal critics, who had been appointed to serve until the next election, won – although he had died two weeks before. I must add that since that time the seats have been filled by live, dedicated men and women.

In 1996, as a volunteer and with the full backing of our AARP membership, I had been active in the passing of a tax measure to support ambulance services in our valley. The tax measure passed along with the creation of the Indian Valley Ambulance Authority. IVASA (sorry about still another set of initials) operated under a Joint Powers Agreement between Indian Valley Hospital and the CSD.

In 2003 the hospital, always in a financial bind, decided that it could no longer afford to keep the ambulance "in house." So the community looked to us in the CSD to find an alternative provider. There was also the need to amend the Joint Powers Agreement to reflect the new situation. The last months of my term as Chair of the CSD were occupied with these urgent tasks. I count maintaining 24-7 ambulance service in Indian Valley as one of my achievements. Another was seeing that the swimming pool in Taylorsville was renovated and reopened by the CSD, with Indian Valley's Recreation District operating it each summer.

It was a sad day for me in October of 2008 when the Greenville AARP dissolved. Our membership had dwindled to less than twenty, with only a few of them showing up to meetings. More than ennui, our ranks had been decimated by the death or debilitating illness of so many and the move to milder climates for others. Elected as Secretary, I was writing the news releases, arranging programs, doing the work of the Treasurer — and aside from chairing the membership meetings, was the de facto President. When I announced that I was burnt out, no one stepped up to keep the group functioning.

At our final meeting, in the tradition that Dick had started thirty years before, I led the discussion of the Propositions which would be on the November ballot that year; and more than the usual handful of people attended. The Chapter had played a key role in many community efforts, had been a chief fundraiser for the swimming pool, the community center, the food pantry and had led the fight to keep utility rates down. I miss it and I hear that Greenville misses its voice.

As to my home design business, I had one job while we were at the Veterans Home and things picked up when we returned to Greenville. There were a few contractors who knew my work and had clients they referred to me. And then there were the sons of those contractors who had grown up in the industry and now looked to me to draw their plans! So, at the ages of eighty- five and eighty-six I had some of my most successful years, financially. On top of which I was doing "pro bono" work in drawing plans for a proposed community center and the renovation of the museum in Greenville.

I really enjoyed designing my very last house although it took almost two years to complete. Most of the delays were not of my doing but arose because of communication between the Building Department in another county and the homeowner who lived in the Los Angeles area. Thanks to my friend Larry Trotter, formerly a building inspector and now a "building facilitator," the problems were finally resolved. The permit was issued in 2009 in time to celebrate my ninety- second birthday!

Today, at the age of 94, I am grateful for these extra innings, for the chance to do a little more — perhaps getting in a run or two! So I am "thinking globally and acting locally." I sit on the boards of the Plumas County League of Women Voters, our local Nutrition Site and the Commission on Aging.

I am grateful that Janet has stayed close through all these years. Seeing Becky and Jessica (nee Cypress) grow up to be beautiful, accomplished women has been a privilege and a special joy.

How fortunate I have been these last innings to have my son Eric as care-giver and companion, fellow writer and supportive critic, *chef extraordinaire* and chauffeur! Before I became his full-time concern Eric was well-known for his empathy and conscientious home-care for a number of aged women in Greenville. "If only we could clone Eric," I have heard people say. As for me, none of these last years would have been possible without him!

Siblings at Leon's 90th birthday: David Rosenfield, Mary L.R. Johnson, Adele Cannon, Leon Rosenfield, Julie Aron, and Nancy Lund

Not Going Gentle

Do not go gentle in that good night
Old age should burn and rave at close of day
Rage, rage against the dying of the light...

Although I understand that Dylan Thomas' poem was written for his father who was going blind, it has come to refer to aging and is therefore an appropriate heading for this final chapter — as it is of my life.

We Rosenfields are a long-lived family. Teeta's death from melanoma at the age of thirty-seven was the anomaly. And cancer was also the cause of Jo's death but that, untimely as it seemed, was at the age of seventy-four. Most of the credit goes to good genes and a sound diet (at least the one we started out with).

A cousin, Helen Adele Ederheimer, lived to the age of a hundred and one, and was bright and chipper almost to the very end. I never made it to New York to meet her, but she always remembered my birthday and our conversation was all about politics after we exchanged the usual report on our health. When she was close to a hundred, she announced that she had been reading about Alzheimer's.

"We didn't have a name for it then but that distant cousin who we always considered a little 'off' was probably suffering from Alzheimer's, and I think that is what I am getting."

"Too late," I told her. "You missed your chance ten years ago!"

It is a cliché to say that we all want a good life and a good death. I have certainly had a good life. A loving family, a very happy marriage, wonderful (if I do say so myself) children who have chosen to stay close, and a circle of friends, now sadly diminished. I would not wish it to have been any other way. But when it comes to death the alternatives are limited.

In the last five years there have been four deaths in my family — first Julie and then Dick in 2006, Leon in 2008 and Adele in 2009. I hope I have learned something from the way each of them faced the end.

Julie — diagnosed with metastasized cancer and iron-willed to the last — decided to banish the possibility of death: only positive thoughts were allowed. Although I visited her as much as my time and distance allowed, there was a false cheerfulness over everything. It was impossible to have any kind of meaningful conversation with her. And although I respected her right to choose this way of death, it was very difficult for me to be so alienated from the sister I knew and loved.

Dear Leon — just short of his ninety-seventh birthday — was unrealistic to the last. I wasn't there but family members tell me that he was very much himself unto the very end. He spent his last few weeks in the hospital, taking advantage of anything that 21st Century medicine could offer. "You know, you can go home and be made comfortable there," I told him, when I called. But, no, he held out hope — a rehab program would set him on his feet.

Death, for dear Adele was a release from the accumulated ill-health which had dogged her for many years and finally reached a point of no return. It had often surprised me that she, an unredeemed and unconverted radical, seemed so passive in regard

265

to her own medical treatment. At least she was spared the indignities of hospitalization and was eased into a long sleep with loving husband Oneil and daughter Jan at her side.

——— ——— ———

So that brings me to the manner of Dick's death, which cannot be covered in a paragraph. Aging, a slowing down was evident over quite a few years, but then in May of '03 it accelerated. Eric was in New Mexico and Dick was keeping the garden going; he wrestled with the long hoses and suddenly was struck by excruciating pain. During the weeks that followed – innumerable doctor's appointments, X-rays, CAT scans, etc. – we learned that three vertebrae had collapsed, but surgery was not an option. Poor Dick got no relief from the drugs that were prescribed. When he was taken off the opiates and given SAIDs, his pain ebbed but he was never the same.

The next three years were not all bad. I took him on long rides around the valley and we would stop in Taylorsville for a frozen ice-cream sandwich or go all the way to Westwood where they actually had real ice-cream cones. There were the family visits. Radia and family came up often from Vallejo. Mahmud, Na'ima and their four kids came from Germany and spent the better part of a month with us to be there for Dick's ninetieth birthday.

——— ——— ———

Ah, the birthday! Dick and I had always said that the celebration of a person's life should be while they are living, not after their death. Accordingly Radia and I planned his 90th birthday to be just that. I made four large posters with photos, clippings and some letters covering his life: the first years until he left Iowa; years in San Diego and his army service as part of a bomber group; photos with him and our three children; and the last one, his years in Greenville.

I rented the Town Hall, expecting the whole town to turn out – which didn't happen – but there were many who came. We set up tables with one of Dick's wooden games on each table — dominoes, taki-ridi tiles, puzzles. It was all very informal, including Jane Braxton Little's part as Emcee asking questions about Dick's life a la *Jeopardy*.

For me, the most memorable point came after a number of people spoke about his contribution to the schools, the seniors and the whole community, and Dick asked if he might speak.

"Everyone in this room deserves the same kind of praise you have given me," he said.

That was Dick. That's the way he felt and the way he lived his life — always giving credit to others.

Leon did have at least two celebrations of his life before he died. He was recognized by B'nai B'rith for his many years dedicated to Jewish youth. And before that there was a really big gathering to celebrate his 90th birthday with former colleagues, friends and family. His boyhood friend, Herbert, came all the way from Texas for the occasion. I treasure the photograph of the six of us — Julie, Leon, Adele, Mary, David and myself — together for the last time.

Adele and Oneil were saluted for all their years of community involvement on several occasions — but I was not able to attend them. Alas, Julie's recognition came after her death, but I think she wanted it that way.

As modest as she was, my sister Jo would have probably rejected the idea of a celebration of her life — but one was held a few weeks after she died. I wasn't able to attend but understand it was most impressive. She had had an impact in many fields beside her long career as a journalist. Support of the arts, a voice for reason in race-relations, and advocate for education, Jo was recognized for her contributions both within and beyond her home in Daytona Beach, Florida.

2006 saw a rapid worsening of things for Dick. Fortunately Eric was there for him, because I fell far short of being an adequate — let alone the perfect — helpmate. The seven stages of mourning are supposed to follow the same pattern as the stages of people facing death, but my mourning didn't evolve; I was stuck on anger.

I felt betrayed. This was not what I had bargained for. I had envisioned our last years as the partners we had been for over fifty years, fading together — peacefully, hand in hand. I think that many people who saw us as a couple thought that I was the one totally in charge, but that wasn't true. I had depended on Dick for many things and most crucially for emotional support. Now it was impossible to have any kind of conversation, let alone the type of meaningful dialogue that would let me say goodbye to him. Now *he* was not there for me.

During that last year it didn't take much to reduce me to tears. Dick would lash out at me for hurting him as I changed his shirt, but then I would be comforted by his saying, "You know you are my all!" Yes, I was luckier than many whose loved one — parent, spouse, child — no longer recognizes them.

I was cried out by the time Dick died. Died in Eric's arms, as was only right. Afterwards I wrote:

DAY 28

Printed cards
Sympathy cards
Cards of condolence.
(I made sure they had a handsome box.)

Most have notes
and that is the hardest part
for they remember Dick as he was
(and as I want to remember him.)

Our grandchild's letter
broke my heart.

She drew Grandpa in his chair
"Throw the ball, don't push —"
and the ball sails into her waiting arms.

Some say he is in a better place.
Any place would be better
than that bed.
(We turned him away from the window —
It will save his ear, they said.)

Thank God they leave God out of it.

Gone

I tell myself it was a spiral
even a year ago — no, further back.
It was a downward spiral.
No way to climb back up
or to rewind the tape.

Finished.

> Two cards yesterday
> but none today.
> Soon they will stop altogether
> and I will put the box away.

> Gone. Finished. Ashes.

> *Not all days are as bad as this.*

Dick and I had always agreed that we would be cremated as preferable to burial. But that didn't mean that I wouldn't want some kind of memorial, a physical place that said "Dick" to me — a place in Greenville, where we had sunk such deep roots, a place where I could sit remembering all our good times. And because

Dick was such a community person it shouldn't be private but a spot where others could also spend a moment or two remembering him.

And so what could be more appropriate than a picnic bench and table in the Greenville Park, with some sort of inscription that would express Dick's dedication to the true meaning of games. The Park is managed by the Indian Valley Community Services and they readily agreed to my plan and permitted me to choose its location. And this was going to be a very special kind of picnic table, handsome, strong and enduring.

I ordered the wood — cedar from Greenville trees, milled by our long-time friend Dave Schramel — and it was built by Greenville High School students in their wood-shop class! The bronze plaque which read "Dick Lund 1915-2006" and below it "Always a team player" was set in concrete by other friends, Jim Hamlin and Brad Smith. The dedication was held in the Park in June '07, with family and friends. And, of, course, we all enjoyed a picnic afterwards.

———

So what have I learned from these deaths? And what would I do differently? I don't intend to impose on my loved ones the façade of denial, or buy into the illusion that medicine can cure everything. Nor do I plan to sink into a world divested of everything beyond my own bodily ills. So what do I intend? I plan to be an active participant in my departure — whenever it comes!

———

I do not expect to see Mama or Dick or any of my siblings in the hereafter; nor do I think that they had any such expectations. But my three children are confident that there is an afterlife of some sort and I am glad that this belief is a comfort to them.

270

Memory of Dick Lund honored in park

Families and friends gathered at the Greenville Park on Saturday, June 2, for the dedication of a new picnic bench in memory of Dick Lund. A bronze plaque set in the concrete that holds the table reads "In loving memory of Dick Lund, 1915-2006, Always a team player." *Photo by Shakir Massoud*

Friends and family members gathered with Nancy Lund at the Greenville Community Park to dedicate a new picnic table in memory of her late husband, Dick, a man who took much pleasure in providing joyful games and experiences for others.

Lund chose the park for the memorial due to all the fun and games Dick so enjoyed with community members and their children.

Lund commissioned the picnic bench and a bronze plaque set in concrete, which was dedicated at the memorial. The bronze plaque reads, "In loving memory of Dick Lund, 1915-2006, Always a team player."

The picnic table was made of locally grown cedar, milled locally by friend David Schramel.

Students of Norman Oilar's Greenville High School FFA Ag Mechanics class built the table.

It now sits near the children's play area, a site Dick would have loved.

As a part of the dedication Lund read from the introduction of World Wide Games, a book that inspired many of Dick's games:

"Fortunately for most people the permanent fascination of games lies simply in the pure joy of playing," she read. "It is this intangible pleasure that distinguishes the true game from, say, the professional sport, where winning rather than playing is all-important."

It was not "godless communism" that turned me into an atheist. The summer that I was fourteen Mary and I read a book that was in the form of a conversation between a scientist and a priest, both on their way to Africa in pursuit of their different vocations. The book was not a polemic but the record of two approaches to looking at the world. Both Mary and I felt that the arguments of the scientist were compelling: evolution explained everything and there was no need for a God to have created the earth and heavens.

271

I am trying to reconstruct a conversation I had with Mama. We were in El Paso and our nurse Obie was still around, so I could not have been more than seventeen. I remember Mama was in bed and I was sitting alongside her. We were smiling over Obie's telling Mama, "You're the best person I have ever known and I hate to think of you rotting in hell because you don't accept Jesus as your savior."

"Why would a just God condemn me to hell?" was her reply.

So it was my turn to ask her, "What do you really think about God?"

"I think God is just another word for good. I think we must live in harmony with what's around us or bad things happen. I believe that we know instinctively what is right and what is wrong. When things get out of harmony you get crime — and wars."

When it came to religious topics, I was always careful not to upset Dick's mother and aunts. And so I was surprised one day when talking with Aunt Min on the phone, she said that she had been asked to describe her thoughts about life and death and found it difficult to put into words. "Nancy, what about you?" she asked.

After a long pause I said, "Well, there are two poems that say it for me. Not Tennyson's "Sunset and Evening Star" but a few lines from Arnold's "Dover Beach" and from "Invictus" by Henley. I'll look them up and send them to you." Which I did.

While "Dover Beach" is in many ways a lament for the loss of faith which once gave man security, the following line offers another kind of solace:

Ah love, let us be true to one another...

And of course "Invictus" spells out a challenge, the determination to live life on one's own terms:

It matters not how strait the gate,
How charged with punishments the scroll.
I am the master of my fate:
I am the captain of my soul.

These two poems still seem to me to cover my philosophy. I no longer describe myself as an atheist, but as an agnostic. I have not read as widely as I might, but David Berlinski's *The Devil's Delusion* has made me doubt whether the scientists have all the answers. Berlinski points out that those who have tried to explain the universe in terms of the Big Bang theory don't fully answer the question of what there was in the universe to precipitate the Big Bang. And if these scientists can't overcome the questions that are raised, some have even posed the possibility of other universes — but not how they might have started!

I accept the theory of evolution — from the interaction of carbon, sunlight and water as the likely beginning of life here on earth. But I am not ready to say that there is no God, nor that there is one. I come back to Mama's idea of harmony and the need to live in harmony with the people of the world and with nature. I have no doubt that we have changed the climate, the air we breathe, the food we eat and the water we drink. And in keeping with my Bo-Peep optimism, I hope it is not too late to restore some harmony with the world around us.

———————

Am I also an agnostic about what form of government is best? Nothing that I see or read has made me change my belief that capitalism is evil — that it rewards greed and leads to poverty and war. Unfortunately I cannot point to any successful alternative.

After nineteen years in the Communist Party I had given up hope that communism was realizable in the U.S., but I still held out hope that elsewhere it had a chance. Later, the examples of Mao, Fidel and Zimbabwe's Mugabe have disabused me of that idea. Why did these leaders, who started out as idealists, became the perpetrators of innumerable crimes — imprisonment, torture, starvation. Wasn't it because they didn't trust anyone — followers as well as people in general — to stick to the ordained path? It seems apparent that dictatorships arise when a single idea is dominant and all other possibilities are rejected.

At one time I was excited about the kibbutz movement in Israel — a socialist plan, on a small scale. I have no such illusions today. A country built on the false premise of "a land without people for a people without a land" is bound to face the reality sooner or later. Today, official Israel is the perpetrator of the worst sort of injustice and violence against the Palestinians — while living in a distorted vision of being the perpetual victim.

Colonialism, with all its injustices cannot wholly explain Rwanda, Nigeria, Darfur, and the Ivory Coast. And yet the examples of Reconciliation in South Africa and in Rwanda gives us hope that healing can take place.

So, yes. I guess you can say I am an agnostic about government. The "third way" — a welfare state as exemplified in Norway and Denmark — looks like the best solution. But up until now they have not had to deal with mass immigration from people from different cultures (and different colors). The state's response to the August 2011 murders in Oslo will test their institutions.

And while I'm on my soapbox let me add — it is time that we stop referring to ourselves as Americans; since we share the continent with two other nations we are not even entitled to call ourselves *the* North Americans. We are the USA.

———————

I started out this memoir right after my 90th birthday — inspired by the interest which some of my younger relatives displayed on learning of my radical past. While I rejected the title of "Bo-Peep" for this memoir I must say that my confidence that everything will turn out right has been a guiding principle throughout my life. And in my life it usually has.

Why has my purse been returned to me — intact — time after time over the years? I have left it hanging on the mirror of the car, at the stadium of a World Series Game, on a deserted park bench — and it has been returned, undisturbed, intact — with no effort on my part! And how come I can neglect to make reservations at the theater but there will be tickets at the box-office when I arrive with guests? See? Bo-Peep's sheep do make it home!

And I remember the time my sister Jo asked me if I wasn't afraid, walking home from the streetcar at night.

"No. Why should I be?"

"What if a man jumped out of the bushes at you?"

"Well, I would certainly be afraid then. But what's the point of being afraid before anything happens?"

———

You might say that these many pages can be summed up in a single paragraph:

I, Nancy Lund, have been through my life a Bo-Peep and a Red — an optimist whose dashed hopes never taught her to be more circumspect and a radical who never went to jail, never was beaten on a picket line, or even cited for contempt. Also a daughter, sister, wife, and mother. And though a lousy housekeeper, I was a pretty good home designer and not bad as a self-appointed guru on aging.

———

If memory is like an attic — crowded with once-useful, now discarded objects, but also some forgotten treasures — should not this rummaging have dredged up at least some insights, some words of wisdom from one who has lived so long? Afraid not. What has worked for me may not be a formula that I can dispense to others. What has worked for me is a core belief that people can change; that — in the long run — living in harmony with our neighbors will make us happier than living in fear and suspicion. And that this is a beautiful world that we get to share for a while and should leave it — if not a better place — at least no worse.

To My Granddaughters

What shall I give you —
You that have so much?

The right to vote?
Your great great grandmother
might have been one of the women
who chained herself to the White House gates.
I know she venerated those who did.

The right to be a doctor or lawyer?
Your great grandmother demanded the right to be an artist
and shocked her family with life-like studies
of nude men and women.
Then taught her daughters they could be anything they chose.

The right to have friends of every race and color?
Your grandfathers sat guard many a night
in the homes of black families who had
dared to move into white neighborhoods
and taught their daughters to see good in all people.

The right to love and be loved
and to know that you need not bear children
until you are ready?
Your grandmothers demanded the right to choose
And your mothers fought to keep Roe safe.

You need not weep, like Alexander,
that all has been accomplished:
Is there a way to end the curse of war
or hunger in the midst of plenty?
And who will save this fragile planet from the plunderers?

In the footsteps of all the women who went before
I see you, your beauty and your strength.
And into your willing hands
I trust the gains that have been won.

What shall I give you?
I give you the tasks we left undone.

Nancy Lund
1996

Acknowledgements

To my niece Jean Bell I owe more than I can say. I am the happy recipient of her editorial skills but above all the encouragement and energy and untold hours she dedicated to getting this memoir completed. In going through the many boxes left by my brother Leon, Jean also retrieved my letters to my mother which added to my recall. Thanks Jean!!

My sister Mary L.R. Johnson not only saved the letters I had written to her over the years but she meticulously dated them and filed them in order. This was invaluable in refreshing my memory of the emotions I felt at the time that certain events occurred.

I am very proud of my talented granddaughter, Hajar Massoud, whose drawing of the little girl on the cover exactly captures the moment that gives title to my memoir. Thanks, Hajar. Thanks also are due to her mother, my daughter Radia, and all the Massoud family, who have regularly housed, fed and nurtured me these past years when I needed to escape the snow and ice of Greenville's winters. And, in case he missed my tribute to him in "Extra Innings," I owe Eric my undying gratitude.

For many years Dick was my proof reader, adviser and rooter and though he is no longer here his belief in me has been a powerful incentive.

Although I rejected the title of "Bo-Peep at 90" as my title, I must confess that it is a role I have played for much of my life. At first my sisters, Teeta and Mary, were the ones who picked up for me, saw that I was on time, found my sweater or my shoes, made excuses for my behavior. And it was Lee Wintner, who I had just met and who I'd never see again, who set me on the path to using my energy and optimism for the benefit of others.

When I left home (at the age of twenty six!) there were many others who took me under their wing. I think of Lil Hunt in those early days in San Diego, Mama Epps that first night alone with a baby, and later, Rosa Lee Carter in so many ways. Whatever success I had as a Senior Legislator I owe in large part to Emma Gunterman who knew all the ropes in Sacramento and was instrumental in getting my proposals sponsored and passed. When we moved to Greenville June Bohne became my guide to all things in the community. The list of those who saw to it that my "sheep" got home is long. They are mentioned here because they gave me so much more than friendship or simple neighborliness!

Once out of the comfortable nest of my parents' home I did become a better partner to my sisters. And I had many wonderful, caring friends who are no longer with us — a few of whom I have mentioned in these pages — Nettie, Lucia, Celia, Bernadette, Ruth Park, and my siblings Teeta, Jo, Julia, Leon and Adele. I am happy that friends Yvonne, Joyce and Julia, younger brother Dave and my sister Mary are still only a telephone call away. In fact Mary is no longer a rival but a collaborator, a twin, albeit an un-identical one.

As a fellow (but much more professional) writer and community person, Jane Braxton Little has been friend, goad, critic and cheerleader. Thanks, Jane! I have been very fortunate, also, to have had the support of other members of my local book group and writers group — friends who know and love books.

———————

With all the help and encouragement I have received through my long life, I like to think that in some small way I have "Paid It Forward."

Appendix

Newspaper Articles by and about Nancy Lund

Selected Clippings

The following pages are a sample of the many articles I have written over the years. The Feather River newspapers have given me the opportunity to express my opinions (and advocacy!) on many issues and I thank them. There are also reprints of pieces about me and my family that I thought would be of interest.

S. D. Reds Force Firms to Hire Negro Employes

Theater Picketed After Stores Sign Racial Agreement

By RICHARD K. GOTTSCHALL

Local Communists, their pressure tactics already successful in three instances, yesterday threw a picket line around an Imperial ave. theater to force the proprietor to hire Negro workers. Police, acting on complaints of Logan Heights business men, ordered extra foot and mobile patrolmen into the area to maintain order.

The New Victory theater, 2558 Imperial ave., was third business establishment to be picketed by the Logan Heights club of the Communist party, according to the club chairman, Enos Baker jr.

STORES TO HIRE NEGROES

Baker declared last night that a conference with personnel and store managers of Safeway Stores, Inc., at Thirtieth and Twenty-fifth st. on Imperial ave. had resulted in an "oral agreement" that five or six Negroes would be hired within the coming week. The Safeway stores were not picketed.

Baker said that after two hours of picketing, the H & H market, 3043 Imperial ave., had signed a written agreement to hire Negro help, and that after nine hours of picketing, Jones Variety store, 3028 Imperial ave., had signed a similar contract.

CLUB ISSUES CIRCULAR

Ted Johnson, owner of the Imperial ave. 5 & 10, at 2589 Imperial ave., reported last night that a group of 10 or 11 of the Logan Heights club has visited his store Saturday morning and threatened to throw a picket line around his business Monday morning if he did not agree to hire a Negro worker.

The Logan Heights club last night was distributing a mimeographed news sheet listing Johnson's store, the Victory theater, the Rasumow Department store, 2522 Imperial ave., and the A. K. Hom grocery, 2485 Imperial ave., as businesses which "have still not agreed to hire Negro help."

SLOGAN URGES BOYCOTT

At the bottom of the yellow-colored sheet is the slogan: "Don't buy where you can't work," and the statement, "Issued by the Logan Heights club of the Communist party."

The news sheet also announces the Safeway Stores agreement and terms it "a direct result of the distribution of a leaflet by the Communist party urging the people of Logan Heights: 'Don't buy where you can't work'."

That the movement to gain a foothold in the political life of San Diego's growing Negro population is openly backed by the Communist party was openly admitted last night by Miss Nancy Rosenfield, secretary-treasurer of the county organization.

SECRETARY CARRIES SIGN

Miss Rosenfield, who appeared at the Victory theater last night to carry a placard in the picket line and bring a fresh supply of the Logan Heights club news sheets, declared that the picket lines were designed to let Negro men employ the skills learned during the war.

"Negro boys and girls have applied for jobs," the brunet secretary said, "and whites have been hired over them." "This is a fight against discrimination of any sort," said Miss Rosenfield. She charged that trade at the Imperial ave. business houses was 80 to 90 percent Negro, but that the proprietors had refused to hire Negro help.

Also backing the movement are the American Students' association, the National Association for the Advancement of Colored People, and the San Diego county fair employment practices committee, Miss Rosenfield said.

According to the Logan Heights club chairman, the American Students' association will meet Monday at 6:30 p.m. at the Clay st. branch of the Y.W.C.A. to select men to fill the Safeway Stores agreement on Tuesday afternoon.

STORE MANAGER EXPLAINS

The other side of the story was voiced by Johnson, the variety store manager, last night. He explained that a group of "10 or 11" had visited his store and asked him if he would fire the white salesgirl currently working in the store and hire Negro help. Johnson said he refused to fire the girl, since her work was satisfactory, and he cannot afford to hire a second person. "She works only part time," Johnson said. The store's trade, he declared, is about 40 percent Negro.

The Victory theater manager, Leo A. Hamecher, said two Negro girls visited him two weeks ago and applied for work. "I told them I had a full crew and couldn't put anyone else on," he said.

HIRES NEGRO JANITOR

Theater patronage, he added, is divided about 60 percent whites and 40 percent Negroes. His present staff at the theater includes a Negro janitor, one Filipino girl and five white employes.

The Logan Heights club chairman retorted "We're not interested in janitors' jobs," to Hamecher's contention that he already employed one Negro. The picket line, said Baker, will be maintained until Hamecher agrees to hire permanently one or more Negroes.

THEATER PATRONAGE DROPS

The agreement, according to Miss Rosenfield, provides for the hiring of one or more Negroes within specified dates, but makes no attempt to dictate to the proprietor what individual he must put to work. However, the agreement states that if the Negro filling the position should prove unsatisfactory, he must be replaced with another Negro.

Theater patronage last night was about 50 percent of normal, according to Hamecher. "We've got him (Hamecher) out there soliciting business now," said Baker, when the theater owner appeared on the sidewalk.

The theater pickets were orderly last night and confined themselves for the most part to bearing their placards silently. Most of the pickets wore servicemen's discharge emblems.

281

BUILDING DESIGNERS AT THE BOARD--Nancy Lund [left] works with drafting student Janet Mc-Been on a nearly completed houseplan. Although traditionally a career for men, Nancy encourages women to become draftspersons.

Drafting her life,homes with skill

By Jane Little
Staff reporter

For some women, equal opportunity is a birthright. They expect it, carrying a strong sense of self-worth through their lives. Nancy Lund of Greenville is a woman who appears to have never doubted her right to be what she is.

"My mother raised six daughters and we are all strong women. There were two sons and my father assumed that we girls would make their beds. But my mother said, "No way!" So that had a lot to do with my feeling about myself."

Nancy is a draftsperson. She has worked at her craft for 30 years, varying the direction in which she has applied herself but never failing to give to her jobs her confidence and her sensitivity.

"When I was out of high school my father said that he'd see that I continued my education if I would promise to get a job as a teacher or a secretary. I told him I'd rather die than do either of those jobs, so I quit school."

During the World War II Nancy applied for an assembly line job and was eventually hired in a defense training program as a draftsperson. "I was very fortunate--my program consisted of four hours of work and four hours of school. I learned a lot and that gave me a beginning."

When her husband went back to school in the Los Angeles area Nancy answered ads for "draftsmen."

"Sometimes I couldn't even get an interview. Often it was a woman secretary who would tell me they had never hired a woman as a draftsman. Sometimes they would tell me that the language would be offensive to a woman and I would say, 'Oh, but you haven't heard me!'"

But she did get jobs and each one added to her skills and range of experience in drafting. "There was always one person on the job who would help me out--lend me tools or take the time to teach me. There was always one person who felt I had a right to be there.".

Nancy developed particular skills as a reinforcement bar detailer, working from 1949 to 1966 in that capacity. She worked with engineers' drawings for bridges, freeway overpasses and other heavy construction, supplying to the placer the precise length and placement of the rebar.

"It was really a man's world--at the time I was the only woman in that field. People would call me and ask to speak to Lund. I had to convince them that I was Lund, not Lund's secretary."

"But I always knew that I would be married and a mother. I never thought of myself as not having children."

Working intermittently when her first two children were toddlers, Nancy took a fulltime job in drafting when her third child was quite young. She hired a fulltime housekeeper whom she paid more than she herself earned. Quick to acknowledge the importance of having had a supportive husband, Nancy says her husband Dick always called himself " a team player."

"In our day it was pretty darn unusual for a man to stay home with the children. When the kids were sick that's where Dick would be. Once his boss asked him why his wife didn't take the kids to the doctor. He said, "Because she makes more money than I do!"

Nancy is presently a building designer, drawing house plans from her office at home. It is a profession which employs both her drafting skills and her sensitivity to the often unarticulated needs of women.

"I try to involve both the husband and the wife in the planning of a house. Women traditionally spend more time in the house so the layout is really much more important to them than to men."

"But women have been intimidated into thinking that they don't have a sense of space. Yet who packs, who puts away groceries? Because of their life experiences women can see the short-comings of different floor plans. I once worked with a plan

that called for an entry between the kitchen and the dining room. A woman would never do that!"

Nancy speaks with intensity, focusing warm but penetrating eyes on her listener. Whether she is serving melon in her cozy, convenient kitchen or sitting at the drawing board in her well-lit and efficient office, she brings energy to her conversations about women--the rights and the myths.

"The notion is that women are good interior decorators and that's the end of their abilities. Of course it's not: Women are practical. They know that an open house means more cleaning. I always encourage women to have homes in which they can function."

Nancy now has two women as students, giving them an opportunity to get into the field of drafting. For years she has encouraged women in her career.

"In our society women have been made to be the consumers but not the designers and creators which they can be. It makes sense for women to lay out homes--they are the ones who have to function in them."

Nancy's own satisfaction with her profession lies in part with its combination of art and math. "My mother was an artist. I've always been turned on by art but not able to do too well without a straight edge and a sharp pencil. And I've always loved math. So drafting combines the two."

There is contentment, too, in putting stability and function together with the hopes of her clients. A woman who works with the dreams of others and the realities of construction, Nancy says, "I think I'm a realist. I'm just as interested in foundations as I am in roofs."

And it appears that along with the house--foundation, roof and well-placed entry--Nancy designs into her plans the dignity for those who will live in the house that she has drafted into her own life.

The Gazette Soapbox
A Column of Personal Opinion
Toward and Age-Irrelevant Society

Many contradictory "truths" are current on the subject of aging.

On November 15, at the Greenville Townhall, Plumas County will join the network of forums and town meeting leading to the 1981 White House Conference on Aging. We will be looking for some sort of consensus on where we are today and where we want to go.

One viewpoint sees the older person in a desperate struggle to obtain the four basic things he or she has always needed: dignity, sufficient income, adequate medical service, and a useful niche in society. Other hold that the aged have never had it so good; what with Medicare paying the hospital bills, Social Security benefits tied to increases in the cost of living, and an SSI check (Supplemental Security Income) for those whose benefits fall below a certain level.

Some people see the segregation of the aged as coming from a society that has emphasized youth and denied its own mortality. Others point to the self-imposed isolation, most strikingly seen in "Sun City." On the other hand, hundreds of thousands of persons over 65 continue to work, provide emotional and financial support to their children and grand-children, and are deeply involved in their communities' political, cultural and social activities.

Today, 10 out of every 100 persons in the United States is age 65 or older. In 1930 it was 4 out of 100, in the year 2020 it will be 16 out of 100. As we face the social and economic trends of the '80's there is a strong probability that programs to expand and improve the quality of life for elders may be limited. If we can form alliances with other groups striving toward the same goals and if we can conceive methods that cost less and provide more, it need not be a bleak future.

And finally, if we can come to grips with the reality of our own aging, recognizing that we all have a present self and - if we are lucky - a future self, we may at last create an age-irrelevant society.

—Nancy Lund
Greenville

284

Indian Valley Record
7/15/81

NANCY LUND, Greenville AARP President

" A town doesn't have to die and be reborn to become attractive. Our community offers a wonderful blending of old timers, whose childhoods and work histories are in this area, and newcomers, who have chosen this place as home.

"I would like to see some development where genuine enterprises in the downtown area provide employment for young people and attractions for outsiders. I look forward to senior housing in he very near future to provide conomical, energy-wise homes for nany of our ill-housed citizens.

"This can become a nucleus for this community, and allow the continued cross-generational interchanges which are so important to the present quality of life in Greenville."

Lund focuses on older women

Nancy Lund is focusing attention on the economic and health concerns of mid-life and older women as she speaks to senior groups and women's organizations in Northern California.

Recently selected as a spokesperson for the Women's Initiative of the AARP (American Association of Retired Persons) Lund feels that awareness, information and organization are the keys to changing the situation in which many women find themselves today.

"The statistics are becoming familiar," she states, and although progress has been made at all ages, women trail men in earnings and earn roughly 59 cents to the men's $1.00.

Women, as a group, receive lower Social Security benefits than men and are less likely to have their retirement income supplemented by a pension.

Women make up 71 percent of

AARP Report

Nancy Lund

the elderly poor. Older women are more likely to be living alone; they are less likely to own their own homes and must struggle to meet rising housing costs with less income.

Single elderly women pay a higher proportion of out-of-pocket expenses for health care than do elderly married couples women are the care-givers — 72 percent of all home care is provided by the woman of the family. Many of these women have outside jobs and family responsibilities on top of the hours spent in caring for a disabled parent, spouse or child.

Lund feels that the volunteer position as spokesperson gives her the opportunity to communicate with an ever-widening audience on these concerns.

"Some of the solutions lie in the field of legislation, expanding services and information is important, and finally, we women ourselves must cooperate in changing the outlook for us, our daughters and grand-daughters!"

Individuals and organizations who would like to hear more about the Women's Initiative are urged to contact Nancy Lund at her home in Greenville (P. O. Box 345, Greenville, CA 95947; (916) 284-6423).

Bay Area Senior Spectrum March 1987

286

Senior legislator sees bill passed

By Lynda Smith
Indian Valley Editor

Nancy Lund of Greenville is excited because a proposal, SB2429, she wrote was picked up by Sen. Henry Mello and last week, after some amendments and changes were made, became a state law when Gov. George Deukmejian signed the bill.

The law, to be added to the Welfare and Institutions Code, is called California Rural Alternative Adult Day Health Care Act, Lund said.

As she prepares to run for a fourth term in the Senior Legislature, Lund said the new law was effective immediately and would affect not only the rural areas but could be applicable in some divisions to the urban areas.

In the measure, Lund defined the need for changes in the licensure and certification standards which regulate adult day health care centers. Athough the standards are appropriate for larger and urban areas, they become unduly burdensome for smaller, rural areas.

Although the Legislature in its Health and Safety Code has declared its intent to encourage the development of models appropriate for rural areas, provide the department with full authority to grant program flexibility and to provide active and ongoing technical assistance to dissolve barriers to the development of adult day health care in rural areas.

Consequently, persons with functional limitations in many rural areas of the state are unable to benefit from adult day health care services.

Therefore, it is the intent of the legislators to establish in this law a rural alternative adult day health care model which meets the special needs and requirements of rural areas and would enable the provision of adult day health care.

Lund said one of the best things about the new law is that it sets aside the regulation of having a specialist on the premises. "We can have a specialist on a consulating basis instead of having to employ or have one on the premises," she said.

That would mean AD health care is an eligible expense for MediCare, which in turn means a center would be reimbursed for daily expenses.

The exciting part is an AD health care center could be set up in someone's home, a social hall or other building with a little as three or four participants, she said.

A broad coalition of people worked on getting the measure passed into law including representatives from the Commission of Aging, Health and Welfare Agency, Department of Aging, Department of Health Services and the Office of Statewide Planning.

Assemblyman Stan Statham's office was also involved, she said.

Entered last year as one of the top 12 priorities, another measure written by Lund, AB1632, which proposed the listing of health care providers to relieve those providing constant care for the elderly, was bumped to a 10-a priority, which passed but later vetoed by the governor.

She is currently working on an admendent to include the list in another measure, written by someone else, concerning weekend care for the elderly, and she will be lobbying for the measure at the 1990 session of the California's Senior Legislators.

The session begins Oct. 14 — Lund's 73rd birthday. The busy, active senior said she couldn't think of a better way to celebrate her birthday unless it would be to go to a theater and see "Steel Magnolias."

Nancy Lund, Greenville's Senior Senator for California's Senior Legislature, is planning to celebrate her 73rd birthday while lobbying at the state capitol in Sacramento.

287

Senator Lund shares a

By Mary Lowman
Staff Writer

Canada has the right idea, Nancy Lund believes, and she's doing everything she can to convince U.S. policy makers to model after the northern neighbor.

The focus is the health care system, and following Canada's lead would mean major changes for the U.S., said Lund, a senior senator in the California Senior Legislature.

"The idea is that every American would have one simple card. It wouldn't change who you go to

for medical care, but the way it's paid," she said during a phone interview from her Greenville home Tuesday.

The idea is encompassed in Senator Nicholas Petris' (D-Oakland) bill, the "Right to Health Care Act," said Lund, adding that there are 37 million Americans without health insurance. "There are other millions who are underinsured, and the costs are skyrocketing," she said.

How ever people pay their medical bills, all that money would go into one big fund.

"Financing would come from the pooling of billions of health care dollars currently coming

from Medicare, MediCal, private insurance, Disability, Workman's Compensation, indigent care, tobacco taxes.

"Private insurance carriers (such as Blue Shield or Prudential) would still pay (a premium) and it would go into the fund. Seniors have $29.60 taken out of Social Security every month, and most of us with any kind of income carry a supplemental anywhere from $45 to $90 a month. And all that would go into the fund.

"No one would be un-insured; there would not be a two-tier system of care for those with insurance and those without," said Lund.

To get the ball rolling, Health Access, a coalition of 200 organizations inlcuding the American Association of Retired Persons, is distributing a model of Canada's health care cards.

"By distributing our Health Security Card to a million Californians within the next few months, we will be giving people something tangible, almost a promissory note that each one of us can make viable. The plastic cards are each individually numbered and have a place for a signature. On the back are listed

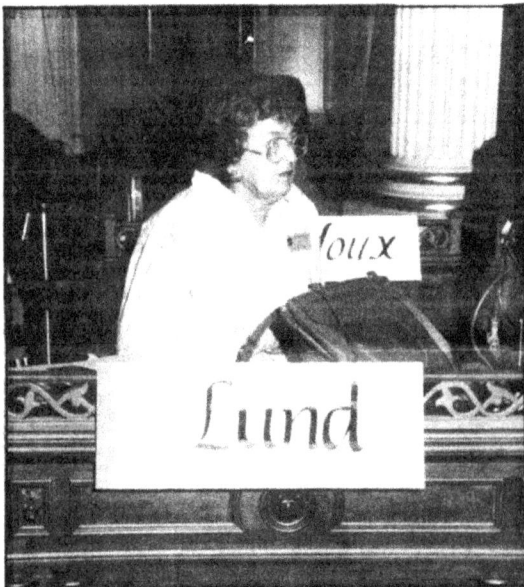

Senior Senator Nancy Lund during a recent legislative session in Sacramento.

a vision of health care

the services which this card will entitle you IF your state or the federal government enacts a universal, publicly-funded Health Care Program," Lund explained.

Lund said she hopes candidates will be committed to the idea of the Health Security Identification Card by the November 1992 elections.

"All the candidates are concerned about one group or another — pregnant women, uninsured, disabled. But they don't address the idea of a single payer."

But the concept is nothing new. "The Senior Legislature has been working on this for eight years," said Lund.

Lund also said a similar plan is being considered on the federal level.

A second problem with the American health insurance system, said Lund, is the the abundance of highly technical medical equipment.

"We have such a high-tech capabilities, and a lot of this stuff is used because we have to pay for it. It reminds me of a cartoon I saw, where the doctor says to the patient, 'It looks like a splinter but we better do some tests'."

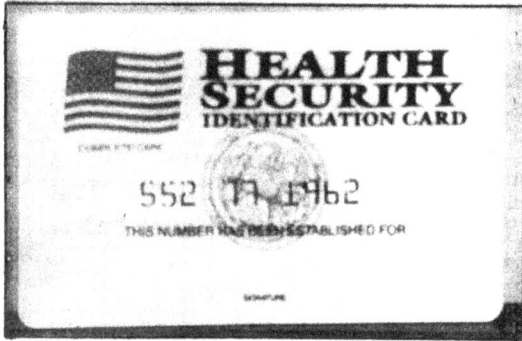

An example of the Health Security card

Patterned after the state Legislature, the Senior Legislature is made up of 40 senators and 80 assembly members who are elected every two years through voting coordinated by the state-wide Area Agencies on Aging.

Lund works closely with Berry Keir of Chico, senior assemblyman, representing interests of seniors in Butte, Glenn, Colusa, Plumas and Tehama counties.

Lund and Keir both have

Health Security Cards available to the public. "With this card in your pocket, you can become an advocate for a hassle-free, care-centered health system," said Lund.

To obtain a card, send 25 cents to Lund, P.O. Box 345, Greenville, Ca. 95947; or Keir, 1670 E. Eighth St., Chico, Ca. 95928.

Lund can be reached by calling 284-6423; Keir is at 894-6324.■

289

Islam, Christian, Jew: a family of varied beliefs

By Alicia Knadler
Indian Valley Editor

Greenville residents Dick and Nancy Lund did not let their different religions stop them from marrying. Dick was Lutheran, Nancy was Jewish, and they were both confirmed in their religions.

They raised their children to honor and respect all religions, leaving them to choose the doctrines they preferred.

For two of their three children that choice was the Muslim tenets of Islam.

Islam is not just a religion, their oldest son, Mahmud, said; Islam is a way of life.

Born as Benjamin, Mahmud converted to Islam and changed his name in the 1970s, followed a few months later by his sister, Rachel, who is now known as Radia.

The Lunds' other son, Eric, is still Eric, and although he is a spiritual person, he chooses not to identify with a specific religion.

The Lunds were surprised by Mahmud's and Radia's choice of Islam, but they did not object, for they trusted their children to make their own choices.

The Lunds' children grew up watching their parents fight for just labor laws and civil rights, and they learned about the personal rewards that come from a life devoted to helping others.

Then again, Dick and Nancy have watched their children grow up with a strong mien of volunteerism in their code of ethics.

Their grandchildren are now showing that same aspect of volunteerism.

Mahmud's oldest son, Jabir, now 19, was helping refugees in Albania during the Kosovo Crisis three years ago.

And their granddaughter, Jessica is a law student who helps seniors and others fight for the services they need in between semesters at university.

The Lunds have become world travelers over the last several years, since their children have lived in different countries.

Radia married Shakir Massoud, who also converted to Islam, and they lived in Saudi Arabia for 10 years.

Although Radia and Shakir wore traditional dress in public, their five children wore American clothes, including T-shirts sporting colorful pictures and sports team logos.

While visiting them for more than two months, Nancy also wore a long robe over her outfits when out in public.

Nancy smiles with a memory. When only 6 years old, Eric observed a major truth in their lives.

Mom was one of eight chil-

Photo submitted

Brothers Hajj Mahmud and Eric Lund may not share the same religious beliefs, but they do share the same values taught to them by their parents. Eric enjoyed a visit at an outdoor cafe with Mahmud and his youngest daughter, Aisha, in Germany three years ago.

dren in a rich Jewish family, and Dad was the only child in a poor Lutheran family.

They did not squabble over religious or lifestyle issues, though. The hardest parts of their lives always boiled down to the decision between rice, Nancy's favorite, or potatoes, Dick's favorite.

Choosing Islam

For Mahmud Lund, Islam was a revelation, and he was stunned that people claiming to be Muslims could do something as terrible as the 9/11 attacks.

To most Muslims, the terrorists are considered nihilists, or people who have no values. Mahmud lumps suicide bombers into that same category.

To people of the Muslim's Islam faith, suicide is the absolute guaranteed path to fire, versus the goodness of the garden promised by Islam Prophet Mohammed.

Mahmud said these terrorist problems all began with the post-Israeli occupation of Jerusalem.

"It is like a cancer that grew under colonialism," he said. "If you pack rats together, they will eventually eat each other."

"And the manipulator, Osama Bin Laden, finds recruits easily in these drastic situations."

Unlike Pearl Harbor, the enemy is unclear. The Afghan people had nothing to do with it, Mahmud said, and it is too far a reach to use the attacks as an excuse to invade Iraq.

He believes that the 9/11 attacks have spurred an interest in Islam, but it is not always the truth that people hear.

The greatest misconception is that terrorism is an integral part of Islam.

Actually, Islamic and western religions hold dear many of the same values, including the rights of women.

"If man is not free any more, the only thing left he can take control of is his wife, or women," Mahmud said, and the head-to-toe robe women were forced to wear is a cultural affectation brought about by colonialism.

His Norwegian grandmother used to wear a veil to church, years later all women used to at least wear hats to church. Today, not as many women wear hats to church.

Culturally, people have changed, but their religions still share many of the same values.

America was founded by people who were rebelling against unfair taxes.

In Islam there is only one tax, a 2.5 percent tax on income above a certain level.

America was also founded by people who wanted freedom of religion, although in reality most would not tolerate some religions.

Mahmud speaks of Benjamin Franklin, who organized a free church, where he even invited Muslim Imams, who teach and give prayers, but are not exactly what

Dick and Nancy Lund enjoyed a special visit from their son, Mahmud, and two of their grandsons, **Bashir, 13, and Jabir, 19, from Germany. Their son's family is of the Islamic faith**

291

Photo submitte

Dick and Nancy Lund spent six weeks visiting their daughter, Radia, and her family in Saudi Arabia. Although Nancy's robe is hitched up for sitting on the ground at a picnic, she and Radia always wore the traditional long robe when out in public. The children romped around in American-style clothes, down to the Chicago Bulls sweatshirt.

Continued from page 14

westerners think of as priests.

There are five things required of the Muslim who practices Islam:

- Believe in Allah and that Mohammed was His prophet
- Pray five times a day
- Fast while the sun is up during the Month of Rammadan
- Tithe 2.5 percent of income if not poor
- Go once in their lives on a pilgrimage, or Hajj, to Mecca

Going on Hajj can have a profound effect on people, and once they have met that obligation, they are permitted to add the honorific Hajj to their names.

Malcom X was a black Muslim, whose tenets included hatred. He was invited by other Muslims to go on Hajj, where he saw thousands of people from everywhere, rich and poor, light-skinned and dark. They were all dressed the same and were all seeking Mecca.

After witnessing so many people together in peacefulness, Malcom completely lost his hatred. He changed his name to Hajj Malik Shabazz,

and he changed his teachings to that of Islam.

Another commonalty between Islam and American values is the belief in justice.

To Islam, justice is one of the greatest treasures that must be protected.

"An event like 9/11 is what happens when injustice is allowed to go on without punishment," Mahmud said. "It creates a breed of people with no values, and going after them causes innocents to be killed."

To follow the teachings of Islam, one must seek to have a nobleness of behavior.

Mahmud never stops learning about Muslims, and he has interviewed many leaders of Islam, including Hajj Dr. Murad Wilfried Hofman, of Germany.

The Islam equivalent to the Bible is called the Qur'an. It is a history book of mankind that contains the meaning of existence, a statement of the unity of God, or Allah, and of creation, according to Hofman.

Hofman was posted in Algeria during their war of independence. It was a war against people who were Muslims, and he saw them accept the terrible war with

patience, and their ability to accept punishment and daily exposure to death was awe inspiring to Hofman.

"It defied my mind," he said.

Hofman wished to know more about these amazing people, so he decided to read the Qur'an, which he believes is the first reformation of Christianity.

In the Qur'an, Jesus Christ became a credible character as a prophet, instead of as a savior and the son of God.

He has studied the sociological evolution of mankind through the last three centuries, and now sees the crash of ethics in American corporate life at the beginning of this one.

The president is now trying to reintroduce ethics into capitalism, Hofman said, and maybe now people will see that Islam has been the answer all along.

Hofman looks forward to a time when the transcendental concerns of mankind are taken seriously.

And, Mahmud continues his quest for knowledge and the sharing of that knowledge through his Website, with help from his son, Jabir.

More information about the teachings of Islam can be found at <www.videos-on-islam.com>.

www.ingramcontent.com/pod-product-compliance
Lightning Source LLC
Chambersburg PA
CBHW031946070426
42453CB00007BA/355